FIFE CULTURAL TRUST

PENGUI

The Stepney Doorste... ...ty

Kate Thompson is an award-winning journalist, ghost-writer and novelist who has published nine fiction and non-fiction titles. She worked at *Pick Me Up* magazine for six years and was subsequently named as IPC's 'True Life Writer of the Year' in 2006. Since then, Kate has worked on national newspapers, including the *Daily Express* and *Daily Mail*. Her debut novel, *Secrets of the Singer Girls*, became a *Sunday Times* bestseller in 2015.

The Stepney
Doorstep Society

KATE THOMPSON

PENGUIN BOOKS

PENGUIN BOOKS

UK | USA | Canada | Ireland | Australia
India | New Zealand | South Africa

Penguin Books is part of the Penguin Random House group of companies
whose addresses can be found at global.penguinrandomhouse.com.

First published by Michael Joseph 2018
First published in Penguin Books 2019
002

Copyright © Kate Thompson, 2018

The moral right of the author has been asserted

Set in 11.88/14.11 pt Garamond MT Std
Typeset by Jouve (UK), Milton Keynes
Printed and bound in Great Britain by Clays Ltd, Elcograf S.p.A.

A CIP catalogue record for this book is available from the British Library

ISBN: 978-0-718-18986-0

www.greenpenguin.co.uk

MIX
Paper from
responsible sources
FSC® C018179

Penguin Random House is committed to a
sustainable future for our business, our readers
and our planet. This book is made from Forest
Stewardship Council® certified paper.

This book is respectfully dedicated to my grandmothers, Joyce Thompson and Monica Bird, who lived and fought their way through the Second World War in the factory and at home. Formidable women, the pair of them!

Foreword

By Sarah Jackson, co-founder of the East End Women's Museum

The way history has traditionally been taught, you'd be forgiven for thinking that women weren't invented until the twentieth century. So often history is presented as a long list of men making laws, waging wars, leading industry, or pioneering new inventions. Where are the women? Off making the tea, presumably. Or perhaps they popped to the shops and just missed the Norman Conquest, or the invention of the steam engine.

Until very recently women were second-class citizens in Britain, seen as naturally inferior to men. And sadly our history books, our museums and our monuments reflect that. While there are statues of women all over the place, most of them are allegorical – Justice and Liberty, for example – and pretty much all the rest are royal. In fact, fewer than 3 per cent of the statues in the UK represent real, named women who didn't sport a coronet.

At the East End Women's Museum we want to balance the history books, and put some of those missing women back in the picture. That means telling women's extraordinary stories, but telling the 'ordinary' ones too, because history is much more than kings and queens, wars and laws. And, in fact – as this brilliant book shows – some of the most surprising, entertaining, moving and inspiring stories are found on our own doorstep, and the streets we call home.

These wonderful stories about women from East London's past are full of strength and craftiness, compassion and anger, dignity, courage and good humour. It's not all rosy. In times of adversity some seem to have survived and thrived by sheer force of will alone. But as the old saying goes, 'Women are like teabags. You never know how strong they are until they're in hot water.'

Most of the women who appear in this book probably never expected to find themselves here. I think it's likely they were too busy fixing problems in the here and now to think much about their legacy, and spent more time thinking about their family, friends, colleagues and neighbours than about themselves.

But they are here not because they were famous, or rich, or royal, or because they invented a new kind of aeroplane, or led a successful military campaign. They are remembered here because they touched the lives of those around them. Their legacy is in their communities, in their families. And this book is a chance for the rest of us to share in those memories, and celebrate the countless women in the East End and beyond who will never have a statue, but probably deserve one.

Foreword

By Professor Dick Hobbs, award-winning sociologist of East London and author of *Lush Life: Constructing Organised Crime in the UK*, and *Policing the 2012 London Olympics: Legacy and Social Exclusion*.

East London, the place that Jack London christened 'the awful east', was dominated by poverty, disease, high levels of infant mortality and casual work.

While casual work was not fazed out of the London docks until the late 1960s, it took the German Luftwaffe to kick-start the post-war slum clearance programmes that decimated the tight-knit communities where socialism and fascism had once resided side by side.

It was the post-war rehousing of East End communities that drew the attention of social scientists, and when Michael Young and Peter Willmott published their seminal *Family and Kinship in East London* in 1957, the focus rested firmly on the role of women. For it was they who took up the task of keeping the extended family together when it spread from Bethnal Green to suburban housing estates. However, this new focus was actually a modern portrait of a phenomenon that had been created long before the working classes infiltrated Essex.

In the nineteenth century Henry Mayhew commented on the plight of East London's seamstresses working for ever shrinking piece rates, and home workers in particular found themselves running a family and working long hours for a declining return in cramped, dirty conditions where disease was a fact of life.

These home workers were part of an army of women working in the rag trade, in cigarette and match factories and in flour and sugar refineries. Women's work was not for pin money. The insecurity of dock work, and the low pay that was common across all sectors, ensured that female earnings were essential to keeping the family fed, clothed and sheltered in an environment where conflict in the workplace, in the home and on the street was the norm.

Violence was part of the everyday narrative of family and working life, and while many local men had 'heavy hands', East End women could also dish it out. In the battle for day-to-day respect, women would fight in the street like men, and would often match male bullies who tried it on with family members. Responsibility for control of the family and the maintenance of hard-won respectability rested with these matriarchs. These were tough, resilient women whose stories are too often told via an over ripe-sentimentality and one-dimensional stereotypes.

We lack a vocabulary to understand the complexity of working-class women's lives, and the unique realities of the East End's political economy have ensured that the culture of East End women is particularly resistant to lazy cliché.

In giving voice to these cliché-defying lives, Kate Thompson has gone some way to unearthing the hidden history of the twentieth century. War, death, disease, defiance and ever-changing networks of dependence frame these amazingly rich lives. We will not see their likes again.

Preface

An unnerving silence fell over the courtyard as a woman in her late fifties stepped out on to her balcony. Dressed in a starched white apron, she cut a formidable figure against the gloom of the Bethnal Green tenement block. In her left hand was a placard; in her right, a scalding hot potato. The turban that sat atop her head cast her face into shadow, but her eyes glittered with a dark defiance. Her name was Kate Thompson and she was ready to go to war.

Her voice pierced the still of the fetid summer afternoon: 'Less rent, more repairs!' Using her placard like a baton, she drummed out her anthem, causing a flock of pigeons roosting on the wash-house roof to flap into the skies in alarm.

'Less rent, more repairs! Less rent, more repairs!' More voices from the surrounding balconies and courtyard beneath joined the chant and soon the sound of the East End tribe pulsed off the dung-stained cobbles.

'Go on, get out of it!' Kate bellowed.

She lifted an arm as strong as a butcher's hook and sent the hot potato sailing over the edge of the balcony in a perfect arc. It landed with ruthless accuracy right in the privates of an unsuspecting bailiff, who crashed to his knees on the floor of the courtyard.

Pandemonium broke out as the visiting landlord, Mr Smart, and his bailiffs were assailed from all sides. Ear-splitting howls filled the courtyard as they were set upon by an apron-clad army, pummelling them with their placards and pelting them with stale cakes from Mrs Selby's grocery shop in the square. The women on the balconies above went wild, showering the men in rotten vegetables and insults. This was an East End sisterhood in action!

The landlord and his bailiffs beat a hasty retreat, followed by a crowd of hissing women and children as Kate offered up a final two-fingered salute from on high. Victory was theirs and the message was clear. Don't mess with a matriarch!

The battle was the culmination of a two-week rent strike action, instigated by Bob Graves, secretary of the newly formed Quinn Square Tenants' Association, but won by Kate and her female neighbours. Kate's Bethnal Green address – 83 Quinn Square, Russia Lane – might sound exotic, but by August 1938, it was one of the most congested, densely populated slums in the East End of London. A place so notorious, policemen would only go there in pairs, and each landing held an illegal gambling den.

None of the flats had their own water taps or toilets, so facilities on the landing were shared between four families. Wash houses were located on the roof and the women of the square had to drag their laundry up six flights or take it to the council wash house at York Hall. The walls crawled with bugs and the damp caused the plasterwork to drop from the bulging ceiling. Not one flat contained a cupboard to put food or clothing in, not that there was much to store in any case.

Outside, the air was ripe; manure, meat and asphalt mixed with sour putrescence from the rubbish chutes. The proud women of the square waged war on dirt, taking it in turns to scrub the communal spaces and toilets daily with carbolic, but with just one tap between four families, staying clean was a challenge.

Perhaps that's why Russia Lane had its own bathing centre,

known as a Personal Cleansing Station, where children would go to be deloused and treated for 'The Itch'. The residents of the buildings would conduct regular smoke-outs to kill bed bugs, and they would also try to control the spread by blow-torching the window frames and doorposts to burn the bugs which lined the crevices. But the vermin of Russia Lane were invincible and great breeders, so they fought a losing battle.

The high, soot-stained walls of Quinn Square concealed over 246 flats, built around a central square, housing large families crammed into every available square inch. Despite their ferocious efforts to keep it clean, many lived in a dilapidated tenement. Residents reported broken steps, lavatory doors with no locks and broken facilities in the wash house. It may have been a slum, but to Kate and her nine children, it was home: a place where poverty was tempered by the richness of community life, and where neighbours were as close as family.

Kate was born in September 1880 in Poplar, East London. Queen Victoria was on the throne, and the empire still had muscle. In the East End, though, the unlit streets and alleys were narrow and horizons were as low as the smoking chimney pots. Hopes were eroded by brutal poverty, and every day was a bitter fight for survival.

Like so many others born into poverty, Kate was respectable; a respect which came not from money or social class, but from conduct and a deeply ingrained pride. Perhaps it was this sense of pride that gave her the will to fight harder than any man. Or maybe it stemmed from a determination to always, at any cost, protect her family, for beneath the corseted bosom, beat a heart consumed with familial love.

At the age of eighteen, Kate married a cooper (barrel-maker) by the name of William Thompson, and moved to

Bethnal Green, where she bore him seven sons and two daughters. Kate is believed to have lost one son that I know of. Infant mortality rates were petrifyingly high and there was a heartbreaking saying offered up to a mother when a new baby arrived: 'Has it come to stay?'

According to the electoral register, Kate was registered to vote from as early as 1923: unusual for those times. Women had been given the vote only five years earlier and even then, it was only for women over thirty whose husbands were householders. Perhaps it was an interest in politics that led her to insist on her right to a decent standard of living, or perhaps it was the other way around. Either way, when the landlord informed them he was *increasing* their rent, he overstepped the line.

Far from being an acquiescent victim, Kate and over 200 other residents promptly formed a Tenants' Association and, helped by the Stepney Tenants' Defence League, flatly refused to pay their rents until the landlord, Mr Smart – or Crafty Old Smartie, as he was known – reduced them to more reasonable levels and made repairs. Kate was not a woman who sought out trouble, but if it knocked on her door, she was not one to shy from a fight. So, with an iron will, the withholding of rent and an instinctive understanding of the value of solidarity and community, Kate and her neighbours scored a victory for the working-class underdogs of Quinn Square. The landlord acceded to their demands to lower the rent and carry out repairs, and the case for arrears of rent made history, paving the way for success for other Tenants' Associations.

Kate and her neighbours were not alone in their protest that smouldering summer. In the late 1930s, rent strikes were breaking out all through the East End, in defiance of the notorious 'slum lords'. After their success, the floodgates were opened and strikes spread to all areas of London, then to municipal tenants across the United Kingdom.

Kate's success in the strikes solidified her role as the matriarch of Quinn Square, a woman called upon to care for the sick, help birth the babies and lay out the dead, whose advice and counsel were sought out by the younger women of the square. When the Second World War broke out a year later, there was no reaching for the smelling salts; it was just another fight to be endured. Rationing and poverty were nothing new to the women of the square, who knew how to feed huge families on sixpenny stews. When incendiary bombs landed on the roof during the Blitz, they were calmly extinguished, and Kate did what she did best: brewed a pot of tea and got on with it.

Which makes what happens next all the more bewildering . . .

Let us walk by Kate's side through the rain-lashed and blacked-out streets of Bethnal Green in March 1943. It's 8.17 p.m. on a dark, wet Wednesday evening, and the air-raid sirens are wailing, but neither Kate, nor any of the hundreds of East Enders seeking shelter at Bethnal Green Underground, are panicking. This is a well-rehearsed routine, performed nightly during the Blitz. Indeed, there is time to down a glass of her favourite Porter malt beer and pull her fur collar round her neck before leaving the Black Horse pub and heading down the Tube, her patched-up boots matching the slap of hundreds of feet against wet concrete. It is busy. Despite having a local resident's shelter ticket, which entitles her to one of the 5,000 bunks, she wonders if she will get a spot to sleep.

Outside the stairway to the Tube, three buses rumble to a

halt, delivering more bodies into the sticky darkness. The crowds intensify. Kate feels breath, hot against her neck, and the press of bundles of bedding pushed into the small of her back. She feels uneasy.

A baby cries, its angry wail rising over the air-raid siren. But then another, less familiar noise screams through the darkness. After three and a half years of war, her ears are tuned to the nuances of aerial bombardment. She can distinguish a Jerry plane from a British one, but this is like no sound she has ever heard before. A vibration ripples beneath her feet at terrifying speed, leaving her ears ringing. The crowd freezes, fearing some new sinister method of warfare. The baby's cries stop abruptly. A sickening moment of silence.

'It's a bomb!' shrieks a lone voice.

The weight of hundreds of bodies trying to get to safety through the small shelter entrance sucks the breath from her body. Kate is picked clean off her feet and propelled at astonishing speed towards the steps underground. Helpless, she twists this way and that to free herself, but she is wedged solid and trapped.

As she reaches the top of nineteen slippery steps which lead to the Underground, a dim twenty-five-watt bulb casts a flickering light over a hellish image. The woman carrying the crying baby has tripped and is sprawled at the bottom of the steps in a stairwell, frantically trying to shield her baby from the surge of people racing underground.

'Stop! Go back!' Kate orders over the roar, but then she too is falling helplessly, faster, faster into the seething pit of flailing bodies. Before she can get back up, others fall over her. The pile-up causes a domino effect. The crush of people frantically trying to get underground only adds to the chaos.

Soon the steps are a writhing mass of men, women and children.

Kate is pinned to the wet concrete floor, waiting to be rescued. At first, it's the indignity of it all, her hat is dislodged and her stays dig painfully into her flesh, but as the enormous crush grows more suffocating, a more terrible thought dawns on her.

Panic builds and desperate cries for help rend the air. All around her, limbs are tangled into impossible shapes, there are muffled groans, hair chokes her mouth and nostrils. Above her, shoes sail through the air, and every now and again, a pair of hands reaches down to pluck a body from the pit.

But there's no salvation for Kate. Not this time. The bodies above her are too tightly interlaced, five, no, *six* people deep. A snapping of ribs. Her eyes bulge. A low moan escapes her lips. The woman on top of her who had been clutching her child protectively now squeezes the life from her. The child's face turns purple as the oxygen slowly leaches from her lungs.

Then, silence. In that moment, Kate knows. In her life she has fought many things: grinding poverty, the Depression, rent strikes, disease, slum lords, corruption, discrimination, the class system, fascism, indiscriminate bombing . . . This is one fight she will not win.

And so we must leave Kate here.

Her death aged sixty-two on a small, damp stairway in one of the Second World War's biggest civilian disasters was quickly hushed up under the Official Secrets Act by a wartime government desperate to avoid news of the scandal falling into the enemy's hands. It was deemed bad for morale. But 173 people – 62 of them children – were crushed to death, most of them within thirty seconds. The sights of that dark night were simply unimaginable. Air Raid Precaution wardens worked alongside housewives and Boy Scouts to save the injured. Bodies were piled into anything with wheels – ambulances, barrows and carts – and were rushed to Bethnal Green Hospital or the Queen Elizabeth Hospital for Children, until news filtered back that there was no more room and the dead were laid out in the corridor. Others were taken to the crypts of nearby churches or laid out on the pavement by the railings of Barmy Park. Authorities moved quickly, washing down the steps, removing the bodies and ordering those that witnessed it to say nothing.

By the time a creeping grey dawn slid through the streets, the only way you could guess at the catastrophic loss of life was by the neat pile of damp shoes stacked by the entrance and a broken pram discarded nearby. Death had visited and its stench hung heavy in the air.

There was no enemy bomb in Bethnal Green that day. The Government had been testing new anti-aircraft rockets from a recently installed Z Battery in nearby Victoria Park. They had neglected to tell local residents. The enforced silence just compounded the survivors' feelings of guilt. Rescuers' hair turned grey overnight; whole families were torn apart at the loss of all those children.

I lament Kate's passing too. As I imagine her last gasped breaths for air on that staircase, I feel my chest tighten with a deep sadness. It seems inconceivable that the life of a woman who had the spirit to take on bullies and fight for the repressed could be snuffed out in a hushed-up accident. She was the lynchpin of her community, the heartbeat of her buildings. Not famous, not even a footnote in the history of the Second World War, she is, to all intents and purposes, a forgotten woman in a forgotten tenement. But to me, she is an ordinary woman who led an extraordinary life. A life that should be celebrated, not silenced.

It might sound odd that I should grieve for a woman I do not know and whose own life ended a full thirty-one years before I came into the world. But that's where history is a great connector. For when I saw her name – *my name* – on a memorial to the dead, I felt an instant, emotional connection to this woman, and the quest to find out more about my namesake has led me on a journey in which I have uncovered the lives of some remarkable East End women.

I have sat in countless front rooms, community group lounges, church group bingo and coffee mornings – even tea dances – letting cups of tea grow cold as I listened, rapt, to some hair-raising stories. The more I listened and learnt, the more I realised, in some ways, Kate isn't dead. Her spirit lives on in her sisterhood of East End women.

I discovered the enormous richness and complexity of working-class life, and the plethora of roles women undertook before the formation of the welfare state institutionalized them. Every street had its own Kate, its own matriarch, who acted as the unofficial leader. The East End, in common with all working-class communities, was a fiercely matriarchal society. Women in crossover aprons and button-down boots were the beating heart of the East End. They ruled the cobbles, kept the children fed, birthed the babies of the street when there was no midwife to call out, and conversely laid out the dead, while intervening in disputes and acting as moneylenders and marriage counsellors. The war only added an extra layer of armour to their strength.

'My mum Flo was only four foot eight, but I saw her punch a man down three flights of stairs for slapping me when I was a kid,' recalls eighty-three-year-old Ron from Russia Lane. 'She lost a sister Rhoda in the Tube disaster in 'forty-three, another sister Maud was decapitated by a lorry in the blackout in 'forty-five and her son Teddy died of TB in 'forty-six. She was so grief-stricken she lost all her hair, but she never gave up the fight. The war brought out the strength in women.'

East Ender Denise – whose own mum was the street matriarch as well as being a mother to seven girls – sums it up like this: 'Every turning had one, she was the "go-to" woman when something needed sorting. If a woman fell behind on her rent, Mum would step in and negotiate with the rent collector to stop her being evicted. If there were ever any dodgy-looking men hanging about, she'd see 'em off. If there was trouble, Mum sorted it. Baby needed delivering or aborting, Mum was the one the local girls turned to. She even got involved if a husband was wanting too much sex from his wife! She was a midwife, nurse, social worker, citizens advice bureau and neighbourhood watch rolled into one.'

It would seem that there was always a tough old bird like Kate on hand.

My 1940s namesake was a far stronger, better lady than me. Indeed, it would appear that a love of a fur collar is about all we have in common. I wish I had one ounce of her strength and common sense. Learning about her grim death on that bleak staircase was a catalyst. I became obsessed with this magnificent breed of womanhood, and found myself wondering why we don't have those sorts of figures in our communities any more when, it strikes me, we need them more than ever.

I became determined to seek out the last remaining

matriarchs, to uncover these shadowy women, chief females, or so-called 'aunties' who have been on the fringes of all the major events in history. I have uncovered the forgotten victims, the unsung heroines, and even those who faced public condemnation and prison for the illegal services they performed. All the glorious richness and diversity of East End life is here. From villains and heroes, to crusading nuns and fascist fighters, with an *EastEnders* actress and a Pearly Queen thrown into the mix. There's even a group of stripping pensioners that make the Calendar Girls look like Mary Whitehouse. A potent cocktail!

Their lives and stories aren't always pretty; they are hair-raising, shocking, painful, ugly and incongruous with our pampered lives. But they are always thought-provoking. And now, I'd like to share them with you. This book isn't just a social history; it's a celebration of the matriarch and an exploration of the ways in which forgotten working-class women have contributed towards the diverse economic, political and cultural shaping of the East End of London.

The title is *The Stepney Doorstep Society* but it could just as well be called the Whitechapel, Bethnal Green, Poplar, Bow, Spitalfields, Shoreditch, Aldgate, Hoxton or Wapping Society. Every single East End neighbourhood had its own strong female collective, a group of women whose influence extended beyond their own doorsteps, to the doorstep of any woman in the community who needed their help. I am sure the same is true of any working-class area of Great Britain.

I am not a historian, or an academic. Instead, I am a journalist, ghostwriter and novelist. To feel my way into an experience of the past and make sense of it, I seek stories, not statistics. All the women in this book have an extraordinary thirst for life and an infectious energy. They continue to march the streets of their beloved neighbourhood with their Zimmer frames and trolleys, patrolling their turf like an army of proud pensioners. They draw from many different religious backgrounds and cultures – some Jewish, some Catholic, some Church of England and others proudly atheist, refusing to believe God exists after all they have seen – but common elements bind them. They have all worked extremely hard all their lives, they have all outlived their husbands by some considerable time, and all are proud to be born either within the sound of the Bow Bells, or in strong working-class communities. Indeed, Marie, who features in Chapter Two, told me that when her granddaughter bought a lovely house out in Essex, complete with a granny flat for her, she enquired whether it came with a shovel.

'Why?' her granddaughter asked, puzzled.

'Because the only way you'll get me to live out here is if you hit me over the head with a shovel, then bury me in the garden with it!

'The only way I'm leaving the East End is in a box,' she sniffed starchily, her steely blue eyes glittering with a fierce determination. This staunch devotion towards the East End, coupled with a bone-dry wit, is another thread which binds the women I've met.

When I first met ninety-one-year-old Kathy from Bethnal Green, she took great pride in telling me about East Enders' reaction to the Blitz, and how her dad saved Bethnal Green Town Hall after it caught fire when an incendiary bomb dropped on the roof. She also took great delight in handing me something in soft white wool from her knitting bag at the end of the interview. How sweet, I thought. She's knitted something for my baby son. On closer examination, it turned out to be not a pair of baby booties, but a willy warmer!

Kathy and her pal Vera took one look at my shocked face and fell about.

'We must've knitted fifty or more of them over the years, babe,' said Vera, wiping her eyes with laughter. I got the train home with a home-made willy warmer and an expanded mind.

Teaming up with the newly launched East End Women's Museum, we are determined to take these forgotten women by the apron strings and pull them from black-and-white into dazzling multicolour, and in doing so, pay homage to the extraordinary and instinctive way they have dealt with their lot in life. The Museum shares my goal. Put simply, to celebrate and amplify the voices of East End women. The women the history books forgot.

This feels like a timely place to mention all the women who I *didn't* get to interview. Those East End women who didn't reach extreme old age, who were damaged, scarred and altered, perhaps not for the better, by the Depression, by the war, by life . . . for there must be legions. This book is about remembering *all* real women, dead and alive.

The matriarchs in this book are the last generation of East End women with intimate knowledge of what it takes to survive poverty and wars in the days before the welfare state. There is a yawning gulf between their experience and ours. Born into the first half of the twentieth century, they have something revealing to say, which can inform our lives today. Not only that, but they are important. Their enormous wealth of social history will die with them, as will their unique, no-nonsense insights into how to live a simpler, happier life. They did not expect many pleasures out of life, so those that they did have were all the sweeter, and enjoyed to the full.

'We didn't have a lot, but what we did have, we shared,' is something I've heard countless times from the mouths of East End women, along with: 'We was all one.'

So let's not waste time. Come and join me on a journey back in time. Let us delve the back streets, prowl the lamp-lit alleys and walk the narrow tenement corridors. Let us catch a glimpse of the matriarch feeding her family by candlelight, rolling up her sleeves to bring new life into the world or silently laying out the dead. Let us sit at her knee and observe her thrift and ingenuity. Let us imbibe her remedies, recipes and pearls of wisdom. Above all, let us learn from the courageous way she took on the Second World War.

Beatty's Remedy

Vinegar dabbed on brown paper and placed on the forehead is a good natural alternative for painkillers if you have a headache. Vinegar is a great cure-all and has been used since ancient times for everything from a sore throat to skin conditions. Try mixing a table-spoon of apple cider vinegar with a teaspoon of honey in warm water and drinking twice a day.

Marie's Remedies

Calamine lotion for itches, bites and skin conditions.
Sugar and water makes a great hairspray.
Rose petals and glycerine for a face cream.
My father was a great believer in the power of Vicks. He used to rub it everywhere: feet, chest and back. He would rub it on the soles of my feet until they were sore, but trust me, it don't half shift a nasty cold!

Beatty's Pearls of Wisdom

If you're going to moan, moan alone.

Beatty's Recipe

Chicken Soup

Bone broth has been declared a superfood in recent years. Containing natural probiotics, it's believed to improve gut health, leading to overall well-being and health, something Beatty and her family have known for centuries, of course. Beatty's mother was similar to many of her contemporaries and used up every part of the animal bar the squeak. 'Economy is the route to wisdom,' as the old saying goes.

Sprinkle salt over your chicken (must be a fowl, and ideally a boiler chicken if you can find one) and leave it for 30 minutes. Set aside the liver. Wash the chicken in water.

Add chopped onion, garlic, carrot and potherbs. Root vegetables are also good to add, particularly something called petrushka, or parsley root, if you can get hold of it.

Poach it in a pan of salted boiling water for two hours, skimming off the scourge as it cooks.

After two hours, the chicken should just fall off, shred it and set aside for a separate meal.

You can drink the broth with a little salt and lemon juice, or add vermicelli noodles or dumplings to make it more substantial.

Chicken liver is delicious chopped, fried with salt, pepper and onion and served with an egg. A cheap and nutritious meal.

1. War Is Brewing, 1936

His face was twisted into a mask of pure hatred. From the tips of his black jackboots, to the brim of his black cap, he convulsed with anger.

'Go. Home. Yid,' he sneered, unbuckling his heavy metal belt.

Drawing herself up to her full height of five foot six, it dawned on her – she didn't stand a chance. She was just nineteen, but what Beatty Inderstein lacked in strength, she made up for in chutzpah.

'I. Am. Home,' the seamstress retorted, jutting her chin out and meeting his gaze with defiant grey eyes.

A vein in his temple pulsed dangerously as he whipped his belt off, 'Why you . . .'

Beatty wasn't sticking around to hear the rest. She took to her toes and ran with all her might. Deep into the maze of alleys that separated Bethnal Green from the teeming tenements of Whitechapel she plunged, her heart thundering against her ribs. Behind her, his jackboots pounded over the cobbles, breath hot on her neck as the tip of his metal buckle licked painfully at her back.

Oh, Beatty. How you going to explain this to Mum? she thought as she dodged an old lady selling grated horseradish from the side of the street.

'Go on, clear out, you lousy lot! We don't want your sort round here,' yelled the old woman, hurling a specked apple at the man's retreating back. 'Go on, gal, you can outrun him!'

'Your mouth to God's ear,' Beatty muttered grimly, leaping

over some nippers playing gobs in the gutter and running for dear life.

With a last-ditch burst of speed, she flung herself round a corner and ducked into a doorway. He thundered past and she slid down the wall in relief. She had escaped her tormentor. This time.

A lone gull wheeled overhead as Beatty pulled down her cloche hat and, keeping to the shadows, ran back to her buildings.

What had Beatty done to unleash such raw hatred in the stranger? Simple. She was Jewish. It mattered not that she was born in the East End, nor that she toiled daily in a tailoring factory and contributed towards her community. To him, she was an alien. Dirt.

By the time Beatty reached her neighbourhood, dusk had settled over the chimney pots of Goulston Street and Petticoat Lane, the skies hazy with smoke. Market stalls covered with everything from live eels to hot chestnuts glistened under the hissing oil lamps and braziers being lit as darkness descended along the Lane.

There was nowhere on earth like Petticoat Lane. Anyone could make a living 'Dahn The Lane', as it was affectionately known, and Beatty never tired of it. Here, an escapologist bound in chains thrilled the assembled crowd; there, a travelling pedlar pushed cures for all from glass bottles. In and amongst them, Irish and Jewish housewives squeezed fruit, eyes bright and beady for a bargain. Unplucked chickens hung from the shop awnings. Birds in cages, rabbits too.

Such a sociable squash of street vendors could certainly stir up a soupy cloud of smells: salt beef, fish and spices, vinegar, manure and over-ripe fruit assaulted the senses. Free entertainment? Not much. What other street had the famous music hall act Wilson, Keppel and Betty doing their 'sand dance' – a soft-shoe routine performed on a layer of sand, mimicking poses from Egyptian tomb paintings – alongside the barrel organ player?

Whitechapel! The place Beatty loved best, welcoming waves of immigrants even before the French Huguenots fled persecution in the late seventeenth century. Where else but here could you find dairies nestled alongside synagogues, breweries and bell foundries? It was a self-contained area; everything you needed all right here nestled in this vibrant, clamorous quarter of London. Whitechapel High Street was a cornucopia of Jewish artistry. Hyman Koranstay the furrier was nestled alongside Miss Filschstein the corset maker and Abraham Sirotkin the bookbinder. They worked hard, but they got by.

Stepping into the courtyard of Brunswick Buildings, deep in the heart of the Jewish East End, she felt her pulse finally begin to steady. The pavements were marked with dusty hopscotch pitches, the lamp posts hung with ropes, but the children were all inside now, called in for teas of bread and jam or, if they were lucky, a nice piece of fried fish from Fat Annie's at the top of Vallance Road. Over the hiss of gas lamps, the sizzle of frying fish filled the courtyard, its comforting aroma curling sweetly into the brackish air.

The buildings, constructed in 1886, might have housed the poorest of the poor, but they bore the hallmark of the proudest breed of Irish and Jewish women. The women of Brunswick Buildings didn't always agree on the way a woman should behave. Some of the old Irish ladies thought nothing of taking their vegetables to the pub to peel. Formidable women in wrap-over aprons with yellow snuff stains under their noses, they would sit outside their doors shelling peas and calling out to their neighbours over a forest of flapping linen. Beatty's mother and her friends, on the other hand, would sooner die than be seen entering a public house.

But, as the now-infamous saying goes, there was more to unite them than divide them, and Jewish and Irish alike were bound by a fierce pride in their homes and their children. Every doorstep in the building gleamed from having been scrubbed with a hearthstone, and the windows were polished to a high shine with newspaper and vinegar. To the women of Brunswick Buildings, pride came before poverty.

Brunswick Buildings was Beatty's territory and she loved the sense of belonging she felt every time she came home. But how sad to have territories in the first place, invisible boundaries that couldn't be crossed. Beatty's eyes strayed up the side of a soot-stained wall and she felt a cold fist close over her heart. Daubed in white paint, right next to an advert urging people to SMOKE PLAYERS 'NAVY CUT' CIGARETTES was another message: DOWN WITH THE JEWS.

Sighing, she trudged up the grey stone steps to home, her head spinning. The violence on the streets and now this! Why couldn't people just let decent folk be? Where would it all end?

To a young Jewish woman like Beatty Inderstein, East London in 1936 was a dangerous and volatile place to live. Fascist blackshirts prowled the streets looking for trouble, armed with brickbats and home-made weapons. Fuelled by rhetoric from Oswald Mosley, leader of the British Union of Fascists, they had one mission only – to rid the streets of people like her. Until 1935, Mosley had been nothing but a peculiar, moustached aristocrat, spinning the tired old line that all Jews were bad landlords and thieves, or ran prostitution rackets, but in February 1936, he changed the name of his party to the British Union of Fascists and National Socialists, indicating a shift from his allegiance to Mussolini's ideas, towards Hitler.

Across the Channel, armies of men were marching Adolf Hitler to power, and you didn't have to be a genius to see another war was brewing. Beatty's Jewish neighbours worked hard to dispel Mosley's anti-Semitic propaganda, but there were plenty of people in neighbouring Bethnal Green and Shoreditch who were desperate enough to fall for his fiery and flamboyant oratory.

Mosley had fixed the East End of London firmly in his sights. Poverty and anger were flourishing in those quarters and young unemployed men and women were looking for a target for their anger. Mosley provided it.

Scarcely a day passed now without a Jewish stallholder down Watney Market having his livelihood trashed, or a brick sailing through a synagogue window. But to Beatty, it was the threat of violence, the fear of what was to come, that worried her the most.

Taking off her hat and smoothing down her hair, Beatty opened the door to her two-room flat, straight into the lounge that also served as kitchen and dining room. She gazed sadly at her mother, Julia, huddled over a small gas stove, enveloped in a cloud of steam, stirring a pot of beans and barley. A powerful twinge of protectiveness plucked at her heart. Life had not been kind to the Inderstein family.

Fleeing the Russian pogroms, her father's parents had come to Britain, along with thousands of other immigrants, seeking sanctuary, peace and employment in the burgeoning rag and furniture trades of Whitechapel, Bethnal Green and Stepney. By the early 1930s, an estimated 183,000 Jews lived in London, with over 52 per cent of them squeezed into the borough of Stepney. They were lured with the promise of lucrative work and comfortable accommodation, but the reality was sixteen-hour shifts in a sweatshop, six days a week, to feed their families. Home was usually a small portion of a divided-up slum or tenement, with kids sleeping four or more to a bed.

Casual employment meant that many Jews were the first to be affected when the Depression kicked in. By 1932, unemployment in Britain peaked at nearly three million and inevitably hit the working class first. Men fought down at the docks for a day's work, children queued outside the Jewish Soup Kitchen, and mothers begged shopkeepers for food on tick. The only place that continued a roaring trade was the pawnbroker's. There was no peace to be found now, unless, as Beatty's best friend, Millie, joked, you counted the food.

'A little piece of this, a small piece of that!' she'd say, rolling her eyes and throwing up her hands, just like she'd seen the street gossips do. Millie was a funny, sparky girl who had been Beatty's partner in crime whenever they played marbles and gobs round the buildings. That was until Millie's father had lost his job, and overnight, they'd been forced to do a moonlight flit. His misfortune spelled the end of their friendship and Beatty had not seen her funny friend in years. Here today, gone tomorrow was the means of survival for so many poor souls.

Happily for Beatty and her two older sisters, Rebecca and Esther, their father had steady employment as a night watchman at Spitalfields fruit and vegetable market. Israel Inderstein was a strong, barrel-chested bear of a man with a luxuriant moustache and smiling eyes, a man who was the breadwinner, but thought nothing of rising early to shine his daughters' shoes before work.

From the moment Beatty came into the world on the seventh day of the seven month, 1917, as German Gotha bombers flew overhead, it became immediately obvious that she was her father's favourite.

'Go down and buy the beigels, Beatty,' he'd grin, chucking her cheek as the cries of the early-morning seller drifted up from the cobbled street outside.

'You're a bright girl. Work hard and the future is yours for the taking,' he promised her. 'Life is what you make it, my girl.'

Not wanting to let him down, Beatty worked hard at her studies at Gravel Lane School in Houndsditch, excelling in housewifery. Her father worked hard; her mother filled their home with the scent of stew and soup, and competed with the neighbours to have the cleanest step. Julia was a quiet, unassuming woman who considered it fast to wear lipstick and scent. Her only ambition was to ensure the comfort of her family and be a loyal and steadfast wife. Their home was filled with laughter.

Until the day Israel Inderstein didn't come home.

How could a man as strong as he drop down dead aged forty-four? A stroke, doctors at Vallance Road Hospital told her mother. But, aged thirteen, this made no sense to Beatty. The death of her beloved father left her broken-hearted and rudderless. Overnight, life had changed. The tight fingers of poverty wrapped themselves around her mother's neck. Julia was forced to leave their home and get a job making cigars at Godfrey & Phillips in Commercial Street, her elder daughters soon following her into work in the many tailoring and garment factories that clustered around Whitechapel.

The bright future Beatty's father had predicted seemed to slip further away when she got a job, aged fourteen, in a dressmaking firm in Alie Street. She went from being a schoolgirl on a Friday to a working woman on the Monday. But even being able to contribute five shillings a week to the household income didn't assuage the deep sense of frustration. Within days of starting her first job laying out silk, it became obvious that Beatty didn't have her sisters' nimble fingers.

'You've a very heavy hand. I've no room for a klutz,' sighed the foreman as he sacked her.

'This is all I'm good for,' she muttered days later, in her second job as an overlocker at Lottereys tailoring firm in Whitechapel, opposite the Rivoli Picture Palace. There Beatty was tasked with putting the buttons on to trousers with a machine. Within a week her eyes were raw and the billowing heat seemed to sap every last sensible thought from her head.

Only with an iron will and working sixteen hours a day, did the Inderstein women keep their heads above water. Their mother struggled but never revealed her fears to her daughters, and *never* allowed them to go to the Jewish Soup Kitchen. 'I have my pride,' she'd say. This deep pride that meant Beatty never came home to anything other than a cooked dinner. By scratching for every shilling and a thrift that enabled Julia to make four separate meals from one chicken, the family were surviving. Just.

'Hello, Mum, got my wages,' Beatty said, nailing on a smile as she pulled the brown-paper packet from her pocket.

Julia turned away from the stove, her brown eyes gentle, until she spotted Beatty's snagged stockings.

'Beatty!' she exclaimed.

'I met a blackshirt coming home,' she confessed.

Her mother's face darkened.

'How many times must I tell you?' she scolded, pointing her wooden spoon at her wayward daughter. 'Those men are dangerous; you must avoid the streets where they meet. Stay away from them, you hear!'

'But you should have heard the tripe he was spouting,' Beatty protested.

'I don't care!' Julia blazed. 'Why can't you go to a dance and meet a nice man like your sisters?'

Beatty glanced over to her elder sisters who were darning at the table, backs curled in concentration and, in that moment, she too wished she could be just like them. But she knew she wasn't cut from that cloth. She wanted to be more than just a good Jewish *baleboste*, or homemaker. Dances bored her. Getting herself dolled up and joining the week-end procession along Aldgate to Whitechapel – as was the custom of all the young women seeking to catch the eye of a suitor – was dreary. She had a greater purpose in life than simply finding a husband. The problem was that she didn't know what it was.

'Who says what street I can and can't walk through?' she railed, burning with indignation. 'Besides, I'm a lousy dancer, what else am I going to do?'

'I don't know where I got you from!' Julia muttered, rolling her eyes and returning to her pot. 'And give those stockings to your sister to darn; they'll be more thread than silk at this rate.'

That night, as Beatty lay on her battered put-me-up, she pulled the coverlet over herself and listened to her sisters' soft breathing in the darkness, their breath pooling in the cold air. The night was bitterly cold, the restless wind moaning in the chimney and rattling at the window frames. There'd be ice on the inside of the panes by morning.

The grief she still felt six years after her father's death was like a dull ache clawing at her chest. He would have understood. He would have known exactly how to handle this mess.

The sounds of the night wrenched her from sleep: a baby's cry in the rooms above, then the soft tread of its mother's footsteps and a Yiddish lullaby drifting sweetly through the aged floorboards, followed by the cracking of glass and the distant crackling of a fascist amplifier.

Discrimination and hatred were seeping like poison through her neighbourhood. In that moment, she knew where she must go. She hated to defy her mother, especially after everything Julia had been through, but to Beatty, it was quite simple. Fascism should never be tolerated, and by continuing to ignore it, surely that was exactly what they were doing. It wasn't enough to simply heckle soapbox racists any longer. She had to take a stronger stance. Her father's voice drifted through the velvety darkness: *Life is what you make it.*

Fear, and if she were honest, excitement, began to build inside her. The East End was a hotbed of politics; you'd have to be blind not to see the communists and anti-fascists marching, the trade unions gaining in strength and rent strikes breaking out all over. Men *and* women were standing up for their rights, and Beatty needed to be a part of it. She'd spent too many hours sitting like a wallflower at the lonely edge of a dance floor. Her father's death had been so cruel and meaningless. She needed some direction back in her life. Who wanted to be remembered for putting buttons on men's trousers? She may not be able to foxtrot, but she could fight! As Beatty finally settled down to sleep, she had a feeling her father would approve.

*

'Where are we going? To a dance?' Beatty's best mate, Ginnie, asked hopefully as they sped through the streets after work.

'Not exactly,' Beatty hedged, as she ducked down into Cable Street in Stepney.

The smell of sweated onions greeted them as they made their way along the long street, which sliced its way through the East End, linking the City to the docks. It was so narrow, you could shake hands with the person coming out of the shop opposite, and usually the air was thick with a yellowy consumptive fog. But this evening, a cooling breeze rolled in from the docks and Beatty relished the feel of it against her face. After twelve hours in a garment factory, the air felt heady with the promise of excitement.

She glanced about her, hoping no one who knew her mother would spot her. It was unlikely. God knows they were poor, but the folk who lived down Cable Street were there because they had nowhere else to go. At ground level, every building was either a workshop or a store, and the rooms above were crowded with poor families. The Jewish lived on the west side, the Irish in the east.

The street had started out as a ropewalk, where workers would twist giant lengths of hemp rope into cables for sailing ships, but by the early nineteenth century, had lost its respectability as a consequence of its proximity to the docks, the brothels and the rumoured opium dens. Pausing outside a shabby-looking building in Swedenborg Square, just off the main thoroughfare, Beatty knocked on the headquarters of the local anti-fascist party.

The door was opened by a man in a serge suit, and Beatty addressed him with as much confidence as she could muster.

'We'd like to join.'

'W—would we?' stuttered Ginnie, glancing at her.

'Yes, we would!'

'Well, you better come in then,' the man said.

Beatty didn't know what she expected to see inside the down-at-heel building, but it was as diverse as her own neighbourhood. Men and women, some even younger than her, Labourites, Jews, Irish and communists, sat about smoking and chatting.

'We are being made a scapegoat,' complained a young tailor.

'That's right, what are the Jewish Board of Deputies doing to protect us?' piped up another voice.

'Pah!' spat a striking young woman, blowing a stream of blue smoke into the air. 'Nothing. The rich Jews will end up finding a compromise with fascism.'

Beatty listened intently as the anti-fascists bandied back and forth with ideas on how to fight back. It was an energetic, grass-roots response to the growing problem of fascism. Beatty was shocked to learn that the very bodies set up to support and represent them, like the Jewish Board of Deputies, were feigning indifference and trying to downplay the problem. But the biggest surprise was the social opportunities the club afforded. There were music and dances, slide shows, film clubs and even rambling weekends and picnics on offer, and she eagerly signed up to them all. But before picnics, came protesting.

'We need to go and agitate, be a presence outside the Albert Hall at Mosley's next rally,' the speaker said at the end of the meeting. 'Who's coming?'

Beatty's hand was up in a heartbeat. She left Cable Street with a fawn-coloured shirt, a red tie and a sense of purpose.

In the build-up to the march, she felt a mounting sense of excitement.

Instinct told her not to tell her mother she was joining a protest march when the day dawned.

'I'm just off to meet Ginnie,' she said instead, shrugging on a coat over her new uniform. 'We may walk up the West End.' It wasn't exactly a lie.

'Get me a penn'orth of bones while you're out, will you?' her mother replied, raking in her purse for a few coppers. 'And tell him to leave the meat on, I'm making a stew.'

'All right, Mum.' Beatty smiled, kissing her cheek, which was covered in a fine layer of soft, downy hair. She smelt faintly of cigars from a long day in the factory. Beatty hated lying to her mum, but Julia would never understand. Her world belonged here, caring for her family, but Beatty's world was out there, in the clamour of the streets.

One hour later, marrowbone was the last thing on Beatty's mind as she and Ginnie joined the enormous crowd of anti-fascists marching their way to the Albert Hall. What a sight! Flags and banners fluttered in the air over men and women, young and old. She spotted tailors and trade unionists, tram drivers and foremen, seamstresses and shop girls. The steady tramping of feet seemed to swell up inside her chest. A platoon of Jewish ex-servicemen with Union Jacks and medals marched in the thick of the crowd, faces grimly determined, as if they were off to fight another war. Beatty chanted and sang along with the crowd, until she and they were one, a more powerful being.

Excitement inched up her spine. *This* was what it meant to belong, to stand up for something you believed in. Every day in the factory, she felt as if more and more of her brain was slowly leaching away. But here, now, she felt for a few glorious moments that they had a voice outside the tenements and sweatshops. The pavements were choked with spectators, cheering them as they marched.

'Good luck!' called a workman repairing the tramway, unscrewing a turncock in the road and passing cool water to the marchers.

As the streets of the East End gave way to the West End, however, the reception cooled. Streets widened as minds narrowed. The stores here sold cashmere and tweed, not live poultry and beigels. The well-heeled pedestrians looked on in disdain with mean glances and tight whispers. A bucket of icy water thrown from a top window missed Beatty by yards. Even the shop-front mannequins seemed to stare out disapprovingly.

Well, blow the lousy bigots, thought Beatty. *If they had people breaking their windows and terrorizing their streets, they'd have a thing or two to say!*

As the Albert Hall hove into sight, the air thickened. A solid wall of blackshirts stood protectively flanking the entrance. From deep within the building, a roar of applause drifted out.

'Hurrah! Hail Mosley! Mosley, Mosley!'

The chants of the anti-fascists rose up to meet them. 'Out, fascists, out! Out, fascists, out! Out, fascists, out!' Beatty and her comrades responded.

They came up against the blackshirts standing shoulder to shoulder outside, and skirmishes broke out all around. Then a door close to Beatty opened. A tiny, slender blonde woman in black slipped out. She shot them a chilly look before advancing into Hyde Park opposite.

'You know who that is, don't you?' remarked the man nearest to Beatty. She shrugged.

'Unity Mitford.'

Beatty had read all about the debutante in the papers, her supposed love affair with Hitler, and now seemingly her support for Oswald Mosley had drawn her back to London. This privileged young woman, and her burning passion for fascism, was alien to Beatty. She doubted whether Unity Mitford had ever done a decent day's work in all her life, much less twelve hours in a factory. Nor did she think she, or the Mitford sisters, had ever had to pick the marrow out of a bone with a knitting needle in order to eat. If the fascist-lover thought she could slip away unnoticed, she could think again. Beatty followed a small crowd in pursuit and began to chase her across the park.

'That's it, run, fascist!' taunted the crowd. For a slight girl, Unity Mitford certainly could run, and before long, she had disappeared from sight.

On the long walk back to the East End, it occurred to Beatty that politics had just become real. She may not have returned home with marrowbone, but she might just have found her backbone. Beatty made her excuses to her mother, a sense of self-preservation telling her it was wise not to divulge where she had really been.

After that, Beatty didn't stop marching. The violence, the uncertainty, the poverty – it all seemed less potent with the knowledge that she was fighting a cause that she truly believed in. She read the newspapers, she was aware of what was happening to the Jews in Germany. This wasn't just about politics; it was about principle and belief, protesting against hatred and the inevitable war, suffering and hunger it would surely bring. To Beatty, it was so simple. *Pride. Tolerance. Respect.* They were the principles her father had raised her with and the virtues she would fight for.

As the mercury on the thermometer rose that long, hot summer of 1936, the tension on the streets intensified with explosive violence breaking out between the fascists and the anti-fascists. Chair legs, bottles, razor blades concealed in potatoes: all became weapons.

By July 1936, the problem was so great, a new group formed to tackle it. The Jewish People's Council Against Fascism and Antisemitism urged the Jewish community to act together and work with like-minded people, not just Jews, but 'citizens of London', encouraging them to band together and fight fascism.

The East End was living on a knife-edge. Word had even spread to Westminster.

'I have known East London all my life – there will one of these days be such an outburst as few of us would care to contemplate,' warned George Lansbury, MP for Bow and Poplar, in a parliamentary debate.

Walking to work one crisp, October morning, Beatty sensed an odd feeling in the streets. The air around Brunswick Buildings was thick with whispers, and the clattering of carts echoed off the cobbles. Then a louder noise roared up behind her. Automobiles were a strange sight down Goulston Street, and Beatty just managed to leap out the way as it drove past. A youth was clinging to the running board, scattering handbills into the air. A loudspeaker was fixed to the top of the car, its message crackling up the long street: 'All out against the blackshirts! They shall not pass! All rally to Gardiner's Corner. Two o'clock, Sunday the fourth.'

After work, Beatty attended an emergency meeting. 'This Sunday, Mosley and his blackshirts are planning a huge march through East London. The police are giving them an escort,' announced the secretary of the anti-fascist party.

'But why?' Beatty asked.

'Something to do with exercising their democratic right to free speech.'

'What about *our* democratic right to safety in our streets?' Beatty protested.

'So come to the counter-rally on Sunday, Aldgate, two o'clock. We won't be marching because we want to, but because we *have* to.'

As more details emerged over the weekend, tensions reached a fever pitch. Mosley had planned the march to celebrate the fourth birthday of his movement. Coachloads of fascists would be arriving in London from every corner of England. The blackshirts were to assemble at Royal Mint Street near the Tower of London, then there were to be four marching columns, ending in four rallies, with Mosley speaking at each of them. Mosley's inflammatory march through the heartland of the Jewish East End wasn't just designed to ruffle feathers; it was to deliver a hammer blow.

Both Beatty and Ginnie – along with nearly 100,000 others – signed a petition drawn up by the Jewish People's Council, which was given to the Home Secretary, Sir John Simon, calling on him to ban the march. He refused. Not only that, but he cancelled all police leave and ordered 7,000 Metropolitan Police to turn out on the day, including the entire mounted division, whose task it was to clear the roads.

After that, you'd have to have your head in a hole not to know about the march. It was being debated on every street corner, in every market and café. Thousands of leaflets and posters, and gallons of whitewash, were used to spread the message of the counter-rally, and Beatty was right in the thick of it. Even the pavements, usually chalked out with hopscotch pitches, were blazoned white with news of the counter-rally.

'Have you told your mum?' Ginnie asked hesitantly, over a cup of Bovril at Curly's Café.

'What do you think?' Beatty replied, eyes gleaming through the steam. In her opinion, it wasn't so much what you did, it was whether you were caught doing it!

'You coming Sunday, girls?' asked the café owner, as he set down two sticky buns. 'This place is going to be a First Aid Centre.'

Beatty swallowed uneasily. Now she definitely wasn't telling her mum. What was the sense in worrying her?

As Sunday, 4 October dawned, the sun rose in a delphinium-blue sky, drenching the cobbles with sunshine. Beatty and Ginnie made their way to Gardiner's Corner, full of nervous excitement. As they walked, an extraordinary thing happened. From out of narrow doorways, courtyards and alleys, men, women and children emerged, blinking in the bright autumn light. Folk streamed from factories, shops and houses, carrying banners and singing. The atmosphere was electrifying, more like a Cup Final than a Sunday morning in Aldgate.

By the time the two girls reached the corner of Leman Street, and pushed their way through the crowds to stand in front of a shop called Critts, they could scarcely believe their eyes.

'Look at all these people!' Beatty exclaimed, taking in the solid wall of bodies jamming the streets. Those that couldn't find a spot on the cobbles were clinging to lamp posts or perched on shop awnings.

Ginnie's eyes sparkled. 'There must be thousands!' she

yelled over the terrific roar of the crowd. Beatty gazed open-mouthed. Housewives in headscarves stood side by side with old boys who remembered the Boer War. Wiry dockers brushed shoulders with Orthodox Jews in black hats. Seamstresses, sailors and shop owners from Hackney to Hoxton. Communists. Socialists. Trade unionists. Jewish ex-servicemen. Men and women, young and old, united in a vibrant human barricade. This was solidarity.

'They shall not pass!' chanted the crowd, and Ginnie and Beatty added their voices, feeling a sense of euphoria building inside as the cries grew louder and more fervent.

A clattering cut over the roar. The crowds stared up dizzyingly to the clear blue skies. A police autogiro circled overhead, monitoring them.

The girls couldn't see it from their vantage point, but a tram was slowly carving its way through Gardiner's Corner. The driver parked smack-bang in the middle of the intersection, stopped and simply melted into the crowds.

'Mosley won't be marching anywhere now!' the crowds hollered.

But in a split second, mayhem broke out. Beatty and Ginnie couldn't see it over the heads of the crowds as they were too far back, but a thick blue line of mounted police were advancing on the intersection. A clattering of horses' hooves and a flash of dark blue. A policeman on horseback, his mouth drawn in a grim slit of determination, raised his leather-bound truncheon and brought it crashing down on the head of a man at the front of the crowd. The deafening shrill of police whistles and screams filled the air.

'Ginnie, stay close.' Beatty reached for her friend's arm. The crush of the crowd left her breathless as they were pushed further back against the windows of the shop. It was obvious the mounted police would never penetrate the tightly packed crowd, but still they advanced, swinging their truncheons about indiscriminately.

Everything went into slow motion, images unspooling like cinema film. In horror, Beatty realised Ginnie had been pushed through the broken window of the store and her face was etched with pain.

'Your hand!' she screamed. 'It's bleeding!'

'I'm all right,' Ginnie replied shakily.

'No. We're getting you to hospital,' Beatty insisted, guiding her through the howling crush. By the time they reached the London Hospital on Whitechapel High Street, there were injured protestors everywhere.

Luckily, Ginnie's cut was shallow and her hand was bandaged up.

'Do you want to go back?' Beatty asked as the colour returned to her friend's cheeks.

'I'm game if you are.'

By the time they returned, the crowds and the fighting had moved to nearby Cable Street and here the sights were even more extraordinary. The Irish dockers had come up from their end of the street and torn up the paving stones to help build a huge barricade made from old mattresses, planks of wood and corrugated iron. A flatbed lorry was overturned in front of it all. Even the neighbourhood nippers were involved; kids who usually played marbles on the cobbles of Cable Street were now hurling them under the horses' hooves.

'Look,' laughed Ginnie, her pain quite forgotten in the unfolding drama.

They huddled in a doorway as women leant out of their windows in the tenements above the shops and emptied the contents of their chamber pots over the heads of the police beneath. Slops, congealed fat and old vegetable peelings rained down from the blue skies, spattering the policemen's helmets. A well-known winkle seller ferried the police's casualties out on his barrow. Excitement beat at Beatty's breast. The ordinary working classes, Jew alongside Gentile, from all walks of life, were beating the bullies. This, *this* was history in the making, and Beatty wanted to witness every minute of it.

'Let's go and see what the blackshirts are doing,' she urged, so they ran to Royal Mint Street and there, in the shadow of the Tower of London, stood 3,000 uniformed and jackbooted fascists, in columns snaking half a mile long. Thwarted and angry, they made an ugly sight. Beatty shuddered. 'We'd better get away from here.'

By the time they made it back to Cable Street, the police were retreating.

'We did it!' yelled the crowd. 'They did not pass!'

After hours of fierce fighting, the Commissioner of the Metropolitan Police, Sir Philip Game, ordered Mosley to turn back and march through the deserted streets of the Embankment. The roads into the ancient heartland of the East End were barred to him. As the sun set over the Cable Street barricades, never had the battered, smoke-blackened street stood so proud. If Cable Street were a woman, she'd be an indefatigable old girl standing with her arms crossed in a ripped pinny and cardboard-patched boots.

Beatty and Ginnie hugged, ecstatic at the sweet victory. Hats flew in the air and complete strangers embraced as the girls made their way up the narrow street, along with thousands of others, to Victoria Park, where the joyous celebrations looked set to continue all night. As a velvet-blue darkness descended over the treetops, a butter-coloured moon rose, bathing the euphoric crowd in its silver light. The singing grew louder. Tall tales were traded. No one who was there would ever forget that day, when the East End said *'Enough'*, least of all Beatty.

Soon after, Beatty attended another march in Victoria Park. Turning around, she felt a larger-than-life presence by her side. A tall Irish man with bright eyes and a look of David Niven about him gazed down at her. His smile ambushed her heart. Beatty did not know it then, but she had just met the man who was to lead her on a life-changing journey.

The 'Battle of Cable Street', as it later became known, was a watershed in the resistance against fascism and a defining moment in the history of the East End. That sunny Sunday, when estimated crowds of around 250,000 turned up to Gardiner's Corner and Cable Street to defend their streets with fierce chants of 'They shall not pass!' dealt a decisive blow to the British Union of Fascists.

This wasn't some wild, foaming-at-the-mouth, razor gang from the Jewish ghetto, as the fascists tried to claim the next day. It was *ordinary* men, women and children – citizens of London – like Beatty, stepping up to reclaim their streets and their pride.

Reminiscences on East End Facebook sites demonstrate the pride with which the battle is still felt all these years on and the place it continues to hold in family folklore.

'My father-in-law Lew from Hackney got stuck in at the battle. He later became a staff sergeant in the British Army and fought all the way through to Germany's borders. Not bad for a boy who grew up with no shoes,' said Freddie.

Patricia proudly recalls her grandfather's reason for turning up to stop the blackshirts. 'Those men stood up for others as a matter of principle and belief. True gentlemen. Working-class winners.'

'Granddad was a communist,' remembers Deborah. 'He had a clubfoot, polio damage in both legs and lost part of his chest in an operation to save him when he contracted anthrax from working at the docks. He was a boxer, a very successful one. During the Cable Street riots, he helped to rescue some documents from the police station. According to my Nan, he rescued his own file, stamped "Subversive". His name was John James Gentleman. His boxing name was "The Hackney Hammer". He is the only disabled boxer that I have ever known to fight as able-bodied. I am immensely proud of him.'

So many words have been written about the Battle of Cable Street, but I like these, by Phil Piratin, who was secretary of the Communist Party at the time of the battle and later to become a communist MP for the area: 'In Stepney, nothing had changed physically,' he wrote in his memoir *Our Flag Stays Red*. 'The poor houses, the mean streets, the ill-conditioned workshops were the same, but the people were changed. Their heads seemed to be held higher, and their shoulders were squarer. The terror had lost its meaning.'

The ramifications were far-reaching. Eleven weeks later, on 18 December 1936, the Public Order Act became law, commencing on 1 January 1937, banning the wearing of political uniforms and strengthening the law on marches, assemblies and the use of insulting language to provoke a breach of the peace.

The battle may not have directly brought about the downfall of Mosley but it helped to widely discredit him, and afterwards his party fell into decline. It was banned from the BBC and coverage of its activities disappeared from newsreels. Strapped for cash, unable to wear his uniform, broadcast or march without police permission, Mosley limped through the rest of the 1930s. When the Second World War broke out, he and his wife Diana Mosley were interned, and they remained in prison, then under house arrest, for the rest of the war.

We should never underestimate the importance of the struggle that Beatty, Ginnie and thousands like them endured. In the 1930s, anti-Semitism was rife and fascists in Britain were given a public platform on which to preach. Police by and large turned a blind eye to the violence at these public meetings. Hatred and intimidation of the kind Beatty experienced in England ran in tandem with the rise of fascism under Hitler and the Nazis in Germany.

For Beattie, the battle was deeply symbolic in other ways, for it brought about an inner toughening and made her who she is today: a matriarch!

The year of 1936 was a restless, uncertain one. As a consequence of the abdication crisis, there were three kings in succession on the throne, and there were hunger marches in the streets. Further afield, the Spanish Civil War erupted. You get the sense that nineteen-year-old Beatty cut her teeth on those turbulent times.

'What can I say? It made me who I am,' she confirmed, when I went to visit her at Jewish Care's Brenner Centre at Stepney Community Centre. 'After that, I held my head up high as I walked the streets. I still do.'

Eighty-one years on, the face is a little more lined, but Beatty, who has just celebrated her hundredth birthday, is still the same spirited, whip-smart woman who chased Unity Mitford through the park and defied her mother to go on protest marches.

'Did you ever tell your mother you went to the Battle of Cable Street?' I asked her.

'Course not,' she retorted with a joyous hoot of laughter.

And the man in Victoria Park?

'John Orwell, a wonderful Irish Catholic man,' she smiles wistfully. Beatty defied her mother once again to marry outside her religion. 'They called us the Kellys and the Cohens,' she recalls with a nostalgic chuckle.

Her union with John was a long and fruitful one. 'We married one year before war broke out and went on to have three children, June, seventy-seven, Maureen, seventy-two and Benjamin, seventy.

'We worked hard, selling handbags on a stall down Petticoat Lane, but John was passionate about his community and I was so proud when he was made the second Mayor of Tower Hamlets in 1966. John died in 1972, but not before he brought about some powerful change: compensation for Aberfan victims, better housing for East Enders, helping to establish community funding. His legacy lives on.

'My John was known as the Singing Mayor or Gentleman John,' Beatty shares proudly. 'Wherever he went, he sang, from council chambers to old people's homes. He really loved the old folk. We both did. He used to go up to them and say, "Come on, boys and girls, what you sitting down for? You're not a cabbage. Get off your bum!" and get them moving and laughing.

'He lit up everyone's world. As Mayoress, I got to meet the Queen and the Queen Mother, not bad for a girl from the slums of Whitechapel!'

Today, Beatty is head of an enormous, tight-knit clan. At her hundredth birthday party, Beatty – or Lady Beatty, as she is fondly known at the Community Centre – holds court, surrounded by her three adoring children, twelve grandchildren, nineteen great-grandchildren and four great-great-grandchildren, plus a small army of friends and other relatives. She has lived through some remarkable times and is herself remarkable. Every line and fissure in her face tells a story of a life well lived.

What does she attribute her longevity to?

'Hard work and family,' she says, without missing a beat. 'I rule the roost!'

The astonishing thing is, she is not alone. The first time I went to visit Beatty at her club, I was met at the door by a sprightly woman with jet-black hair and bone-white teeth.

'My name's Marie Joseph,' she grinned, her quick eyes gleaming. 'I can tell you a few stories about the East End. My poor mum raised seven kids in two rooms. I had to go and sleep at my *bubbe*'s house [Jewish grandmother] as there was no room for me, then come home each morning to take my younger siblings to school. Not that I had any idea I was poor. During the Depression, everyone was in the same boat, you see.'

'How old are you?' I asked in confusion, taking in her staff overalls.

'I'm ninety-four, the young one!' she told me with a playful wink. 'I work here, volunteering twice a week, and I still get up at half-past six for my Saturday job.'

'Do you think you'll ever give up work?' I ventured.

'Give up work?' she scoffed. 'Why? I'm still young.'

With that, the nonagenarian bustled off and I scurried after her in hot pursuit. On our way to the 'memory room' – a beautifully soothing room entirely furnished in 1930s style, complete with art deco mirrors and a wireless – we passed a dartboard with a photograph of Justin Bieber's face skewered to it. I stopped and stared in disbelief.

'What, you think we sit around playing bridge all day?' said Marie with a gleeful laugh. She led me to Beatty, who was sitting with Sally, a performing poet, the baby of the group at ninety-two, and Renee, another sparkly-eyed ninety-one-year-old, born in the old Jewish quarter. Sitting at the next table, devouring a hot lunch, was a 100-year-old communist. Max Levitas is another veteran of the Battle of Cable Street and an East End legend.

Yards from him was a softly spoken ninety-one-year-old gentleman called Henry Glanz. As a fifteen-year-old, Henry was the last child on to the Kindertransport evacuation train. He crossed the border into Denmark hours before German forces invaded Poland on 1 September 1939, leaving behind his family, none of whom survived the Holocaust.

The history contained within the walls of that room was astounding. But look who else is here – Beatty's childhood best friend Millie, whom she last saw playing knock down ginger in 1929.

'I knew it was her the minute she walked in,' says Beatty, shaking her head as she considered their remarkable reunion.

Today, Millie Finger is an immaculately groomed 100-year-old, who has tragically outlived her only daughter and grandson.

'It was hard in those days,' Millie says, recalling the Depression that forced her apart from Beatty. 'People would do anything to earn a few shillings. People were starving.

'We had it terrible, lived in one room, five of us at one time. You never got help like you do now. Never. Bread tickets saved us from starvation some days, but we were always hand to mouth. My mum made cigarettes from home and my dad travelled to markets all round England looking for things to sell.

'I left school at fourteen and went straight to work, which was a little better. I started with eight shillings a week, sweeping up in the factory, and my brother, God rest his soul, Friday afternoon, when we got paid, used to wait for me outside the factory to take the envelope back to my mother. My eight shillings a week bought the family food, and a little more time. Against all this, we had the blackshirts constantly causing trouble, beating up the young Jewish men and spreading lies that Jews were making all the money. What money? We never saw any!'

Beatty laughs wryly and nods her head. 'They can have all my riches!'

Millie goes to the Jewish community centre in Stepney every day, where she can get a hot meal, have her hair done and, more importantly, be amongst friends.

'I don't know how I've reached a hundred,' she shrugs. 'Tough as old boots, I s'pose.'

Beatty and her friends have a combined age of around 475. Individually, they are spirited, together they are positively rambunctious, laughing and teasing each other, but under it all, there is an abundance of love, affection and community.

What do they put in the water round these parts? I felt as if I'd stumbled upon some lost tribe who'd found the secret to defying the ageing process, but in truth, I know. It's their battle against hardship, poverty and starvation, which ironically has secured their passage to long life. They've never over-eaten, surviving off a diet of nutrient-rich bone broths, then rationing. They've strived daily for work and they've walked everywhere. Until last year, Beatty was still walking up thirty-two steps to her third-floor flat aged ninety-nine.

'Children today are spoilt,' Beatty sighs and Millie, Sally, Renee and Marie nod in agreement. 'Too many choices and they don't work hard enough. Me, I've always worked hard and I didn't expect anything to land in my lap. I've lived through two wars and a Depression, and I've not one single regret.'

Since that first visit, I have returned many times, and each time I come away with my bag stuffed full of recipes, stock cubes, sweets and jam, and a heart brimming full of admiration.

Beatty was a small cog in a big wheel, helping to defeat fascism on home soil. In the maelstrom of the restless 1930s, she and her fellow East Enders found an imaginative and courageous way to face their enemies.

Contrary to popular belief, women were not only there that day; they were the backbone of the battle, as author and tour guide David Rosenberg explains.

'Many of the photographic images from the Battle of Cable Street show men but look closely and you see women, standing defiant by the barricades. At Gardiner's Corner, twelve-year-old Joyce Rosenthal and her friend joined a human wall to block the fascists, while other youngsters rolled marbles under police horses' feet. Thirteen women were arrested that day. One, who was taken to Leman Street Police Station, had her blouse ripped by a policeman who was going to beat her, but she looked straight at him and said: "I'm not scared of you." He backed away.

'The courage they showed seems extraordinary, but women have been absolutely crucial to East End struggles for better lives in the factories, on the streets and on their estates, from the matchwomen's strike in 1888 to the Tenants' Defence Leagues fifty years later.'

This particular battle had been won, but it was not enough to prevent the outbreak of war.

Three years after their victory at the Battle of Cable Street, Beatty was expecting her first child when news broke.

'. . . this country is at war with Germany,' declared the sombre voice that crackled from every wireless on the morning of 3 September 1939. The long struggle for peace had failed. Despite the warm weather, fear seeped through the streets like icy water. The East End was about to be hurtled headlong into its most cataclysmic period of history.

Girl Walker's Recipe

A nice young woman from the council came to do a talk at my club the other day about nutrition. On and on she goes, about what we need to be eating to stay healthy. My mate turns to me. 'Who knew, this is where we've been going wrong all these years!' I know how to eat to stay healthy, thank you very much! I'm eighty-four and I can still get on a bike. Meat. Potato. Veg. Eat that and move a lot and you'll be fine.

Girl Walker's Remedy

My mother-in-law was a gypsy and she taught me all the old remedies. Like this: grate an onion over a piece of gauze or muslin and let the juices drip into hot water. Knock that back and once it hits your boots, you'll never cough again. Nasty earache? Bake some salt in the oven, then sprinkle it inside a piping-hot flannel, roll it into a ball and press against your ear for ten minutes for instant relief and to draw out the toxins in your ear.

I suffered with terrible hay fever until I started to rub a little Vaseline in my nostrils.

Girl Walker's Pearls of Wisdom

My mate said this to me, and there's a lot of truth in it. 'Married life is hard. You cook for 'em, you clean for 'em, you do their laundry . . . Then when their working day is over, yours still ain't, 'cause you've gotta have sex with them!'

Like most East End women, I keep a tidy house and when it comes to housework, I always say this: 'Do the corners, and the middle will look after itself.'

2. Evacuation, September 1939

With her platinum-blonde curls and impudent, ice-blue eyes, Marie Walker from Stepney – known to the neighbourhood as Girl Walker – had the face of an angel, but the cheek of the devil. When occasion required it, she could scrap like a bare-knuckle boxer. Her cousins, George 'The Stepney Steamroller' and Billy 'The Blonde Bomber' Walker, would go on to carve out quite a name for themselves as prize boxers, and when it came to Girl Walker, the apple hadn't fallen far from the tree.

'I'm gonna give you a right hiding,' vowed the diminutive six-year-old, raising her fists to the older girl. What Girl Walker lacked in size, she made up for in attitude. 'You're giving me the needle,' she sneered. 'Now sod off to your side of the tunnel.'

She was referring to the Rotherhithe Tunnel, which linked the south of the River Thames with the north. Girl Walker and her mob were used to defending their little patch of Stepney from a group of invaders who came through it from Bermondsey looking for trouble.

'Rozzers!' yelled a distant voice and Girl Walker took to her toes. Skinny legs pumping, she ran through the maze of Stepney streets, until finally, confident she had shaken them off, she came to rest.

Perched on a sandbag, heart punching proudly in her chest, she surveyed her kingdom. York Square, sandwiched between Commercial Road to the south and Salmon Lane in the north, was a small patch of green in a seething, soot-caked neighbourhood. It was also the beating heart of her East End. It

49

had been drummed into Girl Walker for as long as she could remember that Stepney was *her* place; its people, *her* people. Her DNA flowed through every ancient cobbled street, square and alley. Auntie Winnie was at number 3 York Square, Auntie Ivy Margaret at number 5. In fact, every turning within a mile radius contained an auntie, by blood or otherwise.

A whole tribe of Walkers could be summoned up with a wink. The knowledge that she was the eighth generation of this tribe to be born in the East End Maternity Home and christened at ancient St Dunstan's Church in Stepney gave Girl Walker a sense of pride and belonging that was hard to put into words. But she knew she would fight to the death to defend it.

Lately, though, there had been an unsettled feeling over Stepney, the air cloaked with tension. Her three older sisters – Laura, Winnie and Alice – had chats that tailed off whenever she came into the room. One word seemed to dominate every conversation. *War.* Girl Walker didn't know, couldn't possibly know, what changes war would bring, or when those changes came, how swift and savage they might be. As the youngest girl, she knew better than to ask.

Sighing, she kicked angrily at a stone before heading for home. Flamborough Street, off York Square, was much like any other respectable East End terrace. The fronts went straight out on to the pavement, soot-blackened from decades of heavy industry. Carts made from old orange boxes, skates and home-made toys were strewn helter-skelter across the cobbles.

The street served as an extra room and Girl Walker, like every other East End nipper, would often leave the house first thing in the morning with a jam sandwich and a bottle of lemon sherbet, not to return until bedtime. Stray too far, or be saucy to a neighbour, and you'd get a clout round the ear, but this all added to the sense of security that Girl Walker wore around her like a soft blanket. She knew her place, and her place knew her.

Like those of every other East End street, the residents of Flamborough Street were poor. Not that any of them realised it – no one was significantly better off than anyone else, and no one bothered to lock their doors, for what would be the point? There was nothing worth nicking anyhow. Girl Walker did, however, get the sense that she was lucky. Her mum, Alice, was as tough as they came and a force to be reckoned with. Born into the brutal poverty of the Edwardian age in 1906, Alice had clawed her way to respectability and now ran Read's the butchers in Stepney, as well as lending money on the side, which made her a woman of standing in the community. Her bloodstained hands could butcher a lamb before it could bleat and there weren't many that didn't pay back what they owed on time.

Girl Walker's dad, John, known as Jack, was a fishmonger with a cockney language all his own. Thanks to their combined efforts, there was always plenty of meat, fish and vegetables for the pot.

A smile played on Girl Walker's lips as she entered her turning, the scent of wet washing and stew drifting out from open windows. Every morning, before the milkman had even done his morning round, one of the doors would be flung open and a mother would be on her hands and knees, vigorously scrubbing her front step, or attacking her patch of pavement with an old birch broom. God forbid you were last out – there'd be murder! Not taking pride in your home and your nippers meant you had no pride in yourself, and who wanted to be branded the 'dirty cow' of Flamborough Street? Besides which, if you didn't have sparkling windows and a clean step, Mercer's, who owned the housing around York Square, could evict you. Having said that, you didn't want to overdo it. Any woman putting on airs and graces and getting ideas above her station would be mocked for having 'curtains round her keyhole'.

As Girl Walker walked the length of the street, her pleasure at coming home gave way to a niggling feeling of disquiet. Today, sandbags obscured the steps; windows had blackout blinds in place of Nottingham lace. Barrage balloons hovered, where once kites swooped in the skies over Vicky Park. And yesterday, some fellas had even started digging up the park – trenches, they called them. It was all deeply unsettling, like biting into an apple, only to find it crawling with maggots.

A baby slept soundly in a pram outside number 24, tucked up snugly under a snowy white blanket, a piece of string attached from the door knocker to the wheels of the pram to stop it blowing away. If Flamborough Street decided on a name change, Incubator Alley might have been a good option.

Girl Walker felt something primal tug at her heart. Stepney was home. It was more than just ancient brickwork, faded wallpaper and wonky pipes that froze in winter; it was where she belonged, with all the other nippers.

As she neared number 2, her heart fell to her boots. Her mum was standing on the doorstep with another woman she recognised from the neighbourhood, hands on hips, her mouth as tight as a white-knuckle fist.

'There she is!' screeched the woman, resting arms on her shelf-like breasts. 'Your Girl Walker hit my daughter,' she announced, eyes glittering malevolently.

'This true, Babe?' Alice demanded.

Girl Walker knew better than to lie to her mum. 'Yeah, but she started it,' she protested.

'See!' crowed the other woman.

'Get inside,' Alice growled, pushing Girl Walker inside the dim passage.

'Ain'cha gonna hit her?' screeched her complainant.

'Not to please you, I won't!' Alice snapped, slamming the door shut in the woman's face. A second later, Girl Walker winced as her mother delivered a stinging clout round the back of her head.

'What've I told you about fighting, Babe? Now get in the kitchen for yer tea, I need to talk to you.'

Settled in front of a doorstep slab of bread and butter and a cup of tea laced with sterilised milk, Alice twisted the hem of her apron and surveyed her daughter. In the dim light, the flames of the gas mantle playing over her face, Alice's expression was unreadable, but her eyes were as dark as treacle.

'What is it, Mum?' Girl Walker asked, uneasily sipping at her tea.

She heard the snag of her mother's breath in her throat and then a tight click. 'You and your sisters, you've got to go away, Babe,' Alice said gruffly.

'Away? W-where?' Girl Walker stuttered.

'To the countryside.'

'But I don't wanna leave you, Mum,' Girl Walker protested, her eyes filling with hot tears. 'I wanna stay here, in Stepney.

Angrily, Alice dashed her youngest daughter's tears away with a tea towel.

'Pull yourself together, Babe. You've got to go. No choice. They've closed your school down. It's decided. Done.'

In that moment, Girl Walker felt as if the warped floorboards beneath her feet were crumbling away.

Don't cry. Please don't cry, she willed, pinching the back of her hand under the table. Growing up, she had never been allowed to cry. It wasn't the Walker way. Alice raised her to be tough. She had once made the mistake of calling out to her mum in front of the whole street:

'I love you all the money in the world and two bob.'

Alice's reply?

'I don't know where I got you from!'

Now Girl Walker was six – a big girl. Her future had been decided, and there was not the slightest thing she could do about it. Scraping back her chair, she fled. Outside, she leant against the wall and felt a sour lump travel up her throat. Late-August sunshine bathed the cobbles and the mothers of the street were settling in their usual spots outside their front doors, to shell peas into their apron laps while supping an evening glass of Porter. The Stepney Doorstep Society was gathering, their lively voices lapping at the brick walls. As the sun bent to the horizon, the skies over the cluster of smoking chimney pots were brilliant, striated with bands of gold and peach. Skeins of smoke drifting over from the factories were lit up a dazzling pink in the fading light.

How was she supposed to leave all this? Her street, her East End, her world, to go to the countryside, wherever the hell that was?

Squinting against the gathering dusk, she made out the stout figure of her nan, Old Boots, as she was affectionately known, her face wreathed in smiles. Not for the first time, Girl Walker wondered why it was that almost everyone she knew in the East End had not one, but two, and in some cases three nicknames. Take herself – her mum only ever called her Babe, her dad called her Snowy, Winnie called her Sooky, and Laura and Alice called her Marley. The only thing no one ever called her by was her actual name!

Old Boots was a 'good old girl' as they say in the East End, with bow legs and a penchant for snuff and other people's weddings. There was barely an East End wedding bash, or funeral, come to think of it, that she hadn't attended.

Mainly it was for the free food, but she was a talented piano player and could always be relied upon to hammer out a tune or two on one of the pianos that were invariably rolled out on to the cobbles on such occasions. Unbeknownst to Girl Walker's mum, she always took her granddaughter with her to Wilton's Music Hall just off Cable Street, a notorious place of ill repute, when she was employed to play the organ there. Girl Walker kept her trap shut about these visits and Old Boots bribed her silence with an arrowroot biscuit and a lemonade.

'All right, Babe,' grinned Old Boots, as she hobbled gamely up the street.

'All right, Nan. Where you been?'

'Funeral, two turnings up. Poor old girl.'

'You knew her?'

'Nah,' sniffed Old Boots, raking about in an old leather pouch for her snuff. 'But the family did her proud, put on a lovely spread.'

Girl Walker scuffed the toe of her boot and sighed, staring at a sparrow that was pecking at a patch of dried horse dung. Her nan lifted up her chin.

'What's up, Babe?'

'They're sending me away, Nan, and I don't wanna leave.'

'Leave it with me; I'll have a word with your mum.'

But Girl Walker knew once her mum's mind was set on something, there was no changing it.

As she stared at the baby in the pram, she wondered if she tethered herself to the front-door knocker with a piece of string, she might also be allowed to stay at home.

The next day, Girl Walker felt like a rock in a streaming torrent of water as she stood clutching her gas mask and a small case, amongst her three sisters. Excited children and nervous mothers bumped and rocked all around her. Even with her sisters, she felt anxious. Nervously, she fingered the edge of her cardboard label. She was all packaged up like a parcel, but where was she to be sent off to, and to whom?

Alice looked about the crowded school playground and sniffed uneasily as she tucked a stray curl under Girl Walker's woolly hat. She wasn't one for long or teary goodbyes, and Girl Walker could see her mother was itching to get back to behind her butcher's counter. Alice felt more at home amongst the sawdust and giant swaying carcasses than she did here in this frenzied, emotional turmoil.

'Right, girls, what have I always taught you?'

Girl Walker could repeat her mother's five strict codes of conduct in her sleep: Speak the truth and shame the devil. Work hard. Have a running-away fund. Never borrow money. If you lose your way, never ask a copper or a priest, ask a tramp, and then give him tuppence for a cup of tea. She repeated them dutifully. Satisfied, her mother nodded and kissed them all in turn briskly on the cheek.

'Be good . . .' and turning to her sisters, 'and look after Babe.'

I love you all the money in the world, Mum, and two bob, thought Girl Walker, silently pleading with her mum to cuddle her. But Alice was gone, stomping her way through the crowds. Girl Walker looked around the playground in bewilderment at all the weepy, misty-eyed goodbyes, and hugged her arms about herself.

On 1 September 1939, Operation Pied Piper began. One and a half million children, pregnant women and schoolteachers were evacuated in four days. A further significant number of children were also evacuated to friends or family in private arrangements. It was a colossal undertaking. Seventy-two London transport stations laid on special trains to distribution centres in the surrounding countryside. Never before had the country seen such mass mobilisation and movement of children. The effort was prodigious. The Anderson Committee had put complex plans in place in October 1938, almost a whole year before war broke out.

While it became compulsory to carry a gas mask and make sure your house was properly blacked out after dark, the Government had decided that evacuation should be voluntary and, unlike Alice, some mothers simply couldn't countenance being parted from their children. Many East Enders told me that during the war, they had remained in London right by their mother's side, with the prevailing belief being, 'If we die, we all die together.'

At the beginning of the war, or as it later became known, the bore war, with no real action occurring anywhere but at sea, to civilians on the home front 'safety' was a subjective concept. To many mothers, safety was having your kids attached to your apron strings, not in a remote countryside billet.

But Alice clearly did not share those mothers' beliefs. Though unemotional in her approach, this steely woman resolved that evacuation was the only way to keep her daughters safe from harm.

As Girl Walker's train lurched out of Paddington Station some hours later, great plumes of gritty smoke billowing up over the London skyline, the kids in the train went wild. London might have been choked with bereft mothers, but inside the train, East End nippers were behaving like they were off on a beano! Cheers and whoops filled the carriage, hats and caps flew up in the air. Girl Walker's sister Alice squealed as she dropped her orange. Girl Walker stood stock-still, bewildered in the chaos.

Some 170 miles further west, in Torquay, another bewildered East End evacuee was struggling to come to terms with her new life. Eight-year-old Babs Clark and her big sister, Jean, thirteen, wished they were anywhere but on the English Riviera. They might have been in the so-called 'safety' zone, but it certainly didn't feel that way.

'Eat it!' ordered Babs' Aunty Ivy, dolloping the flaccid vegetable on to the plate in front of her with a wet slap.

Babs stared down and felt her stomach heave. This was the sixth night on the trot Ivy had served up the *same piece* of cold marrow, and now it was turning into a battle of wills. Glaring up at her aunt, she pushed the plate away and folded her arms.

'Well, you're going to go hungry then, child,' she replied, flicking her tea towel over her shoulder and turning round with a tight, self-satisfied smile.

Babs and Jean glanced at each other and shared a mutual look of suffering. If it was just lumps of soggy marrow, Babs could have borne it, but since they had arrived, her mum's brother and his wife, Ivy, had made it abundantly clear that Babs and Jean were neither wanted nor welcome at their new home in Torquay. It wasn't just soggy, week-old vegetables, it was the pushes, shoves and slaps that she served up alongside them. Babs cast her mind back to their tiny house in Shoreditch and wondered with a fierce scorch of homesickness what her mum, Bobette, and nan, Barbetta, would make of it.

Ever since she had come into the world in 1931, Babette, or Babs for short, had both the richest and poorest childhood on record. Rich in love, poor in the purse, but it had never seemed to matter, because somehow, her mum had always known how to make things better. God knows, she'd had a hard enough life herself. Bobette, known to all as Bobby, had been three months gone with Jean when her husband had been killed in the mayhem of the General Strike in 1926. He had been on the footplate of a lorry, directing it out of the docks, when a picket van had smashed into it. For some women, losing their husband when three months pregnant during the Depression, with no access to free medical care or handouts of any kind, would be enough to finish them off, but not for Bobby Rosena Britten. Born in 1900, this woman was made of a different calibre and it was the bitter fight for survival that turned Babs' mum into a matriarch. She hadn't cried. Instead, she'd picked herself up by the bootstraps and resolved to make a go of it.

Bobby moved in with her mum, and took over the running of her greengrocer's stall. After Jean arrived, she was brought up by Barbetta, while Bobby worked seven days a week hauling a barrow of veg around the streets of Shoreditch until eleven o'clock at night. Babs' mum was a tough old bird, with muscles any docker would be proud of. Fear of the workhouse drew her and her barrow out in all weathers and, in time, she saved enough to become a moneylender. Even a second marriage to Babs' dad, William Henry John Nichols, known as Nick, hadn't quelled Bobby's fear of poverty – or her fierce independence.

Bobby rarely talked of her past, or indulged in self-pity – crying was for other women, women with more time on their hands – but repressing her grief had left her with an unfortunate tic. Babs always knew when something was wrong when her mum let out a little dry cough. Like that warm August day last month when they had been walking down the street and Babs had spotted a large poster on the wall. One word had stood out over the rest. *War.* 'Here, Mum, what does that poster mean?' Babs had asked. Almost immediately, her mum did *that* cough and Babs wished she'd never asked.

Now, stuck down in Torquay with a cold and loveless aunt, Babs vowed to be as strong as her mum and nan. At every opportunity she got, she wrote letters to her mum, pleading with her to come and get them, but every time, Aunty Ivy got to them first and did a censoring job the British Army would have been proud of. It was Jean who finally managed to get word back to the East End and reveal the whole truth about poison Ivy.

'I've written to Mum, but given it to my teacher to send,' she whispered furtively to Babs late one night.

'How long do you think we'll have to wait?' Babs replied.

In the event, not long. Aunty Ivy's face was a picture when she wrenched open the door to find her sister-in-law standing on the other side, quivering with rage.

'What are you—?' she began.

'No one treats my Jean and Babsy like that!' Bobby interrupted, suppressing a dry cough. 'How dare you?'

The muscles Bobby had built up hauling heavy barrows about also, it turned out, came to good use when it came to protecting her daughters. The air turned blue as Bobby weighed in.

'Take that!' she screamed, drawing back her fist. Aunty Ivy hit the deck. The next day, Babs and Jean were safely ensconced in new lodgings with their mum.

'I'll not leave you again, girls,' Bobby reassured them. With Babs' dad working away as a driver in the Navy, Bobby decided it would be easier and safer if she were to stay in

Torquay with her girls. Babs didn't care where she was, as long as she was with her mum.

'Please, Mum, no more marrow, though,' she begged.

Babs wasn't the only one discovering the dark side of leaving the East End. Girl Walker's evacuation was rapidly turning into something like the plot of a penny dreadful.

'Get in that cupboard and don't move a muscle.' Her sour face and vinegary breath was the last thing Girl Walker saw and smelt before the door banged shut. A thick, impenetrable darkness engulfed her and almost immediately, she started to tremble, her feet knocking against a broom that was kept in the cupboard under the stairs. The door was flung open. Light flooded in.

'I. Said. Don't. Move.'

The woman who had taken in Girl Walker and her sisters four weeks ago smiled cruelly. Quick as a flash, she threw something on to her lap. A leopard-print slipper? Girl Walker's exhausted brain swirled. Thoughts rushed at her, woolly and disjointed. She'd had nothing to eat over the past twelve hours but a mouldy crab apple she'd found in the garden, and she struggled to make sense of anything. She was so hungry. So tired.

'If you move again, that slipper will turn into a real-life leopard,' her host goaded, poking her hard in the chest. 'And GOBBLE YOU UP!'

Wrenched from the life she knew, and dropped into this home in Windsor, Girl Walker was utterly traumatised. It had started with sharp kicks under the table from the lady charged with her well-being, but as the days progressed, this strange woman seemed to get a sadistic pleasure out of inflicting pain and suffering.

Girl Walker stayed in the cupboard for hours, drifting in and out of sleep. As she slept, she dreamt of Flamborough Street, of the doorstep society mums, the street games of hopscotch and Hi Jimmy Knacker, of Old Boots bashing out the tunes. But mostly, she dreamt of her mum and, in her dreams, she vowed to make it home. One phrase rang out loud and true in the darkness: 'Speak the truth and shame the devil.'

Finally, Alice found her and with a gasp, hauled her out of the cupboard.

'I wanna go home,' Girl Walker whimpered to her big sister.

Without a word, Alice drew her up the stairs, her body rigid with anger. The foster 'mum' loomed out of the darkness, a guttering candle in her hand, a shawl draped round her shoulders, and Girl Walker shrank back.

'She's coming to bed with me,' her sister snarled.

Without a word, she turned and shut the door to her bedroom.

While Girl Walker waited and prayed word would reach home, things went from worse to nightmarish. The tickling on her head that had been troubling her soon developed into a full-blown itch.

'Impetigo,' announced the doctor.

Girl Walker felt a deep shame sweep over her as a nurse at the clinic shaved off all her beautiful, treasured blonde curls and smeared her scalp with a thick green paste that signalled loud and clear, she had 'the itch'. Back home in the East End, respectable mothers fought a continuous battle against bugs and were scrupulous in their hygiene – anything to avoid having to send your kids to the dreaded Cleansing Station. If her mother could see her now, she knew she'd have a blue fit. There was no greater shame.

Days bled into weeks, or was it months? Girl Walker gave up counting. The only thing that gave her any comfort was the certain knowledge that one day, her mum would come and rescue her from this hellhole. And it wasn't just her mum she missed, it was her East End kingdom. There were no street markets, no nippers playing knock down ginger, no washing flapping on the line here in Windsor. Where were the barrows piled high with meat, fish and clothing, the pub on every corner, and the quarrels and laughter? She stared out the window. Nothing but row after row of identical pebbledash houses huddled under a curdled sky. Stepney was only twenty-five miles away but it might as well have been in another country.

As she drifted off to sleep, Girl Walker thought she was imagining it. But as she blearily came to, the noise from outside grew louder. It sounded like . . . No! It couldn't possibly be. A woman's voice, getting louder and more agitated by the second.

'Girls! Get your things packed and get yerselves down here. NOW!'

Unbeknownst to Girl Walker, one of her sisters had been caught nicking and the police had been summoned, her mother ordered to come from London. She was up in seconds, her heart thumping as she cast off her coverlet and ripped aside the blackout blind at the bedroom window. There, stood on the patch of lawn outside the cottage, was five foot two inches of anger wrapped up in a scratchy wool coat. Her mum! Relief coursed through her as she leapt from the bed and bundled her meagre belongings into her small case.

As she charged down the stairs and out to the front of the house, she longed to throw herself headlong into her mum's arms, but that was impossible. Alice had the landlady in a tight headlock and was marching her towards the pebble-dash wall of the small cottage. Girl Walker had never seen her mum so angry. Her mouth was clamped shut in a tight line and she blew noisily out of both nostrils.

'How dare you lock my daughter up?' Alice said icily, her voice dangerously low.

'I . . . This is preposterous! I did nothing of the sort,' the landlady spluttered in a reedy voice.

'Let her go lousy, would ya?'

'Of course not . . .'

'Where's her f***ing hair then?' Alice roared.

Girl Walker trailed her hands over the top of her shorn head.

'She's a liar,' squeaked the landlady.

Girl Walker winced and stepped back. Alice could see through people like an X-ray and the one thing she wouldn't stand for was being lied to.

God knows Girl Walker had had enough clouts from her mum over the years for being saucy, but she knew it was nothing compared to what was about to be dished out. Revenge: Stepney-style.

Blackout blinds the length of the street twitched and a hushed silence descended over the neighbourhood. The landlady's face made contact with the wall with a sharp thud. The flesh on her cheek grated off like cheese as Alice calmly rubbed her face, first one way, then the other, the entire length of the pebbledash wall.

'That's for what you done to my girls,' Alice said when she'd finished, dropping the landlady like a sack of spuds on the floor and dusting off her hands. 'Nobody hurts my kids and gets away with it!'

The landlady was hysterical. Pieces of pebbledash were embedded in her cheeks, and a steady stream of blood and snot spattered on to the grass. But try as she might, after the weeks of pain and torment that woman had put her through, Girl Walker couldn't summon up an ounce of sympathy.

It was inevitable, but a police constable was on the scene in moments, blowing on his whistle.

'Come on, Mother, let's calm down, shall we?'

'Don't you "Mother" me!' Alice vented, giving way to her anger. 'That woman is wicked. Look at the state of my daughter!' she bellowed, pointing a finger at Girl Walker's head.

The landlady screamed hysterically as Alice called her all the names she could lay her tongue to. The suburbs had never seen such a dust-up. The constable shook a weary head.

'I'm taking you to the station and putting you on the first train back to East London.'

At first Alice looked as if she were going to go quietly as the constable ushered them to the car, but at the last moment, she turned, and drawing back her fist, she slammed her bunched knuckles firmly into the landlady's face, delivering such a knockout blow Girl Walker could have sworn she heard her back teeth rattle.

'Go on, then,' Alice said, calmly turning to the copper and offering her stretched-out wrists. 'F***ing nick me. Then nick her, and we'll see who comes off worse.'

Thus, Girl Walker's evacuation came to an abrupt end. Knowing when he was up against sterner stuff, the police constable declined Alice's offer and instead, bundled them in the car, gunned the engine and delivered them as fast as he could to the nearest station. Many, many hours later, Girl Walker returned home to her beloved Flamborough Street.

Seventy-nine years on, she hasn't strayed far – less than a mile, to be precise. Girl Walker, or Marie as she is known these days, hasn't changed, but the world around her has. The East End community she grew up with has all but gone, the teeming streets replaced with soulless luxury housing and glass corporations. York Square and the streets surrounding it remain, however, listed and protected, but sadly the house prices put it way out of reach of the average East Ender. Today, characters like Old Boots have vanished, to be replaced with bearded trendies sipping lattes. But eighty-five-year-old Marie remains, indefatigably defending the streets she loves, bristling cockney pride running through her like a stick of rock. She is a true child of the East End.

We meet after she answers an advert I've placed in a local paper, asking for those with memories of the old East End, and the first time I catch sight of her, she is standing outside her home, vigorously scouring her wheely bin with hot soapy water.

'Why does no one clean their bins any more?' she asks me, before I'd even had a chance to say hello. 'I do this out here so it encourages others to raise their standards. In the old days, within two minutes of my doing this, every woman on the street would be out scrubbing her step.'

Marie and I have since become friends and she never fails to make me laugh with her sage observations on life. On the expensive luxury housing complex casting a shadow over her home, she remarks, 'I wouldn't give you tuppence for it.'

The only way Marie is leaving the East End is in a box.

'My granddaughter bought a beautiful house out in the countryside, with a little cottage next to it. "That's for you, Nan," she said. "Does it have a shovel?" I replied. "No, why?" "'Cause if I move out here, I'd have to kill myself and

66

you'd have to dig a hole in the grounds to bury me in. What the hell am I gonna do in the countryside?"'

In the East End, she visits a number of LinkAge Plus clubs weekly where she can play bingo and darts, but Marie's at her happiest when she's meeting new people.

'I'm always out and about,' she says, her blue eyes gleaming with a reckless mischief. 'The other day, I took myself down the South Bank, and as soon as I spotted a man with a flag, I jumped on the back of the tour sharpish. Got myself on the London Eye for free! Done a couple of nice theatre trips that way too an' all. Who's gonna suspect a grey-haired grandma?'

Marie chuckles when she recalls her mum calling her a saucy mare. She still is one today, in the loveliest way possible. No one makes me laugh like she does and, despite the lack of education due to the closure of her school during wartime, she is also whip-smart. But none of this reaches to the centre of her charm.

She is clearly the head of her family, and her two daughters, son, six grandchildren and five great-grandchildren adore her. Their lives are tightly entwined and she sees her family regularly when they come up from their homes in Essex and Kent to visit.

'Family is everything,' Marie insists. 'You have to look after them, but I always say, don't put your kids before your husband!' She leans forward conspiratorially. 'They'll grow up and move out, and where does that leave you, if you've neglected your husband?'

The closing of her school, the bombing of her streets, the decimation of her family and neighbourhood – Marie firmly blames it all on one man: Hitler. Despite this, there is no rancour in her heart.

'Don't get me wrong,' she says, shaking her head. 'For years, I hated the Germans. I once threatened never to speak to my daughter again if she went on holiday to Germany, but then a funny thing happened. I got chatting to a German fella at Fenchurch Station. "The last time I spoke with an English woman, she spat in my face," he told me. He was ever such a nice man and the more we spoke, the more I realised, they never wanted that war, any more than we did. So I says to him: "I'll let bygones be bygones if you will."'

Marie and her mystery German kissed and with that single kiss, a lifetime of hatred and bitterness was eased.

'He walked off with tears in his eyes, and so did I,' she concludes.

But of all the staggering events Marie has lived through, the Government evacuation scheme, which forced her apart from her people, was one you sense she will never recover from. It seems incomprehensible today that children could be packed off to church halls and strangers allowed to take their pick of them.

A look at the newspapers of the time reveals the propaganda surrounding the scheme: 'If I had been a little boy or girl, I would rather have enjoyed yesterday's evacuation,' gushed a reporter in the *Daily Herald* at the beginning of the first phase. 'Is there a child in the world who does not like (a) picnics, (b) train journeys, and (c) mysteries? Yesterday, a, b and c were all rolled together in an alphabet of excitement.'

Many did have a wonderful experience, staying lifelong friends with the people they were billeted with. It's equally true that many did not.

One eighty-seven-year-old lady wept silent tears as she told me of the serious sexual abuse she suffered as a nine-year-old evacuee. 'Sorry, dear,' she apologised, plucking a white handkerchief from the sleeve of her blouse, 'but I still think about it most days.'

'Evacuees had a major impact on rural communities. The idea of all the evacuees being taken in by the middle classes in the countryside is something of a myth,' says Professor Martin Parsons, who interviewed over 5,000 former evacuees to establish the Centre for Evacuee Studies at the University of Reading.

'The majority were taken in by agricultural labouring families, so living in a cottage with an earth floor, no electric or hot water and a privy in the garden was a shock to many of the children. In addition, for some of them, it was also hard work. Unfortunately, as a result of this, a few children were abused and overworked.

'Although the Government implemented the evacuation scheme for what they believed to be the right reasons, it was totally unaware at the time about the long-term effects it would have on the children and their families.

'Research indicates that the psychological effects of separation extend to three generations. Many evacuees and parents failed to reconnect after the war, especially in situations where the children had been away for the whole duration and where the standard of living they had experienced with their hosts was better than at home. Many of the children had gone away as youngsters and returned as adolescents and some found it difficult to settle down, to the extent that some returned to their former evacuation areas to find work.

'The sociological pressures, especially in areas with a strict "stiff upper lip" mentality like the East End of London, made it very difficult for mothers to show their real emotions about being separated from their children.

'A significant number of ex-evacuees have spent the rest of their lives searching either for a home, a lost childhood or something intangible. Sadly, despite their resolve, few evacuees remained unscathed.'

Psychological damage aside, some evacuees were in reality no safer in their new countryside homes than they were in the cities, especially those located in Bomb Alley in Kent, and also – as Babs, Jean and Bobby were about to find out to their peril – in Torquay.

It was a chilly autumn day on the English Riviera, just the sort of day to blow out the cobwebs, Bobby decided. Babs had put the trauma of her experience with Aunty Ivy behind her and was enjoying the fresh tingle of sea air on her cheek as she gazed up at the fat loafy clouds patching the pale-blue sky. Suddenly, from those clouds, two planes came out of nowhere and flew down low over the beach.

'Look, Jean, what are those funny sparks coming out of them?' Babs asked.

'They aren't sparks, they're bullets,' Bobby shouted over the roar of the engines, pushing her daughters down on to the sand. Turns out they were two German Messerschmitt planes and they were machine-gunning everyone on the beach. Praying for dear life, Babs pressed her face into the sand as the deafening thud of bullets sprayed up sand around them.

When it was safe to get up, Babs felt her legs wobble as she stared in bewilderment at her mum.

'Sod that,' Bobby sniffed as she brushed the sand off her coat, 'we'll be safer off back in the East End.'

But as Bobby packed their belongings and the girls finally headed back to the East End, they had no idea how wrong they were. For Babs and her sister Jean, life was set to take a blood-chilling turn.

On a cloudless and picture-perfect Saturday afternoon in September 1940, the skies above the south of England suddenly darkened. People who were quietly going about their business shopping, mowing their lawns or basking in the drowsy sunshine stared upwards at the unfamiliar yet horrifying sight: 348 German bombers escorted by 617 fighters were heading directly towards London. The Blitz had begun.

Gladys' Recipe

Blackberry and Apple Crumble

Blackberry picking is one of the simple pleasures in life. Never buy them when you can pick them. Rationing taught us to plunder nature's pantry. Once you've picked them, put them in a bowl of salted water to kill all the maggots and flies.

1. Preheat the oven to 200°C/400°F/Gas 6.
2. Peel, core and chop three cooking apples into small chunks.
3. Layer the apples, blackberries and sugar in a large pie dish.
4. Place 8oz flour in a large bowl and then rub in 6oz butter until it resembles breadcrumbs. My mother used to get chopped suet from the butchers and that would add a lovely flavour to cooking. Add 4oz oats and 2oz sugar and mix through.
5. Use a spoon to sprinkle the crumble topping evenly over the fruit. Bake for 45 minutes.

Gladys' Remedy

My mother swore by two things. Andrews Liver Salts to clear out your kidneys and Syrup of Figs to keep you regular.

Gladys' Pearls of Wisdom

Everyone's for themselves these days. When was the last time you sat back and reflected on what you've done for others?

3. The Blitz, September 1940

Bedtime. Eight-year-old Gladys Hale was tucked up beside her brother John, but sleep was impossible: sirens screamed, pom-pom guns boomed and, over it all, she could hear the sickening drone of the German bomber. The drone grew louder . . . closer . . . louder still. Gladys clamped her hands over her ears and whimpered. Her skull felt like it was about to crack open.

WHOOSH!

Gladys sat bolt upright. What the . . . ? She tried to breathe but the air was red-hot and choked with acrid smoke. As the dust cleared, she gazed about in dismay. Their iron bed was crushed and mangled under bricks and masonry. One of the bedroom walls was missing.

Gladys turned to John. Two white eyes stared back petrified from a face encrusted with soot.

'W-what happened?' she stammered. Arms reached out, scooped them up. Gladys' mother stood quivering with fear the other side of the bedroom door, unable to confront the possibility that her children had been killed. So it was a neighbour who reached in and plucked Gladys and John from the debris.

'There, there,' she soothed.

'F*** you, Hitler,' Gladys swore, immediately clamping a guilty hand over her mouth.

Gladys' reaction was understandable. She had, after all, just been bombed in her bed.

Gladys lived on the Grosvenor Estate in Westminster

with her mother Mary, her father Jim who was a bus conductor and her six siblings. Until war had come, there had been a familiar, gentle rhythm to a life lived in the shadow of Parliament. Turning a skipping rope with her pal Mary on the street after school. Swimming on a Saturday at the handsome tiled baths on the Buckingham Palace Road; feasting on shrimps, winkles and whelks on a Sunday.

All their groceries were purchased fresh on a daily basis: bread from the baker's, milk from the little Welsh dairy, even salt and vinegar were bought from a man on a horse and cart, who came round calling his wares. 'Penny a pint of vinegar. Ha'penny a lump of salt.'

Every penny was watched and worked for and Mary had her standards and a fierce pride. It had been drummed into Gladys that a respectable family *never* lived beyond their means, *never* borrowed money, and certainly *never* purchased anything that they could make themselves.

After the first night's bombing, their home was patched up and schoolgirl Gladys learnt a sobering lesson: war is cruel and relentless. The Luftwaffe returned that night, and the next and the next to deliver their deadly cargo of bombs. A veil of nervous exhaustion fell over the neighbourhood and the air was thick with the stench of death. There was a brick shelter right outside on the courtyard, but Gladys' mother wasn't taking her chances in any of those filthy things. 'If it's going to get you, it'll get you,' was the matter-of-fact mantra she lived by. When the bombers got too close for comfort, Gladys and her siblings hid under the bed.

Each morning, the women and kids of her neighbourhood would be out sweeping up the glass, arranging the debris into piles, attempting to create order out of chaos. For mothers like Mary, it wasn't just a case of keeping her kids alive night after night; it was also the daily grind of trying to find running water to boil for a cup of tea, or juggling rations to stretch to many hungry mouths. Amongst the mothers of the Grosvenor Estate, anger was festering like a cancer.

One Friday, Gladys came in to see her mother and father huddled over the wireless.

'*Germany calling . . . Germany calling . . .*' rang out a strangely nasal voice. Traitor William Joyce, also known as Lord Haw-Haw, had moved from England to Germany and was doing his level best to demoralise and depress the nation with his propaganda broadcasts from Hamburg. Back in 1936, Joyce lived in Britain and was a rabid supporter of fascism and a key member of Oswald Mosley's British Union of Fascists.

'Hello, you lot in your stinking rat holes,' he jeered.

Rat holes? Something inside Gladys hardened. 'The only rat is you!' she shouted, shaking her fist at the sky. 'We'll show you, Hitler!'

'That's enough,' Mary sighed, turning off the wireless, her face doughy with exhaustion.

Gladys wasn't the only one close to breaking point. Eight days after the Blitz broke out, on 15 September 1940, the fear, the deprivation and the danger swirled together to bring matters to a boiling point.

Out on the balcony, a local lady by the name of Mrs Herd was crying her eyes out. 'It's my Ernie,' she sobbed, holding aloft a telegram. 'He's been killed.' Ernie had been a prisoner of war in Germany and had been killed during a British bombing raid.

A group of neighbours had gathered round to comfort her. Suddenly they were interrupted. A shriek tore across the flats.

'There's a Jerry coming down!' shouted a young boy standing in the courtyard.

The group gazed up at the dirty sky towards nearby Vincent Square. A figure suspended from a parachute drifted down.

'The wing's fallen in Flat Iron Square,' yelled the boy excitedly.

The air suddenly became electric as, one by one, doors along the balcony flew open. Women in wrap-around aprons and headscarves started to trickle out, and Gladys watched in fascination as an angry lynch mob of housewives formed in front of her very eyes. Mouths tightened to slits, fists bunched into balls, the air over their flats turned blue, then black . . .

'Let's get him,' one muttered darkly, her knuckles turning white as she gripped her broom handle.

'What we waiting for?' asked another. Running inside her flat, she grabbed a coal shovel.

There was a small stampede as the women of the neighbourhood ran in the direction of nearby Kennington, armed with brooms, shovels, brushes and sticks, while Gladys and the neighbourhood kids ran the other way to claim the wing. The thud of feet on the hard ground echoed up the balcony. And then they were gone, anger and adrenalin pulsing in their wake.

Individually, these women were tough. Together, they were terrifying. Gladys shuddered to think what would happen when they caught up with the pilot.

One woman reached him first and with an angry cry of, 'That's for my boy at Dunkirk!' smacked him hard with her coal shovel. Oberleutnant Robert Zehbe was already wounded when he parachuted down in Kennington. He struggled to his feet and tried to run, but his harness was too much for him and the lynch mob laid into him, months of anger, grief and fear coalescing into a burning ball of hate. This pilot might not have been responsible for the death of so many sons on the blood-drenched sand of Dunkirk, or the bomb that nearly killed Gladys in her bed, but he was German, and that was good enough.

According to eye-witness reports in the South London press, police constables from a temporary station across the road tried to break through the mob, but they were flung back. Eventually, an Army lorry drew up and half a dozen soldiers with fixed bayonets jumped out and forced a way through the crowd. They rescued the German airman and took him under armed guard to a nearby hospital, but he died the following day.

The incident was the talk of Gladys' neighbourhood for weeks to come. Her own mother hadn't got involved, but she refused to sit in judgement on them either. Despite her tender years, Gladys understood. Perhaps because of the destruction of her neighbourhood, and the decimation of what was left of her childhood, she understood – and felt – the rawness of their anger and grief. And there and then, she knew. The Germans may have started it, but if the women of her neighbourhood were anything to go by, they would sure as hell finish it.

Three months into the Blitz, on 8 December 1940, Gladys' pal Mary, along with her mother, brother and around forty to fifty others, were killed when the street shelter they had been sleeping in took a direct hit. At a mass funeral, an exhausted and shell-shocked neighbourhood gathered around to honour their dead, watching bleakly as rows of cardboard coffins were loaded into the backs of charabancs (motor coaches) and taken to be buried. What struck Gladys most was the starkness of the burial. No handsome black horses to pull the coffin as there had been before the war, no flowers – just plain cardboard coffins, covered in Union Jack flags.

Gladys felt hatred blacken her heart as they drove off. What had sweet little Mary ever done to hurt anyone? She was only eight years old. Where was the sense in any of it? She had been taking refuge in the supposed safety of a shelter, while Gladys, under her bed at home, survived. Then another, more macabre thought occurred to her. She had heard that most of them were blown to bits. Was Mary even in that coffin?

There was little pity from her mother over the death of her best friend and Gladys quickly learnt to put up and shut up. No one else was complaining, after all. Mary did not express herself through hugs and kisses, but she could show her love through cooking.

'Jam tart,' she said, setting down the rare treat on the table with a flourish at teatime a few weeks after Mary's death. Gladys eagerly picked up her spoon, just as the siren started up. Jerry's timing was immaculate.

'Under the bed,' Mary muttered, ushering them through into the bedroom for the now familiar routine.

The noise was terrific tonight, even more so than usual. The drone of the German bombers was followed by whistles and then the horrendous boom as the bomb made impact. An almighty BOOF shuddered the foundations and Gladys squeezed her eyes tight.

'Please God, don't let it be us,' murmured Mary from her chair next to the bed, 'but God help the poor soul who got that.'

After a while, Gladys stuck her head out.

'Can I come out, Mum?'

'No,' came the reply. 'I do wish your father was here to help me. I need him here, instead he's outside helping others.'

Fifteen minutes later . . .

'Mum,' Gladys piped up again. 'I must go to the toilet.'

'Go on then, quickly!'

Crawling on her hands and knees, Gladys passed by the kitchen and was suddenly gripped by an overwhelming curiosity.

I've had enough of this, I'm having a look, she thought, pulling herself up.

Gladys stood transfixed at the kitchen window ledge, her pale-blue eyes wide with horrified fascination. A full moon hung in the sky, brushing the rooftops silver. Planes darted through the searchlights and a fierce crimson glow drenched the skies blood-red. It was too much for her brain to take in. Guns blasting. Barrage balloons. Panic, heat, movement.

A man's voice suddenly tore through the darkness.

'London's afire! London's afire!'

With a start, Gladys realised it was, too. Great tongues of flame roared into the sky, catching at the spire of a church opposite. The breath caught in her throat as it engulfed the building whole.

This is how the Great Fire of London looked, Gladys said to herself, before turning and crawling back to the bedroom.

'Mum, it's all red out there,' she gabbled as she scrambled back under the bed, to where her younger brothers and sisters were huddled, wide-eyed with fear. With Gladys safely back under the bed, Mary sat guard in a small wooden chair by the bedstead, quietly crocheting, as Hitler unleashed hell outside.

The Blitz began on what became known as Black Saturday: 7 September 1940. Over the following eight months, more than 43,000 civilians were killed in truly terrible ways. Babies were swept from prams by the force of bomb blasts, mothers were killed running to safety, girls like Gladys' friend Mary were buried in the supposed safety of brick street shelters, and whole city centres were obliterated. British citizens saw their streets transformed from a home front to a battlefront as the earth spewed blood and fire. Bombs crashed through the roof of Beatty's building in Whitechapel. They fell on the narrow streets of Girl Walker's Stepney, and they carpeted Babs' Bethnal Green. Death rained from the skies.

Gladys' memories paint a visceral picture of wartime women's anger reaching a boiling point. We may not agree with the lynching of a German pilot, but these authentic stories take the true temperature of the times, revealing what happens when frustration and fear spill on to the streets. Constantly being under fire shocked women out of their normal rhythms.

The Blitz was Hitler's attempt to bring Britain to heel. He believed it would have such a devastating effect on civilian morale that the Government would be forced to negotiate peace terms. But he underestimated the British character – and particularly that of our matriarchs.

It was 6.15 p.m. on Sunday, 29 December 1940, and 'moaning Minnie' – as the air-raid siren had been dubbed – went off, its mournful wail rising and falling over Flamborough Street. By now, the Walker family were well used to the Blitz, having endured three months of nightly bombardment. It never once occurred to Alice to take her children and leave the East End, especially not after the mistreatment of her youngest daughter during the first round of evacuation. Alice had faced down poverty and lived through the bombs of the Great War. The Blitz was just one more test to survive.

Sometimes, she and her girls sheltered under the railway arches, emerging tired and gritty-eyed into a smoky dawn. But tonight, as they were about to find out to their peril, was to be different.

Outside, it was a clear, frosty night and moonlight drenched the cobbles.

'Bombers' moon,' Alice muttered grimly, clutching her daughter's hand.

Girl Walker gazed up at the sky and felt her jaw drop open. A cruel full moon hung over the jumble of rooftops. Searchlights swooped through the skies, cutting great silver swathes through the night. Girl Walker blinked, then blinked again . . . More Jerry planes than she had seen since the Blitz began were flying overhead. You couldn't put a pin between them. As the last notes of the siren faded away, the bombs began to drop.

Incendiaries exploded like fireworks, flares blossomed and trembled. Just then, a strong westerly wind blew through the narrow East End street, bringing with it the distant clanging of fire-engine bells and an acrid stench. All the neighbourhood dogs started up.

'Run, Babe!' screamed Alice over the noise, and hand in hand they pelted up the street, past the heavily blacked-out Queen's Head pub and on. They drew level with the arches, already heaving with shelterers, but abruptly turned left.

'I'm taking you to Mrs Riley's.'

Girl Walker scarcely had time to digest this information before she was bundled down below ground and a door yanked shut over her head. The last she saw was her mum's face disappearing from view.

Bang! Blackness descended. A match crackled into flame, and a neighbour's face appeared through the darkness.

'All right, Girl Walker,' remarked Mr Lather, sucking hard on his pipe. 'Nice night for it.'

Girl Walker looked about the shelter. On 25 February 1939, the first of 2.5 million Anderson shelters had begun to be issued to people with gardens in vulnerable areas. Anybody earning less than £250 per year received a free shelter.

The one Girl Walker sat in was a stuffy, fetid hole. An oil lamp cast a flickering glow over the confined space. Immediately, she was put in mind of the cupboard under the stairs at her old billet in Windsor and felt adrenalin sluice through her veins.

Up above, she heard the unmistakable boom of bombs, followed by the distant thud and crump of a collapsing building, a noise which seemed to pass through bone and blood and lodge straight in the soul.

'Ooh, that one didn't have our name on it. Some other poor sod's copped it,' said Mrs Riley cheerfully as she got out her knitting. 'Sounds like we're in for a right hiding tonight, though, eh, Girl Walker! I said as much, didn't I, Mr Lather?'

Mrs Riley was right. Up above, German aircraft were dropping 10,470 incendiary bombs over the City of London, followed by 136 bombers, ready to deliver 127 tons of high explosive bombs. The night sky was so clear, Luftwaffe pilots could count the fires from their aircraft.

Soon, the whole City was burning and, thanks to the strong westerly wind, the fires soon joined together to form mighty white-hot conflagrations. The streets that had been engulfed by the Great Fire of 1666 were once more alight.

Ancient buildings and city walls groaned and crashed to the cobbles, blocking already narrow streets. St Paul's Cathedral took a battering as firewatchers worked frantically to extinguish the incendiaries that threatened to engulf its famous domed roof in clouds of smoke.

Over 9,000 firemen battled to save the City, but with a low ebb tide, they found it impossible to draw water from the Thames, and soon even the hoses began to burn. The City seemed doomed. And so too did Girl Walker as she trembled in the darkness, rigid with fear.

'How about a sing-song, see if we can't drown out them bombs?' suggested Mrs Riley. '"Run Rabbit Run", anyone?'

Her words were drowned out by a high-pitched whistling. It grew louder and louder, and in that moment Girl Walker knew. This bomb *did* have their name on.

The colossal blast seemed to lift the shelter from its earth foundations and the corrugated iron walls buckled and groaned. The pressure inside the Anderson changed, causing a vacuum that left her ears shrieking. When the noise gradually faded, it was replaced by a silent scream. *No. No. No . . .*

Mr Lather rattled the door to the shelter, but it was stuck fast. Mrs Riley's house and yard backed on to a railway siding. The bomb must have hit the train tracks.

'We must have the luck of nine blind bastards,' he muttered. 'Bet half the railway's on top of us.'

Suddenly, the walls of the confined space seemed to slide even closer together. Panic, dark and electric, filled the tiny space. Rather than being a safe, womb-like space, the Anderson now felt like a coffin.

'W—will they find us?' Girl Walker gibbered, gripping the edge of her seat, overwhelmed with claustrophobia.

'Course they will,' Mrs Riley soothed, giving her a cuddle. 'They'll dig us out, love, just you wait and see.'

Mrs Riley was a cheerful soul, and kept up her reassuring chatter, even when the oil light flickered out and died. Candles were lit and in the soft light she sang and rocked Girl Walker in her arms.

Mrs Riley rationed their sandwiches and a flask of cold tea to nibbles and sips, and a bucket was on hand for their toilet needs. The hunger and indignity she could cope with; it was the darkness she hated. When the candles finally burnt out, they were plunged into an underground coffin, so black she couldn't see a hand in front of her. Girl Walker fought back wave after wave of panic.

'Have they forgotten us?' she wept into the darkness.

'Course not,' Mrs Riley replied. 'We're going to be all right, girl, you'll see, they're coming for us. I'm gonna keep talking so you know I'm right here.'

Girl Walker lost track of time, as the shelter grew hotter and stuffier. She drifted into a fitful doze and woke to find herself clawing at the walls. Mrs Riley turned greyer by the hour, her cheeks hollowed out with exhaustion, and eventually even her cheerful patter began to dry up.

The darkness was endless, the silence stultifying. Girl Walker had the feeling she was slowly sliding into East End soil, as if roots had wrapped themselves around her ankles and were tugging her deeper into an inky pit. Was this hell? Was she dead? Only the rasp of Mr Lather's breath and the hot, marshy odour from the makeshift toilet told her she was still alive.

'I can't hear anything,' she croaked, as hours bled into

Pickets on duty
outside the
Estate Office

An apron-clad army. Rent strike pickets on duty outside the landlord's office during the Quinn Square rent strike.

Women on the barricades along Cable Street.

Three-tier bunks ran for miles up the length of the tunnel, sleeping thousands.

An underground shelter library. After Bethnal Green library was bombed, librarians calmly transferred 4,000 volumes underground.

The day after the Tube disaster in which 173 people were crushed to death, these central handrails were hastily installed to improve safety down the steps, but it came too late for the dead.

Even children proved their worth during the war years. Here are the Schoolboy Gardeners of Russia Lane converting bombsites into thriving allotments.

Holders of this ticket were entitled to sleep in one of the 5,000 three-tier bunks that ran along the tunnels at Bethnal Green Underground Station.

Metropolitan Borough of Bethnal Green

Valid until ....

Not Transferable. No. **4**.......................

LONDON CIVIL DEFENCE REGION

SHELTER TICKET

National Registration No. ....

Name..................................... Age.......

Full Postal Address ....

....

Nature of Employment.......................
Signature   Date

....

Shelter at...
Bunk No. N. 181........ Between **5** p.m.
                              and **7** a.m.

                                    Controller.

The woman I believe to be my namesake, the other Kate Thompson, who got involved in the 1938 Quinn Square rent strikes, seen here (circled) on a beano in 1935. Eight years later she was dead.

Beatty and John Orwell, proudly showing off their first child, June, born in November 1939, just two months after the war began.

Beatty proudly clutching the banner (left) as she marches in support of the Labour Party in Bethnal Green. Today, she is believed to be the longest-serving member of the Labour Party.

Beatty, John and June, enjoying a rare moment off from the war.

Proud and defiant – a young Marie Joseph who was there amongst the giant crowds at the Battle of Cable Street in October 1936.

All togged up in their finest. Girl Walker (right) with her pal Sheila, out and about in the East End.

A young Girl Walker on a day trip, replacing Stepney with the seaside.

Girl Walker's formidable mum, Alice, behind the counter of her butcher's shop in Stepney.

Babs Clark (left) with her mum, Bobby (centre), and older sister Jean (right). In trying to protect her daughters, the war pushed Bobby to the limits of her endurance.

Kay Coupland was just eighteen when she joined the Women's Auxiliary Air Force (the WAAF) on ambulance duty in the East End. Seen here on her wedding day.

Doctor Evelyn Goldie, a much-loved woman doctor who practised in Poplar from 1930 to 1981, reaching an almost legendary status in the borough for her dedication to her patients.

days. 'They're not coming for us. Maybe they think we're dead?' An awful thought occurred to her: perhaps everyone up above was dead!

Mrs Riley squeezed her hand weakly as hope slipped away.

But Girl Walker was wrong. Above ground, the air was thick with acidic yellow smoke roiling into the horizon as rescue parties worked frantically to free them. A crane had been drafted in to lift a heavy metal railway girder that had fallen over the top of the shelter. The whole street had gathered round to watch.

By the time the door was wrenched open, Girl Walker was nearly blinded by the sudden brightness as it streamed down into the Anderson. Then there were hands, pulling her free, wrenching her into the light, and a great cheer went up. She felt reborn.

Girl Walker had gone down that shelter on the evening of Sunday, 29 December 1940, and emerged *three days later* into the gritty dawn of New Year's Day 1941.

Standing round the entrance to the shelter stood the entire street, including her mum, dad, Old Boots and her sisters, Laura, Alice and Winnie. Fortunately for her sisters, they had been sheltering with other neighbours along Flamborough Street. Two in five houses in Stepney were damaged through the Blitz. Statistically speaking, Flamborough Street was bound to cop it. Why, Girl Walker wondered as she staggered free, did she have to be the one member of the family to be buried alive?

'Come here, Babe,' said her mum at last, her voice cracking as she pulled her into her arms. Her apron stunk of blood, smoke . . . and fear.

Alice – notorious moneylender, butcher and all-round

tough matriarch of Stepney – still didn't shed a tear when her daughter was freed from the bombsite. But Girl Walker could have sworn she saw her bottom lip wobble. Just for a second.

Girl Walker turned back round to look at the shelter, and screamed. It was the stuff of horror flicks.

Mr Lather calmly took off his right leg. Half-slithering, half-rolling out of the shelter, he pulled himself to standing and hopped off back up the yard towards what was left of the house.

'Where's his leg?' she babbled hysterically, gripping her mum's arm.

'It ain't real, Babe,' Old Boots laughed, picking up his false leg, complete with sock, and waving it in front of her grand-daughter's face.

'He's got another one inside. I'll show you if you like!'

But Girl Walker was by that point, understandably, beyond reason. Mr Lather's false leg provided a farcical end to an intensely traumatic ordeal.

The Blitz was the first time women and children found themselves in the firing line. Never before had the popula-tion smelt death at such close quarters. But rather than buckle under the pressure, the 'gentler sex' as they were up until then regarded, were proving themselves in ways unimagin-able to today's generation.

Kay Coupland was just eighteen when she went from a job in dressmaking to working on ambulance duty for the Wom-en's Auxiliary Air Force (the WAAF) the same night Girl Walker was buried alive.

'The twenty-ninth of December was particularly bad for fires – even the hoses were burning,' she recalls. 'We were sent on a job to a point in North London with sweeping views and, oh my! The whole of London was on fire! Countless churches and all the spires were blazing. Suddenly, there was a terrific clap of thunder and fingers of lightning lit up the sky. Rain came down in buckets, drenching the fires. It felt like divine intervention. "Now we'll see what God can do," I said to my colleague.

'There were more sad times to come,' Kay continues. 'My good pal, Joan, who worked with me in the WAAF, was killed soon after that night. One minute she was working right by my side on the switchboard and we were talking, the next moment, I turned around and she was dead on the floor with barely a mark on her. A piece of flying shrapnel had caught her in the neck. The tragedy is she had only been married a few weeks when her husband, a pilot in the RAF, had been shot down and killed during the Battle of Britain, and now she too was dead. I didn't have time to grieve for her or dwell on the dangers, I just had to get on with things. I wasn't brave,' she insists. 'I just had no choice.'

Kay's modesty about her work in the Blitz as an eighteen-year-old is humbling. For just under one year, she worked at the Eastern Fever Hospital in Hackney, ferrying casualties to hospital from the bomb-shattered streets of the East End. She has since settled in Blackpool, but the women of the East End left a profound impression.

'It was the East Enders I felt most sorry for,' she recalls. 'The raids were terrible in that quarter, but those proud cockney women were bloomin' marvellous. I'd never seen anything like the scenes I saw in areas like Bethnal Green and Stepney, with everyone pulling together. There was always a street "auntie" on hand, instinctively directing the clear-up operation, a big sister looking after a horde of kids while the mum went off to work in a factory. I even saw one young woman sweeping the glass off the streets in a siren suit, red lipstick and heels. That's real style!

'You had to hand it to them. They were poor, God love them, there was more week than money, but they were so proud, and they really knew the value of community, which served them well during the Blitz. I only found that in the East End, mind you, not the West End.'

Even when she was off duty, Kay still managed to find herself in the thick of danger.

'I was in the famous West End nightspot Café de Paris when it was bombed. It was nightmarish. I could see people's mouths opening as they screamed, but I was deaf. I left in a trance through a hole in the wall with my ears ringing. It was chaos. There were people running past carrying bodies, feet sticking out of rubble.'

However horrifying this sounds, the war did at least give Kay the opportunity to fulfil her ambition of working in medicine.

'At school in 1930, we had to write an essay entitled "What I Think the World Would Be Like in 2000". I wrote that everyone would have a telephone and travel by air – flying would be the thing. I also wrote I wanted to learn about foreign diseases.

'My teacher called me up and I read it to the class, who promptly rolled about laughing. I think they thought me very fanciful. My teacher wrote in my report: "Kay is prone to flights of fancy. Her essay made very interesting reading, but the poor child shall have to come back to earth."'

'Fanciful' Kay wasn't the only one proving her mettle in the dark crucible of the Blitz.

*

Dr Joan Martin also found herself thrown into the front line of treating casualties. Joan was twenty in 1936 when she became one of 60 applicants out of 150 to win a place at the Royal Free Hospital, the only London medical school at that time to take women. Joan began her clinical training at the hospital, which was based in Gray's Inn Road, London, just as war broke out.

As the blacked-out Metropolitan line train rattled down the tracks towards West London, Joan leant back in her seat and yawned, trailing her fingers through her Scottie dog Andy's coat.

It was Sunday evening, and she and Andy had spent the day at her parents' home in Ilford, Essex, and were returning to her student lodgings in North Kensington. Joan adored her parents, for it was they who had encouraged her to pursue her dream of becoming a doctor, and their sacrifices that were helping to make that dream become a reality.

Henry Martin, a devout Methodist minister, and his wife, Violet Pratt, a trained nurse, had devoted their lives to service and duty and encouraged their elder daughter to do the same. It had been Henry who had introduced Joan to real poverty, taking his daughter with him to visit sick and injured mill workers in his parish in Huddersfield, West Yorkshire, in the 1920s. The blackened sandstone buildings and shoe-less children, the strikes and the aching poverty, all had opened her eyes to the true nature of suffering. But it was the death of Joan's three close childhood friends, cut down in their prime, that had sliced the deepest. Polio, pneumonia and encephalitis claimed the lives of her friends one by one, without mercy.

'I don't want to have any more friends,' she had wept to her father. 'What's the point when they just die?'

Henry was a pragmatic man. When Joan was a young girl, he had shown her how to use a compass in order to be able to navigate her way through life. In the face of such bewildering grief, he had applied the same logic.

'Well, what are you going to do about it?' he'd replied simply.

There and then, a six-year-old Joan had resolved to find a way to make people better when they became ill.

Thanks to Henry and Violet's scrimping and saving – along with grants they had managed to obtain and a scholarship – eighteen years on, she had done it. Despite the privations of the war – or maybe even because of them – her heart was filled with a desire to help. Joan was poorer than she had ever been in her life. Each day, she budgeted sixpence for some cheese, an apple and a cup of coffee for her lunch in the hospital canteen, and one-and-sixpence for her evening meal in a little restaurant nearby. But hunger was a small price to pay to get the chance to become a fully qualified doctor.

Joan had watched as many of her fellow students suspended their training and moved out of London when the bombing began. She understood their fear, but she had given her word. Joan's deep faith in God had sparked a motto in her. At school, they had taken part in a symbolic passing of the flame ceremony at the end of each term. *May the spirit of this flame dwell in you, and kindle other hearts.*

This prayer resonated deep within her. No matter what, she would *not* leave London.

Suddenly, an enormous bang roused Joan from her thoughts and Andy leapt on to her lap. The tracks seemed to vibrate from the force of the explosion and the train juddered to a halt. A voice tore through the darkness.

'Farringdon's taken a direct hit. Evacuate the train!'

With her heart galloping, Joan and Andy followed the stream of other people jumping off the train. Outside, the stench of cordite hung over the tracks. Gingerly, she made her way over the greasy rails and on to the street. It was there that Joan was rendered speechless with fear. There were fires everywhere. It wasn't something she admitted to readily at work, but she had a deep fear of fire, ever since she had seen and smelt the burnt flesh of a child she had visited in hospital with her father.

Fighting down her panic, Joan looked up to the end of the street. One side of the road was a solid wall of flame. The deafening roar of water filled the air as a fireman battled to bring the rolling inferno under control.

'Get in a shelter,' ordered an ARP worker. 'There's one up the road.'

Joan followed the stream of passengers hurrying for the bomb shelter, but dogs weren't allowed in. There may have been a raid, but she wasn't about to leave Andy. No, there was nothing for it but to carry on home on foot. She walked on through the flames and bombs, her Scottie dog padding by her side.

'Let's keep going, eh, boy?' she said, her breath ragged in the smoky air. 'Just keep putting one foot in front of the other.'

Through the darkness loomed the figure of a sailor. On seeing Joan, he dropped his kitbag and pushed back his cap, bewildered.

'Do you know the way to Paddington?'

'Let's go together,' suggested Joan, reasoning that there might be safety in numbers. Back in 1940, walking through the darkness with a strange sailor wasn't considered respectable behaviour for a young woman, but the Blitz was ripping up the rulebook and so-called normal behaviour was pushed out the window.

The trainee doctor, the sailor and the Scottie dog carried on their journey through fire and rubble, afraid but united in their desire to stay alive and comforted by their mutual presence. By the time she made it home hours later and pushed her key into the lock, her face blackened with grime, Joan was beginning to learn important lessons about what she might be capable of. Over the course of the war, these lessons were to be pushed to the very reaches of her sanity, but for now at least, she was home safe.

The next morning, Joan was back on duty. During the Blitz, the Royal Free used only its ground-floor wards and these were only for casualties, the worst of whom, sadly, she was becoming more than used to seeing. The Blitz was rapidly turning her from a trainee doctor to a budding surgeon. Today, however, she was detailed to work at an outpatients' clinic near the hospital.

'Good morning,' sang out a clipped voice.

Consultant paediatrician Ursula Shelley was a tall, dark, striking woman who looked as if she had stepped straight out of the pages of *Vogue*. Her beauty hid a razor-sharp brain and a ferocious work ethic. The glamorous doctor had become something of a mentor to Joan.

'Right, let's get on with it, we've a lot to get through,' said Ursula.

Joan had no sooner started treating a mother and child than a bomb dropped nearby. Instinctively, she lunged forward, pushing the mother and child under her desk. The windows of the clinic splintered.

'Everyone all right?' called Ursula's voice from next door.

'Y-yes,' Joan called back shakily.

'Good,' she replied crisply. 'Get on with your work then.'

Bombs dropping nearby were not to delay patient care. Ten minutes later, a sister from the casualty department bustled in.

'What do you think you're doing?' she blazed. 'There are people with their guts hanging out in casualty. All medical staff are needed.'

A wartime medic must be prepared for all eventualities, Joan realised. Within ten minutes, she was back in the casualty department of the Royal Free, surrounded by frantic clergymen, blood and guts. The bomb had hit the Church of Scotland near the medical school where a conference was being held. Not all the clerics were behaving as coolly as Ursula under fire. One was on his knees in the middle of casualty, praying hysterically in his blood-soaked cassock, his face a mask of dust.

Ursula looked up, irritated, from where she was staunching the flow of blood from a puncture wound.

'Pray to God, man, but for God's sake, pray quietly.'

By the time the injured were patched up and the dead removed from the rubble of the church, Joan had been working flat out for over twelve hours. Not a drop of food or drink had passed her lips. She was bone-weary and hungry.

She felt a tugging on her shoulder. Turning, Joan took in a little old lady, coated in dust, who had been sitting patiently waiting to be seen. 'Doctor, don't you remember me?'

It was the lady who worked in the medical school canteen, who often slipped Joan a free doughnut which, despite only costing sixpence, was beyond her slender means. Joan smiled, and felt a rush of affection and relief at seeing the sweet old lady's face. Bomb blasts were odd things. In moments, you could travel from death and delirium, to reminders of pure humanity.

All the discomfort, the fear, the bone-numbing exhaustion and the horror she had witnessed, all were eclipsed by a purer sense of purpose. *This* was why she came into medicine. Her parents' sacrifices had not been in vain.

'Come on,' said Ursula with a weary smile. 'I'm taking you for dinner.'

Over the remainder of the Blitz, Dr Joan's calling was thoroughly tested. In the space of eight months, she narrowly avoided an exploding gas works and a parachute mine, helped to evacuate patients and rescue equipment from the hospital during a raid, and joined the London Ambulance Service, moonlighting at night, to earn extra money. Sleeping and eating went by the wayside, as the trainee doctor saved life after life after life.

As any fan of *Call the Midwife* will know, women have always played a critical role in the public health of East London. Viewers might not know, however, the story of Dr Evelyn Goldie, a much-loved woman doctor who practised in Poplar from 1930 to 1981, reaching an almost legendary status in the borough for her dedication to her patients.

Best known for her soft Scottish brogue, Dr Goldie knew the names of every single one of her patients and would go to extraordinary efforts to make sure everyone got the care they needed, including cycling through the Blitz and crossing the River Thames in an old rowing boat in the middle of an air raid to tend to them.

Evelyn Goldie qualified in her hometown of Aberdeen in

1926. In those days, apparently a woman was good enough to qualify as a doctor, but not to actually work as one! She had no choice but to move to London in search of work.

The newly qualified Dr Goldie arrived at the Methodist Mission in Commercial Road, East London, and stepped into a world of slums and poverty, but also immense courage and community. After four years there, she and another pioneering woman doctor, Minnie Stevens, set up a surgery in Poplar on the corner of Chrisp Street Market at 72 Grundy Street, on the site of an old barber's shop. Minnie left after three years but Dr Goldie stayed – for fifty-one years.

In Poplar, like the now-famous nursing sisters of Nonnatus House, St John the Divine, the suitably named Dr Goldie found her calling and quickly became a treasure to the community she served. Like the sisters, she delivered heartfelt healthcare to the poorest members of society.

'People would go daily to Chrisp Street Market, get their shopping and stop off at the doctor's. It was part of the social life of Poplar, and no one minded waiting,' her daughter Heather told me. 'Mother never had an appointments system or a receptionist or anything like that. She'd open her surgery doors at eight thirty a.m. and in they'd file. It was a case of first come, first served, but no one was ever denied care or turned away. She treated them all – including the Jewish, the Chinese of Limehouse, and the dockers and their families. The surgery door swung open and shut, until the last patient was seen at seven p.m. I remember waiting for her to come home. She rarely arrived before nine p.m., sometimes even staying overnight at the surgery on a camp bed. She truly was open all hours, never once refusing to see a patient.

' "Why are you late when you shut at seven p.m.?" I'd ask.

"I stay on until eight thirty p.m. in case anyone needs me," was the reply.'

And the people of Poplar did need her. Dr Goldie tended to outbreaks of smallpox, polio and diphtheria. Few people in Poplar went to hospital unless it was desperate – instead they went to Grundy Street. There was always a patient queue of old women in slippers, headscarves covering their curlers, with badly ulcerated legs; dockers nursing nasty bumps from unloading goods down the docks; and kids with burns, bumps and cuts. Dr Goldie would go to those that were too sick to get to the surgery, bumping down the cobbles on a big old boneshaker of a bicycle. She would park up her bike then tackle five flights of stairs, always in a dress and heels.

'My mother was a real lady in that way,' Heather laughs. 'She didn't believe in flat shoes; she was always beautifully turned out and people came to expect it of her.'

Conditions in the tenements of Poplar were dire. There was one toilet to serve five families on the landing. Tiny flats housed families of up to twelve who crammed into two rooms, children sleeping top-to-tail and babies in drawers. Wood was stored in the bath and a lid covered the tub, turning it into a table that was used for meals.

Dr Goldie witnessed their daily struggle and sacrifice, and vowed to match them. This was a lady who genuinely loved and admired the people of Poplar. Like the nuns of Nonnatus House, her lifelong guiding principles were compassion and duty of care to her community. Before the National Health Service began, she charged people just sixpence, or often didn't charge at all, so it was she became known as 'the sixpenny doctor'. The dockers and stevedores would often pay her in goods liberated from the docks – a dozen eggs or a banana. It was about survival and she understood that.

But Dr Goldie was put under an almost unbearable strain during the Blitz. She had her two children evacuated to Cornwall and stayed with her people in Poplar. This was her most challenging time in medicine. Often, the Blackwall Tunnel, which she used to get from her home in Blackheath to Poplar, was flooded or sealed off after a raid, so she would find someone to row her across the Thames so she could open up the surgery on time. Once she got caught in a raid on the way home from work and saw a German pilot fly down so low over the Thames she could see his face. One can only imagine what a young Luftwaffe pilot made of the sight of Dr Goldie, crossing the river mid-raid in a dress and heels.

'Mother ran to the nearest brick shelter during a raid, then when the all-clear sounded, she grabbed her doctor's bag and headed out on her bike, dodging rubble and craters,' says Heather. The Luftwaffe were not going to put a stop to Dr Goldie's daily rounds!

Her mother's courageous career in medicine rubbed off on Heather, and in 1961 she too graduated as a doctor, working alongside her mother.

'Two years before she retired in 1981, my mother found a lump in her breast, but never told anyone as she wanted to carry on working,' Heather says. 'By the time she retired and got it looked at, things were very far advanced. I knew it was the end of her days when I saw her in flat shoes.

'She died four years after retiring, at the age of eighty-one, but she knew exactly what she was doing. Poplar and her job were her life and that was what she wanted to do for as long as she could. Over fifty-one years, she must have seen thousands of patients in Poplar, even treating five generations of the same family. How she remembered all their names, I shall never know.'

*

Kay, Dr Joan and Dr Goldie are the Second World War's greatest unsung heroines. Collectively, these women's actions have come to personify so-called 'Blitz Spirit'. But what does that phrase mean exactly? Joshua Levine, author of the best-selling *Secret History of the Blitz*, advises caution when digging into this emotive and politically charged period of history:

> So how did the people of Britain behave during the Blitz? Did they sing 'Roll Out the Barrel' in communal shelters, shaking their fists at 'bloody Adolf', before cheerfully dodging the debris the next morning on their way to work? Or did they loot from bombed-out houses, fiddle their rations and curse foreigners, while hoping for a negotiated peace that would save their wretched lives?

Joshua argues they did both, presenting the light and shade of this complicated time.

> Life was dangerous, hard, and lived in the shadow of invasion and death. It was also exciting and shot through with optimism.
>
> People pulled together and helped strangers; they broke rules and exploited neighbours. They bonded with, and stole from, one another, they grew to understand, and to dislike, each other. They tolerated without complaint, and complained without tolerance. They were scared and fearless. They coped and they cracked. They lost all hope, and they looked to the future. They behaved, in short, like a lot of human beings.

Let's compare the lives of two East End women who lived half a mile away from each other during the Blitz. Sally from Whitechapel, who's now ninety-two, was drawn to the excitement and sense of adventure.

'I know I shouldn't say it,' she admits, 'but I enjoyed the war years because you met up with people and there was a different kind of freedom. I missed it when it was over. The whole community drew together during the Blitz and lived as one, and it brought out the best in people.'

For ninety-year-old Emily from Bethnal Green, however, the opposite is true. 'I have never felt such heart-stopping terror in all my life as I did during the Blitz and I'm not ashamed to admit it,' she states. 'I get annoyed when people say, "Oh, I had a great time during the Blitz." I didn't. I never knew if I was going to see the next day.

'Centuries-old houses offered no protection. There was no room in our tiny back yard for an Anderson shelter, so we used to share with the family that lived at the back of us. To me, the pulsating throb of the enemy aircraft overhead sounded as if they were saying, "*For you . . . For you . . . For you . . .*"

'I still feel the heart-gripping fear now if I stop to think about it.'

Strangely enough, the myth of the Blitz didn't extend to acts of criminality, of which, according to our matriarchs, there were many.

'Everyone who stayed and defended London was a true hero,' insists eighty-seven-year-old Vera from Bethnal Green. 'Apart from the villains, that is. No one talks about them much, but there were certain men in the East End who used to pretend to be wardens and then would go in and plunder from bombsites, taking gold rings from the fingers of dead women. It was disgusting. Not that you dared say anything, mind. You'd end up with a nail through your hand.'

Marie from Stepney, aged ninety-six, agrees: 'My sister-in-law Nancy used to run a pub in the Elephant and Castle and after the all-clear sounded, in came the gangs. They'd bring in all their stolen and looted gear to sell. One time, a bloke even brought in a human hand with the rings still on! The Blitz brought out the worst in the villains.'

It is equally true to say that it brought out the best in our women. Setting aside the paradoxes of personal experience, there can be no doubt that Gladys, Girl Walker, Kay, Dr Joan, Dr Goldie, Sally, Emily and all the women who lived and worked through the Blitz demonstrated courage and forti-tude as their lives were turned upside down. In the words of Joshua Levine:

> Women were encouraged to step outside the home, to become independent, to contribute actively to the war effort. Yes, they were paid less than men to do their widely varying work. Yes, they were still required to run the home. And yes, when it was all over, they were expected to step aside and allow the men to replace them. But for the dur-ation, their lives opened up in extraordinary ways.

Ninety-year-old Len from Bethnal Green paid tribute to the women of East London this way. 'Do you know who the real heroes of the Blitz were? The mothers of the East End. Night after night, they sat there being bombed, but they had no weapons to defend themselves or their children, no rifles with which to fire back or grenades to throw. Nightly, they hid from the bombs, then each morning they had to get up and care for children or clock on to work. It was business as usual, see.

'Me, I was just a skinny fourteen-year-old boy, working as an apprentice cabinet-maker on Brick Lane when the bombs started to drop.

'The Blitz was the happiest time of my life. From about

six or seven p.m. onwards, you'd hear the drone of the enemy planes, the sirens would start up and off we'd go. Everyone would muck in together, no matter if you were a millionaire or a skinny cockney kid in tatty trousers like me. Money and status don't matter when you could be dead in the morning. For the first time ever, society was on a level pegging and I felt equal.'

But dear old Len is wrong in one respect. East End women did have one weapon with which to fight back: humour.

'One shouldn't laugh but there were some, albeit unintentional, funny moments during the Blitz,' recalls ninety-one-year-old Dot from Bethnal Green. 'I was fourteen and working in Horn Brothers garment factory in Hackney at the time. I had lied about my age to get into the Land Army but someone grassed me up, so back to the East End it was. Every night, I sheltered in a huge basement under a school near my home in Bethnal Green.

'One evening coming home from work, I met my mum and we got caught short when the sirens went off, so we dived into the nearest brick street shelter. We were sitting there a while when Mum nudged me. "Here, Dot," she said, over the wailing siren. "This shelter's about as much use as a chocolate teapot." She pointed upwards and I was stunned to see the shelter had no roof!

'The school basement shelter was much safer – well, it had a roof at least. The shelter warden there was called Mr Nutt – poor chap was so bow-legged he couldn't have caught a pig in a passage. I still remember sitting down in that shelter Christmas 1940, singing "Silent Night" with some visiting curates, with the bombs crashing down all around us, and my friend and I trying to stifle our giggles.

'Mum sung a terrific song which kept all our spirits up. It went like this:

> *I went round to see my girl Mary Brown,*
> *She was having a bath and couldn't come down,*
> *I ask her to slip on something that's quick*
> *So she slipped on the soap and came down in a tick.*

'Looking back, humour was our best weapon for survival.'

With their humour, along with an inherent and razor-sharp instinct for survival, honed through centuries of desperate poverty in the East End, cockneys were born ready.

After 267 days, on 11 May 1941, the Blitz ended. More than a million houses were destroyed and damaged in London, and 43,000 people nationwide had been killed. London alone received 18,800 tons of explosive. Despite this, Hitler's attempt to bring Britain to her knees had failed.

Decades on the Blitz still holds a unique place in the history of our country. Britain was the first country to successfully resist Adolf Hitler, after all – thanks in no small part to our matriarchs, who still remember certain details as vividly as if they happened yesterday.

Gladys, who opened this chapter, today volunteers at the Imperial War Museum by speaking with schoolchildren about life under fire. The steely matriarch wants people to understand the sacrifices her generation made.

We meet in a McDonald's at Greenwich near the *Cutty Sark*, a popular tourist destination. Streams of giggling tourists are at the next table taking selfies.

'Kids today haven't got a clue,' Gladys remarks crisply. 'I didn't have a childhood, it was stolen from me by the war.

The moment I saw my best friend's body carried past me in a cardboard coffin, was the moment my childhood ended.'

Gladys has a patriotic pride and a dignity about her, which she wears like a robe, an almost regal posture that is very commanding. Swirls of white hair are piled high on her head. Her penetrating blue eyes seem to see straight through you, and flash and darken at the mention of war.

'Everyone lost a loved one. When Mary died, I wasn't offered counselling or allowed to cry. I just had to get on with it. Come to think of it, looking back, I was never shown much love by my mother, but that's probably because she was too busy trying to keep us kids alive. She did raise me to respect my elders, be honest and work hard, and for that I thank her. To this day, I've never lived beyond my means and I'm fiercely independent.'

Gladys worked first as a divisional supervisor for British Telecom for twenty-four years, and then in communications for investment banks. She also worked at the Palace of Westminster, where she is proud to have been one of the few women allowed to climb over the palace rooftops. 'Something Hitler never managed,' she grins.

Gladys worked hard until she was seventy-two, when she suddenly found herself fighting colon cancer.

'At the hospital, the nurse spoke down to me. "Aren't you lucky to be getting this treatment for free, dear?" she says. Free? Don't make me laugh. I've been paying for it in income tax since the NHS first started.

'The problem is, once you reach a certain age, people think you're not important. You cease to exist as a valid member of society. You're a "dear", not a "person". There's such a lack of understanding. We need to be teaching manners, morals and respect to our younger generation. Attitudes towards older people *must* change. We have lived through so much. We have stories to tell, and advice to offer. After all, when you don't know your past, you don't know your future. We're missing a trick by not utilising the skills and wisdom of our older generation.'

Gladys' anger is palpable as she leans forward over the table.

'That wisdom was hard won in the ashes of the Blitz. But back then, communities pulled together. We lived collectively, not individually.'

Gladys is right. For as we will find out in the next chapter, at the height of the bombardment, a secret and ingenious East End community was forming, which took our matriarchs into the dark belly of London . . .

Minksy's Recipe

My husband died young of emphysema from smoking, and he ate a lot of hydrogenated fats. Over the years, I've seen a lot of friends die from eating the wrong thing, so I said to myself, 'I'm going to know what is the best thing to eat, so I won't die young of disease.' I got a book out the library about nutrition and I educated myself.

Now, I always start the day with a bowl of porridge and blueberries. I eat lots of raw food like tomatoes, which contain lycopene that stops you having strokes. I mix turmeric with black pepper and boil it up in water for 45 minutes, then I take about three tablespoons daily for my arthritis.

White bread's no good for you; I only eat wholemeal bread. And don't talk to me about sugar! Do you know it's the biggest killer in the world? I am keeping well, to stay alive for the sake of my children because I love them. I don't want to go the same way my husband did.

Minksy's Remedy

Cut an onion in half, take all the outer skin off and roast it in the oven. Sounds a bit odd but eat that once a week and you'll be singing from the rooftops. It's full of anti-inflammatories. Yellow Basilicon Ointment is an old-fashioned remedy that my mother-in-law used to use on her dry, cracked skin. It's marvellous stuff.

Minksy's Pearls of Wisdom

Do what brings you joy in life and makes your heart sing.

4. Secret Underground Towns, 1943

'Crash, bang, wallop! Let's be having yer!' boomed the compère as he beckoned Minksy up on to the makeshift stage. The bouncy blonde bombshell was just sixteen, but there was no trace of nerves as she patted her platinum waves and swanked her way into the spotlight. A hush fell over the occupants of Bethnal Green Underground Station as she parted her cherry-painted lips:

> *I had a little back room to let, the rent was half a crown,*
> *A smart young lodger took the room, in the name of Brown . . .*

Minksy belted out the tune with all her heart. Who needed a microphone? The acoustics of the curved platform roof carried her song the length and breadth of the station. Reaching her favourite part, she gave a coquettish grin and lifted the hem of her dress teasingly:

> *I tiddly highty, tickle me under the nightie . . .*

A gale of laughter echoed up the tunnels as the crowd joined in with the chorus, even starting up an impromptu conga line, which snaked up the station platform.

> *Tickle me under the nightie . . .*

'There's only one winner – Minksy Agombar!' announced the compère, handing round a cap into which the grateful shelterers tipped their coinage.

'You're a caution, Minksy,' hooted a woman in the crowd,

dabbing the corner of her eye with her hankie. 'I forgot myself for a minute there.'

Thanks to Minksy, the drudgery and fear of war had been suspended, if only for the duration of a song. Her win also meant there'd be grub tonight. Counting up her winnings, Minksy dashed excitedly through the heavy steel door and pelted up the stairs of the Tube and over the road, to where her mum Hetty, dad Bill, three sisters and brother were sheltering in the railway arches behind the Salmon & Ball pub. Here, it was even more crowded and her breath hung like steam in the damp, coal-scented night.

'I only won, is all, Dad!' she babbled, tapping him on the shoulder. 'Tea's on me.'

Bill Agombar turned, his craggy face lighting up on seeing his eldest daughter.

'Fancy that!' he grinned, holding up seven fingers to Jack the Potato. 'I taught you well, my girl.'

Soon, Minksy and her younger sisters, Marie, Jeannie and Patsy, and brother, Billy, were tucking into a handsome tea of piping-hot jacket potatoes, split down the middle and doused with vinegar, salt and pepper.

As she licked the salt from her fingers, Minksy gazed affectionately at her father. She knew he could be a right old rogue when the fancy took him, spending most of his earnings down the pub and making life a struggle for her mother, but when it came to his talent, she was a chip off the old block.

Minksy Agombar was the eldest of five. Born in Bethnal Green Hospital in January 1927, she had been named Henrietta after her mother. But from the moment she had been brought home to 11 Shetland Street in Bethnal Green, and a neighbour had stuck her face in her pram and cooed, 'Look at'cha, Minky Minksy Moo,' the nickname had stuck.

Growing up, Minksy had inherited the best of her parents' talents. Hetty was a gifted seamstress and Minksy had fallen out the cradle able to sew. A talent with a needle and thread was bred in the bone round these parts. But it was her father's singing talent, honed at his knee, which she cherished most. William, or Bill for short, was descended from French Huguenot silk weavers who had fled to East London escaping persecution.

In the Agombar household, like most residents of Bethnal Green, music and song were important, but for them, it put food on the table. Work as a road sweeper was difficult to come by between the wars, and though Bill did his best, tea was often a roll dipped into a watered-down Oxo cube, or a kettle bender – a cup of crusts with some hot water, salt and a knob of marge.

If you can sing or sew, you can earn, was the mantra drummed into Minksy. And so it was that Bill went out to sing for his supper in the pubs, clubs and music halls of East London, taking his eldest daughter with him. While most girls her age were out on a Saturday afternoon playing whip and top or two balls, Minksy was down the pub, watching her father sing and, on occasion, even getting up to join him.

The showmanship began the minute Bill set foot outside their home. A well-rehearsed routine between himself and a local gay man, known to all as Freddy the Fearless Fly, took place every time Bill and Minksy boarded a bus to Hackney. Contrary to what people might think, drag acts were commonplace in the East End, with charismatic performers with names like Diamond Lil and Silver Shoes keeping everyone's spirits up.

'Oi, where's that three ha'pence you owe me?' Bill would call from across the top deck of the bus to Freddie. 'You must be keeping two homes.'

Freddie, without missing a beat: 'I am, dear, I am. Between my legs.'

Bill treated the streets as his stage, warming up with banter so that by the time he reached the pub he was on full steam. On a good night, he brought the house down with all the old-time cockney classics.

'Blimey, fella! I'm s'posed to be the comedian,' Arthur Haynes had laughed as he'd listened to Bill sing at a pub next door to where he was performing at the Hackney Empire, 'but you've really made me laugh!'

'Put yer money where your mouth is then,' Minksy had flashed back, holding her father's cap out. The chink of coins had been music to her ears. The following day, they had feasted like kings – conger eel doused in vinegar and peppercorns, winkles and watercress, followed by a piping-hot tray of Hetty's bread-and-butter pudding. Happy days. Unless her father got sidetracked on the way home . . .

'Where's your wages?' Hetty Agombar would demand to know then.

'Shut up, *you*,' her father would reply, swaying gently. 'I use my God-given voice to put food on the table.'

Bill never once called his wife by her real name. 'You' was the only name he used. *You. I'm going down the baths. You. Where's my tea?*

Hetty Agombar might have been degraded, but she was *never* downtrodden.

'I only saw a statue called Count Agombar today,' Bill announced excitedly when he came home one evening. 'Do you think I might be related?'

'Lose the O out of Count and you will be, pal,' she muttered.

Despite his obvious flaws, Minksy adored her father. Being separated from him and her mum when she and her siblings had been evacuated down to Little Saxham in Suffolk at the onset of war had been terrible. But now the Blitz was over, and she was back in Bethnal Green, where she belonged.

By 1943, the nightly raids were over and relative peace had been restored, but the Agombars, like most East Enders, had become accustomed to shelter life, and with the sirens still going off from time to time, they felt happier crammed under the arches behind the pub. They had their own Anderson in the back yard, but where was the community when you were tucked away down there? When it took a direct hit during the Blitz, that had sealed it for the Agombars. Down the Tube or in the arches was the only place for them.

With their jacket potatoes finished, Bill decided it was time to sing for the shelterers.

'How about "Sweet Sixteen", Dad?' Minksy suggested.

Minutes later, they had the shelter spellbound as their silky voices harmonised into the cold night air.

Bill gently bumped his daughter's shoulder. 'How's about getting your sister up?'

Before long, it was a real family affair, as Minksy, Marie and their mate Cathy belted out a Carmen Miranda number they'd remembered from watching *That Night in Rio* at the pictures, 'I, Yi, Yi, Yi, Yi (I Like You Very Much)'.

'Aye. Aye. It's the Andrews Sisters,' shouted Jack the Potato from behind his stall.

'Someone's nicked your banana!' yelled a wag from the back of the arches.

Minksy broke off. 'Shut your cakehole! You're the only

bloke I know who goes on holiday and comes back with a sunburnt tongue.'

The shelter fell about and Bill winked at his eldest daughter. She might not be treading the boards up West, but Minksy Agombar was learning her trade in swagger and song in the crowded wartime shelters of London's East End, and there was no finer training ground. Shelter life was a richly lived and intense affair, where entertainers like her helped to while away long, cold nights of boredom and fear.

By 1943, Bethnal Green Underground didn't just host singers like Minksy Agombar in their theatre built over the tracks, but Russian baritones singing opera, tap-dancing troupes and plays. There was a fully staffed crèche, doctor's quarters, a wood-panelled library with 4,000 volumes, a café serving up bacon sandwiches and hot pies, three-tier bunks for 5,000 and chemical toilets.

It was a secret subterranean community plunged deep below the earth. But these facilities only came about after a bitter struggle between the people and the Government, which has come to be known as the Battle of the Underground. And you can be sure our Bethnal Green matriarchs played a crucial role in this historic battle. After the long, shadowy years of propaganda and myth, only now are we getting to the truth of this strange tale.

As we saw in the previous chapter, after the first night's bombardment, when waves of German bombers set off from France bound for the distinctive loop of the Thames, it was clear that no one in London – and later, all cities and towns across Britain – was safe.

At that stage, Bethnal Green Underground was a desolate, half-finished Tube station, a building site, whose doors were firmly bolted to keep out civilians. Minksy's dad Bill, amongst other casual labourers, had been working on connecting it to Liverpool Street Station as part of the Central Line, but when war broke out, building work was immediately suspended. It lay discarded, the platforms covered in railway sleepers, rubble and rats.

At seventy-eight feet below ground, it made the perfect deep shelter, but at the outbreak of the Blitz, the Government was clear. Tubes were for transport, not shelter. Rather than bringing people together in large shelters where they might be killed en masse, fall prey to fear and panic, or succumb to a shelter mentality, in which they never emerged above ground, it was felt that people should be spread out, in garden shelters, or in small localised shelters. The Government and the London Passenger Transport Board (LPTB) were adamant. The Underground should only remain open as a transport system. Life and war work were to carry on as normally as possible. But the Blitz was proving to be anything but normal.

On the first night of the bombing, hundreds of residents of Columbia Market Buildings in Bethnal Green were sheltering in its vast basement. Despite the intensity of Black Saturday's raid, there was great community spirit in Columbia Buildings, with residents even carrying on with a wedding party. It was a wedding night the bride and groom would never forget. In a million-to-one chance, a fifty-kilo bomb whistled down a ventilation shaft measuring just three feet by one, exploding instantly and killing fifty-seven, including baby twins.

Anne, now ninety, who was born and raised in Columbia Market Buildings, along with her thirteen siblings, was there that night.

'Noise, confusion, smoke and screams, then my mum

rushing me away,' she says in a shudder. 'My elder brother went to help. He picked up a baby and it literally fell apart in his arms. Such shocking scenes. The King and Queen came round soon after to visit; he was in his Army uniform and I remember thinking how pale he was.'

Six miles further east in Canning Town, 600 men, women and children were crammed into South Hallsville School in Agate Street, which had been set up as an official rest centre, waiting for transport out of the East End. The refugees were exhausted after the first night of bombing; many were in a state of shock after losing their homes, with no possessions, save for the filthy nightclothes in which they sat. They huddled together, bewildered and angry, soothing crying children, desperation growing by the hour as bombs crashed down around them. It's hard to imagine a worse kind of hell.

Whitehall authorities were warned many times that these refugees were sitting ducks. By the third night, the rescue coaches were still nowhere to be seen and mothers pleaded with officials to get their children to safety. As day turned to night, the Luftwaffe returned, dropping a bomb that split the building in two.

Hundreds of tons of masonry crashed down on the shelterers. Whole families were wiped out. Romford Road swimming baths was drained and used as a temporary mortuary, where workers were given the gruesome task of piecing together body parts. Back at the school, rescue workers tried their hardest to dig out the bodies, but after twelve days, they were ordered to concrete over the crater, with bodies still entombed inside. The council's official death figure was 73, though locals still believe that figure to be far higher, more in the region of 450.

A raw and terrifying anger swept the East End and the

mutters turned to angry cries. *Why aren't the Tubes open? Where are the deep shelters?* East Enders felt as if they had been hung out to dry.

The propaganda machine worked overtime. 'The Cockney is Bloody But Unbowed' claimed the *Daily Herald*. King George VI visited the districts of all our matriarchs – Babs' Shoreditch, Girl Walker's Stepney, Beatty's Whitechapel and Minksy's Bethnal Green – in an effort to boost morale. One woman from Bethnal Green, who preferred not to be named, confessed: 'I saw the King and Churchill touring the East End, giving the V for victory sign. I flicked it round and gave the sign the other way round. I didn't need my morale raising from them, thank you very much.'

Bethnal Green was an inferno, a nightmare of noise and fire. Soft tissue and limbs littered the streets after a raid. People dug through the rubble-strewn wreckage with their hands for loved ones. Desperate pleas of 'Have you seen . . . ?' rent the air, and in the silence between the cries, more bombs screamed into the furnace.

In the first two weeks of the Blitz, ninety-five high explosive bombs and thousands of incendiaries dropped on the district, causing serious damage to Bethnal Green Hospital, the Queen Elizabeth Hospital, Columbia Market, the Central Library and the power station, as well as destroying thousands of homes.

The exhausted residents of Bethnal Green squeezed themselves into cold brick street surface shelters, dusty cupboards under the stairs, draughty church crypts, Andersons, railway arches and trenches. Or simply took their chances in their own beds.

What they needed most were safe, dry, clean, deep shelters. What they got from the Government, aside from

Anderson shelters, were brick street shelters. It was hard to see how a brick shelter, built above ground, would protect someone if the worst happened.

Glad, an eighty-one-year-old from Poplar, has vivid memories of sheltering in one. 'My wonderful mum did an amazing job of hiding her fear from me and my five siblings during the Blitz. She raised six children in Poplar by the docks, the worst hit area. She used to calmly usher us all to the nearest street shelter after the sirens went off. God knows how she did it on her own with six kids.

'I remember her once in the shelters reading us bedtime stories to try to drown out the thump of bombs. When the bombs got louder, her fingers would curl around the spine of the book, gripping it tighter and tighter until they were blood-red. That's the only way her nerves betrayed her.'

'I sheltered in one,' says Ray, eighty-four, from Bethnal Green. 'They were dark and squalid, not fit for human habitation. It housed about thirty, forty at most, with nothing in them but hard benches lining the walls. No one trusted the brick street shelters. It was no safer than staying in your own home. The general viewpoint was that *they* wanted you in there, so if a bomb dropped on the street, it was easier to just dig you all out of one place, rather than having to dig through all the houses individually. Everyone had their pride. The street shelters weren't fit for a dog.'

The 'they' Ray refers to, were the authorities, revealing the 'them and us' attitudes that were beginning to form in this dark, turbulent period. The aftermath of the bombing of a street surface shelter was sometimes described as a 'Morrison Sandwich' in honour of the Home Secretary.

'A bomb landed near my buildings in Russia Lane, and I ended up digging out people I knew from a brick shelter that had been hit,' recalls Len from Bethnal Green, struggling to control his tears all these years on. 'Terrible, it was, just terrible seeing the look on the faces of the dead women I pulled out. Bits of their bodies were splayed everywhere. They weren't safe in that brick shelter – the concrete ceiling had caved in and flattened them. I broke down and cried my eyes out at the sight of them, but the next day I got on with it. I tell you what, though, I swore after that not to use the street shelters. I took my chances and stayed out in the open, dodging shrapnel.'

Others weren't prepared to take their chances like Len. The day after the first heavy bombing of London, a huge group attempted to gain access to Liverpool Street Station. The station entrance was being guarded by police, but the crowds simply roared past. Three nights later, on 11 September, 2,000 people rushed down the stairs at Holborn Station before going to sleep on platforms and in corridors. Others simply bought a ticket to travel, then bedded down for the night.

Phil Piratin, a thirty-three-year-old communist councillor for Spitalfields East, the same man who helped to spearhead the Battle of Cable Street, was busy protesting once more. On 14 September, one week after the Blitz broke out, he led a party of seventy-seven from Stepney and invaded the plush Savoy Hotel, off the Strand, which had transformed its underground banqueting hall into a shelter – refusing to leave until the all-clear had sounded. Piratin wasn't daft. He chose the Savoy on account of the American journalists who were staying there, who wouldn't be subject to the same censorship that British journalists were.

The police soon arrived, and Piratin pointed to a mother from Stepney with four children whose husband was in the

Army. 'What would you do,' he asked the police inspector, 'if your wife were put in the position of that woman over there?' The inspector expressed sympathy but still proceeded to take the name and address of every Stepney intruder. When the all-clear eventually sounded, the occupation ended. 'Everyone left elated,' says Piratin, 'and there was publicity in the Sunday papers.'

It was this publicity, perhaps, which shamed Churchill into a U-turn on Government policy. On 25 September, eighteen days after the Blitz began, the Government conceded defeat and declared: 'The use of Tube stations as shelters has now been officially recognised.' The people had won. Not that Bethnal Greeners needed official permission from their Prime Minister to seek safety. They had already taken over the Tube.

Phoebe, eighty-five, speaks with pride of being one of the first families to take over Bethnal Green Tube: 'My dad, Morris, was a Jewish café owner. He was a gregarious man, larger than life. Terrible gambler he was too – he'd bet on two flies crawling up a wall! But he weren't willing to gamble on his eight kiddies' lives.

'When the raids were really bad, the Tube was locked. It was a disgrace. People just wanted to be safe, and there was a perfectly good deep shelter sitting empty while thousands got killed up above. Our people took action.

'A neighbour acquired the key to the Tube somehow and in we went – squatters' rights – and we never left. To start with, it was horrible. It stunk of sewers and it was full of rats, but we had to be somewhere safe. We made history and I feel very proud of that fact.'

Phoebe was closely followed by Gladys from Bethnal Green and thousands more. In they streamed, giddy with relief, down the steps and through the heavy steel flood doors on to the concrete platforms, where they staked out a patch on which to sleep.

'What's that noise?' Phoebe's mum cried when she reached the platform.

'I can't hear anything,' came the reply.

'Exactly!' she said.

Deep in the bowels of the earth, they were finally cushioned from the tremendous noise of the bombs.

'There was no adequate shelter in the East End, so civilians took over the Tubes. What choice did we have?' shrugs Gladys, now eighty-six. 'It was happening night after night. Most of the houses in Bethnal Green were so old, it was only the wallpaper holding 'em up. Not having a safe place to shelter was soul-destroying. No one was trying to break the law; it was simply a case of do or die, self-preservation really.

'To begin with, before they fitted it out, it was hellish. Concrete, bare boards, cold and it stunk of stagnant urine . . . It was a building site really, and I was terrified. You had to start filing down the concrete steps from about four p.m., to mark your spot. But at least you couldn't hear the bombs and the camaraderie was terrific, with everyone laughing, joking, eating their dinners and singing.'

Babies asleep in suitcases, neighbours gossiping, couples rowing – all life went on at Bethnal Green Underground.

'We caught everything going down there,' Gladys laughs. 'Scabies, head lice, you name it. You couldn't take proper baths. Occasionally, we'd go to York Hall baths and pay sixpence for a bath. As the Blitz raged on, we tried more stations, from Liverpool Street Station right up to Oxford Circus. I must have slept on every platform on the Central Line! Bethnal Green was the best, though.'

'To begin with, it was awful,' agrees Alf, eighty-eight, who also slept down there as a boy. 'They hadn't finished the building then, so we just slept in the concrete pits, later to become the tracks. We either slept in the "suicide pit" between the rails, or in the dips either side of it, where the live rail would one day run.

'A stout, no-nonsense shelter warden by the name of Mrs Maud Chumbley ruled us kids with a rod of iron. She'd be waiting by the entrance to the Tube when the sirens went off and order us in a deep, sergeant-major voice to: "Shut it, keep moving and keep quiet." She'd been a nurse in the Great War, and by God we did what she told us.

'We slept cheek by jowl with other families, but people tried their hardest to respect each other's privacy, holding blankets up for women to change behind. We paid tuppence to store our bedding at the bundle shop outside the entrance to the Tube. During the early evening, there was tremendous camaraderie, men played accordions and everyone sang. There was also great banter. Women and children were down there from about six p.m. The husbands would come down to check they were all safe, before going off to work the night shifts. "Remember to shut the windows and put the cat out," the women would joke. Like it mattered. Chances are your home wouldn't be standing in the morning in any case.

'My mum Elizabeth had to leave the Tube at five a.m. each morning, regardless of whether there was a raid on, to start the first of her three cleaning jobs in the City, but at least she managed a couple of hours of kip, albeit in a railway tunnel.'

Alf shakes his head in dismay as he recalls this. 'However did she do it? Women were solid back then.'

The Bethnal Green Doorstep Society took the tight-knit community they had enjoyed above ground and simply embedded it below ground. Life continued much as it had before. The twentieth-century equivalent of TripAdvisor, Bethnal Greeners spread the word and the people came. Three months later, in December 1940, Bethnal Green Council paid a token rent of £510 per annum to the London Passenger Transport Board to use the Underground as a shelter, and the authorities began the task of making it fit for occupation.

From then on, the Tube was transformed into an efficient, self-disciplined and many-layered working body. The council installed a proper ventilation system and chemical toilets. The walls were sprayed for bugs and whitewashed, and Boy Scouts helped to install three-tier bunks. Staying clean was always going to be a challenge, though, and medical officers did regular patrols to ensure hygiene. Tower Hamlets Local History Library & Archives holds records of this time, including a letter of complaint from one aggrieved woman to the council about a particularly 'verminous' family, and another lady complaining about the rats.

The council official's response was swift and blunt. 'Madam. There is scarcely a Tube shelter without them.'

At the height of occupancy, 7,000 people slept at Bethnal Green Underground and the shelter became an important safety valve for the community. Shelterers referred to it as an 'iron lung'.

The facilities, organised by the Women's Voluntary Services, were extraordinary for their time. As well as a staffed crèche, enabling mothers to go out to work, there was a library offering 4,000 volumes. After Bethnal Green Library was damaged by a bomb, librarians calmly transferred their books seventy-eight feet below ground and carried on stamping books and hushing noisy children, much as before.

The life-affirming story of Bethnal Green's underground library casts an illuminating spotlight on why we won the war. The fact that we clung so fiercely to our proud literary heritage, while above ground London was burning, adds a layer of civilisation to our country that Hitler overlooked.

Pat, an eighty-eight-year-old matriarch from Bethnal Green, made full use of the facilities.

'I used to borrow *Milly-Molly-Mandy* from the library and take free tap-dancing lessons. Us kids all used to hang out together in great packs, roaming for miles up and down the tunnels and playing kiss chase. It was great exercise and our parents never worried about us down there.

'I even remember watching a baritone singer in the theatre one night. He sang in Russian and I had never heard anything like it. I was entranced and it sparked a lifelong love of music. Sheltering underground opened my eyes to another way of life. You never had time to be bored and I never saw anyone miserable, ever. In the morning, mothers would feed their kids what little food they had from their rations, then emerge blinking into the smoke-filled dawn, hoping to find their home still standing for a quick wash before heading off to the factories for work. Business as usual! Hitler never banked on that.'

Pat wasn't the only one whose childhood rolled out at Bethnal Green Underground. Phoebe, who was first through its doors, laughs uproariously as she recalls a rite of passage that went wrong underground.

'I begged my mate, Alice, to pierce my ears down the Tube one night for my fourteenth birthday. She used a needle still threaded with cotton, put a cork behind my ear and stuck the needle in. It went in like a dream. She had the needle halfway through my other ear, when the lights went out. A bomb had dropped that had cut the power. I ran up the platform screaming blue murder with a needle stuck in my ear. "What's all the commotion about?" yelled a fella. "Some of us are trying to get some kip here."

'Despite that, I loved Tube life. I used to play Ludo and Snakes and Ladders down there. The adults had great parties and sing-songs of a Friday night. I even had my first sip of Guinness down the Tube! It was that place that kept our morale up.'

Living cheek by jowl down the Tube might sound alarming to our ears, but in wartime it had its compensations.

'There was one elderly couple who used to come down together every evening, and slept in bunks side by side,' recalls Gladys. 'They were devoted to one another. One night, the woman came alone. Her husband had been killed in a raid. The Salvation Army came to see her in her bunk and played "Abide With Me" to comfort her in her hour of need. The whole station fell silent. It was so moving.'

The story of Bethnal Green Underground offers up a valuable picture of shelter life, and reveals what happens when a community is tested. It also goes to prove how, far from descending into troglodyte and lawless enclaves as the Government first feared, the Tube became a thriving, self-governing community, thanks to formidable shelter wardens like Mrs Chumbley, to say nothing of Pat, Gladys and Phoebe's fearless mothers. In a forgotten grey corner of London, the mothers of Bethnal Green weren't trying to break the law, just keep their children alive.

'In mass emergencies, supportive behaviour towards strangers is common,' explains Dr John Drury, Reader in Social Psychology at the University of Sussex. 'This common fate that these mothers experienced led them to share identity with others. Strangers were no longer "others" but "us".

'The myth of so called "shelter mentality", that when people form a crowd they would become barbaric, fearful and irrational, is contradicted by what happened at Bethnal Green Underground during the Second World War. Feeling psychologically part of a crowd would have made the shelterers feel supported and safe, and the validation they got from seeing others who felt the same way as them, would have felt emotionally good.'

Little wonder then, that all these years on, some women I interviewed still feel great nostalgia and happiness when they refer to their underground home. I visited Bethnal Green Underground and stood on the platform where Minksy, Pat, Gladys, Alf and Phoebe all bedded down for the night. I fancied I might feel the reverberation of Pat's footsteps as she played kiss chase up the tunnels, or if I listened hard enough, I'd catch the distant sound of Minksy's song and laughter drifting up the platform, or a whiff of Mrs Chumbley's carbolic.

But no vestige of scent or sound remained. The secret underground town has long vanished. No more joyful singing competitions. No conga lines. No babble of cockney voices rising up from the bowels of the earth. Just silent commuters staring down at their phones. Up above ground, the bundle store where Alf and his mum stored their bedding at tuppence a go is a Starbucks.

But wait! One thing remains in Bethnal Green and it's as British as bread and butter – the irrepressible Minksy! She may no longer be singing 'Sweet Sixteen', but she's still knocking them out at ninety-one. We meet in E. Pellicci, an Italian family-run café where the Krays used to hang out, just around the corner from Bethnal Green Tube. Thankfully, it's more famous these days for Maria Pellicci's delicious home-made spaghetti and gigantic, gut-busting fry-ups – and the warmth of the welcome.

The handsome café is tiny, but packed to the rafters, the windows steamed up from chatter and laughter. This Bethnal Green landmark has been trading from 332 Bethnal Green Road since 1900 and is a matriarch in its own right. Its glorious yellow Vitrolite façade and art deco-style panelled interior is preserved with a Grade II listing.

Any star worth their salt has sampled the Pellicci hospitality and been pictured in the family album – from boxing legend Sir Henry Cooper, to Michael Gambon, Hollywood star Colin Farrell and a host of *EastEnders* stars. But it's authentic cockney Minksy whose star quality shines the brightest. She is a tiny little thing, with skin as white as pearl, and a laugh as dirty as a drain.

'I've been coming here since 1947,' she confides over an enormous plate of liver and eggs, with a mountainous side order of hand-cut chips.

'Anna Pellicci jokes with me. "You still here?" She slams her palm down on the Formica table with a great shriek of laughter, full of the same spirit that entertained war-weary shelterers.

'I started singing at my dad's knee aged three, and I'm still singing now,' she says, sapphire-blue eyes the colour of old glass shining with emotion. 'I just love it. It gives me great pleasure.'

After the war, Minksy kept on singing and was even sponsored by the Tate & Lyle sugar factory in Silvertown, to perform with an entertainment troupe, singing in old folk's homes and hospitals. Remembering the lyrics to song and verse has clearly helped this nonagenarian's memory and is the key to her vitality.

With our interview concluded, Minksy polishes off her liver and eggs, before whipping a microphone out of her bag. Anna Pellicci raps a teaspoon on the counter and calls for silence. A hush descends over the steamy café.

'Who fancies being transported away from the grey miserable British winter, to sunny Spain?' she bellows. A roar of approval is all Minksy needs and she's off, giving it both barrels.

> *Oh this year I'm off to sunny Spain*
> *Y Viva España,*
> *I'm taking the Costa Brava plane,*
> *Y Viva España . . .*

Suddenly, Minksy might be sixteen again, the same girl who sang behind the smoky arches. Minksy's Friday afternoon sing-alongs in Pellicci's café are clearly a regular fixture, as no one bats an eyelid. Soon she has the whole café singing along. Clearly life in the wartime shelters has done nothing to diminish Minksy's appetite for life. In fact, if anything, it's fuelled it.

But for all the joys of underground living, the robust community and camaraderie, as ever in wartime, something was always just around the corner to remind East Enders of the breathtakingly cruel nature of warfare. The theatre of war in Bethnal Green was about to offer a staggering new twist.

Babs' Recipe

Auntie's Bread Pudding

An old aunt showed me how to make this. She used to prepare it in a big old tin basin in the scullery. No need to weigh anything. Just use up all the old stale bread you've got to hand. Soak the bread in water, then squeeze out the excess and use it to line the basin. Then chuck in a chunk of about half a pound of margarine or butter, sultanas, mixed spice, as much sugar as you can spare, and two eggs. Cook it on a really low heat for a few hours. My aunt's used to last for days and she sent all us kids to school with a lump of it wrapped in brown paper.

Babs' Remedy

Mix up a few drops of olive oil and lemon juice, and drink. It does wonders for a sore throat.

Babs' Pearls of Wisdom

Someone up there has it all mapped out for you. Never leave the house without a clean pair of knickers in your bag!

5. The Bethnal Green Tube Disaster, 3 March 1943

8.17 p.m. and the drone of the air-raid siren filled their home. Babs didn't need to hear it to know when they were going to have to sleep down the Tube. Her mum's nervous little cough was all the warning she needed to get her bundle of bedding.

'Right, come on, girls,' ordered Bobby, hauling her scratchy wool coat wearily over her thin shoulders. Turning off the gas lamp, she reached for the bag that was always packed and ready by the door, containing the family essentials, including ration books and insurance documents.

Outside it was pitch-black, the rain bashing the bricks. The siren's mournful wail rose up in great waves over the rooftops of Old Ford Road. Bobby, Babs and her big sister, Jean, scurried to the stop for the bus that would deliver them to Bethnal Green Underground shelter, just as the bus slid away, showering them in a spray of filthy water.

'Bugger it,' Bobby muttered over the siren. 'We'll have to wait for the next bus.'

Babs had already been through so much since this strange war began: grappling with an abusive aunt; getting machine-gunned on the beach . . . Just twelve, yet she had confronted danger and violence in its most extreme forms. Sleeping down a Tube station felt quite normal, all things considered.

They waited in silence, bodies hunched over against the rain, until the outline of a bus loomed, its headlamps partially dimmed to comply with the blackout. At the entrance to Bethnal Green Underground, they joined a queue of other shelterers by the railings at Barmy Park, all waiting patiently to go down the steps to the Tube.

Suddenly, the crowds seemed to swell. Three buses had stopped at once, spilling yet more bodies on to the pavement. The picture houses, cafés and dance halls of East London were emptying, their occupants seeking one thing only – sanctuary down the Tube.

Babs couldn't make out faces in the darkness. Just dark, hunched-over outlines clutching bundles of bedding, packing her in so tight, her breath came in short and shallow gasps. The stench of damp wool and unwashed bodies . . . *Hot. Sticky. Dank.*

Searchlights fingered the dirty skies above their heads. Her heart picked up speed and, shifting uncomfortably, Babs squeezed her fingers tighter through Jean's.

'It's all right, Babsy,' murmured her big sister's voice in the darkness. 'I won't let go.'

'Busy tonight,' remarked a lady in the queue.

'It's 'cause our boys bombed Berlin, couple nights back,' sniffed a man. 'Jerry'll want retribution. You mark my words.'

The crowds stiffened then shuffled forward a couple of feet as the queue moved.

Nearly there. Just a couple more minutes, thought Babs, her heart punching in her chest. *Wonder if we'll get something to eat.*

The thought was blown clean out of her head. A fearful whoosh rippled over the station, lifting the hairs on her head, followed by a loud explosion. It was like no other noise she had heard before. Babs froze, felt the flesh on her back shrink. The crowd surged forward, picking Babs up and taking her with it. And then, she was falling . . .

'Please come down the Tube, Minksy, please?' begged Dolly.

Her sixteen-year-old friend stood before her, her face as

white as bone in the darkness of the arches. Minksy tried to answer but her head was spinning. So much noise. So much confusion. They'd all heard the bang. It was loud enough to take the roof off the shelter. Now people were pelting towards the entrance to the Tube, just over the road from where they were standing. Shouts tore through the darkness.

'It's bombs! It's bombs! Get down the shelter! Quick! Quick!'

'My mum's down the Tube,' said Dolly, growing tearful as she tugged at Minksy's arm. 'I have to find her. Please come with me.'

Minksy glanced back anxiously to the shelter behind the Salmon & Ball, to where her mum, Hetty, stood.

'I can't, Doll. You go with your mum and I'll keep with mine.'

'But she'll be worried about me. Be a pal, Minksy, and come find her with me.'

Her fingers were tight on Minksy's sleeve, pulling her further out the shelter towards the Tube.

Minksy wavered. She, Dolly, and Minksy's little sister, Marie, had been through so much together. They'd all been evacuated to Suffolk and returned at the same time. Pals through thick and thin. Dolly deserved her loyalty.

'All right,' Minksy relented. 'I'll come help you find your mum.'

She walked towards the Tube with Dolly. One step, two . . . a terrible premonition, an emotion so powerful and dark, seeped over her, stopping her dead in her tracks.

'I can't, Dolly,' she mumbled, backing away, her clear blue eyes swimming with tears. 'I can't. I love my mum. I've got to stay here, with her.'

Dolly shot her a last desperate look, before turning and running towards the morass of people crowding the Tube entrance. Minksy watched Dolly's bright blonde curls bobbing in the darkness, until the crowds consumed her and she vanished.

Legs. Arms. Twisted limbs. The seething crowd propelled her at speed towards the entrance to the Tube. Confusion swirled. *Where was her mum, her sister?* Babs tripped over something. *A bundle? A body?* And then she was stumbling towards the steps.

People were tumbling, one after the other, down the dark, wet steps, plunging headlong into the inky darkness. With no central handrail to break their fall, they went down like dominoes, piling up, one on top of the other. Where once people ran to sanctuary, now they were being swept to their deaths. A solid wall of tangled bodies was forming, growing higher with every second.

Desperate cries, thuds and grunts tore through the gloom. *'Stop! Help! Go back'!*

But there was no turning back. The sheer weight of the crowd was too much. There must have been hundreds attempting to get underground. Another voice, louder this time, reached her ears.

'I can't come, I've got my sister with me!'

'Jean!' Babs cried, and using all her effort, thrust her hand through the darkness towards the sound of her sister's voice.

'Babs!' she cried.

Fingers reached out and wrenched her free. At the last moment, Jean pulled her from the crush, like a cork coming free from a bottle. Babs shuddered as the cold night air rushed back into her lungs.

The two sisters stood bewildered in the rain as the shrilling of police whistles grew louder.

'Jean,' Babs trembled, an awful thought dawning on her. 'Where's Mum?'

Minksy stood, forgotten, in the unfolding drama and watched as if in a dream, rain battering her face like fists. A human chain had formed around the Tube, holding people back so that the emergency services could get through.

Rescuers worked frantically, plucking the dead and injured from the pile. Shelter warden Mrs Chumbley was wrenching children from the mangled crush. A steady stream of workers with stretchers raced past, but it quickly became obvious there weren't anywhere near enough to cope with the bodies, so they laid them down on the pavement, with no time even to take pulses.

ARP wardens in tin hats hammered on passing cars, flagging them down so they could transport the injured to hospital. Housewives and even Boy Scouts helped injured children on to barrows and ran with all their might in the direction of the hospitals. And all the while, the line of bodies being lifted limply from the crush grew sickeningly longer. Down in the bowels of the station, around 1,000 people were bedding down as usual. None of them had a clue of the horror unfolding right above their heads.

Minksy stared, terrified, at the bodies laid out on the wet pavement by the railings.

'Dolly, Dolly, where are you?' she wept, as her eyes ran along the line of corpses. She recognised a big strapping sailor she knew locally, home on leave, lying alongside a six-year-old boy who played out in her neighbourhood. Both gone. Their skin chilled and lilac, the light gone from their eyes. The clamorous stench of death rose up in waves from the pavement.

As she began to focus on the familiar faces, her hands

flew to her mouth and she stumbled back. A woman, not much older than her mum, crushed so badly her face was mauve, blood trickling from the corner of her lips, eyes bulging in surprise, mouth frozen open in a scream.

Minksy felt her heart cleave in two. She barely registered the hand on her shoulder, pulling her back.

'Now that's not for your eyes; you mustn't look at that,' said her father gently.

In a trance, she allowed him to lead her back to the arches. He stood her by the warmth of Jack's potato stall, then returned to the Tube to help.

Minksy sat, white-faced and shivering, despite the heat from the coals. In her heart, she knew. Dolly was dead and the sights she had witnessed would stay with her until her grave. A warm and innocent place in Minksy's soul darkened and shrivelled. After tonight, she knew she would never see life in quite the same way again.

Just yards from Minksy, Babs sat on a bunk, equally shocked. She and Jean had been ushered over to the arches behind the pub.

Confusion. Pandemonium. Noise.

'Wait here,' ordered Jean over the hubbub. 'I'll see if Mum's back here.' With that, she disappeared into a room at the back of the shelter. When she re-emerged, she was deathly white.

'She's not here. Come on,' she muttered, 'let's get out of here.'

They walked, scared and confused, back towards St John's Church, which faced the Tube. Survivors were being taken to the church, bodies down to the crypt.

Suddenly, out of the darkness, strode a familiar outline.

'Mum!' cried Babs, feeling her legs buckle with relief.

On seeing her girls, Bobby closed her eyes briefly, her

hand clutched to her chest in relief, but the steely mother was not going to break down. She didn't have the time for shows of sentiment. Instead, she took their hands firmly.

'We're going home.'

As they hurried for home, Bobby realised the vow she had made her girls that they would be safer back in the East End was beginning to sound a little hollow. Drawing level with the railings to Barmy Park, Babs saw people lying on the pavement. She slowed down to stare.

'Here, why are those people lying down on the pavement?'

Bobby shot Jean a look.

'They're . . . They're . . .' Emotion shattered the words in Jean's throat. 'They're tired,' she managed.

'But they're all gonna get wet,' Babs persisted.

'They're having a little sleep is all, now leave it, Babsy,' her mum ordered in a voice that brooked no argument.

As the bodies started to arrive, they looked as if they had simply fallen asleep: no cuts, no blood, scarcely a broken bone between them. Junior doctor Joan stared dumbfounded as the trickle of corpses soon turned to a flood.

After her training at the Royal Free Hospital during the Blitz, the twenty-seven-year-old had thought she had seen all there was to see. But she was wrong. For tonight, at the casualty department of the Queen Elizabeth Hospital for Children in Hackney Road, the recently graduated doctor was about to face her biggest test yet. And what lay ahead, was a night of undiluted hell . . . They'd not long started the night shift when Joan had received the phone call telling them to expect thirty faints from a Tube shelter.

'It's a put-up job,' she'd remarked knowingly to the two young male students from the London Hospital working under her that night. 'They're trying to see how quickly we get the ward organised.'

So with great enthusiasm, Joan and the two students had taken down the cots and begun putting up beds. They'd scarcely finished when the doors swung open and a body arrived, followed by another, and another . . .

For a moment, Joan stood stunned into silence.

'Good grief,' she breathed. The dead were all pale lilac in colour and their clothing . . . It was sopping wet. No sign of a bomb blast, or shrapnel wounds.

'Come on, then,' she said, snapping out of her torpor. 'Help me move them off the stretchers, the ambulance men will be wanting their stretchers and blankets back.'

With huge effort, as their waterlogged clothes made them heavy, Joan and her helpers managed to roll them off the stretchers. They'd scarcely moved one body, when another arrived. As the bodies began to pile up, two things quickly became obvious. Most of the dead were women and children – and they were fast running out of space.

'We don't have much more room,' she said in desperation to the ambulance men as they delivered yet more bodies.

'Please, Doctor. You have to take 'em,' begged one, tears washing runnels in his grey, hollowed cheeks. 'The London, Bethnal Green Hospital, even the church crypts . . . They're all full.'

Joan nodded bleakly, and watched in mounting desperation as the casualty ward transformed into a morgue.

'What can we do?' asked her young student breathlessly, when the ward was too full of bodies to lay any more down.

There was nothing else for it. 'Let's put them in the consulting rooms,' Joan said, 'and the corridor.'

At that moment, the Senior Casualty Officer burst in. She took one look at the heap of dead bodies and looked like she might pass out.

'This . . . This is preposterous,' she spluttered, her voice rising. 'You can't do this. Y-you don't know what you're doing. This is disrespectful.'

'What else are we to do?' Joan asked, keeping her calm. 'I can hardly turn the ambulance men away.'

'But . . . But . . .'

Joan could see she was growing hysterical, which was the last thing they needed.

'With respect, I don't think you are in a fit state to work,' she said bravely. 'Perhaps you should go home?' Her senior promptly signed herself off work.

Joan looked at her two young male students. 'Looks like it's just us then.' Like it or not, the junior doctor had just found herself in charge of the casualty department.

As the trio worked, laying the bodies out as respectfully as they could, Joan did all she could to ensure they hadn't overlooked the faintest sign of life. A moth's breath even, but there was no hope. However these poor souls had perished, the end had clearly been swift and brutal.

At the sight of a young woman, she paused, haunted by the sight of her cold white fingers, tightly curled as if she had been grasping something at the moment of death.

'Dear Lord . . . What happened to you?' Joan breathed.

After an hour or two, she got her answer.

'Live casualties coming in,' announced the registrar.

A nine-year-old boy with a broken arm sat waiting to be treated. As Joan bandaged him up and arranged for a hot, sweet drink to be fetched for him, she smiled gently.

'Are you able to tell me what happened tonight?'

The poor mite nodded, pale as stone.

'The siren went so we ran to Bethnal Green Tube shelter. There weren't no people on duty,' he said, the words spilling out of him. 'Something happened on the stairs going down, we just piled up.'

He started to shake. 'I had to climb over the bodies to get to the top and some ambulance fella caught me, brought me here.' He swallowed hard. 'Please, Miss. I don't know where me mum is.'

Joan shook her head, stunned. These poor souls had been asphyxiated in a crush. Suddenly, so much made sense. The woman's curled fingers, no doubt clutching tightly at the hand of a child as they were separated, the emotional ambulance men, tending to the bodies of their own. Joan had been working in the community of Bethnal Green long enough to know that everyone knew each other.

She had already witnessed such terrible suffering here in the East End – malnourished children with rickets, others covered in scabies and bug bites. There was no medicine she could give this boy who had lost his mother. Joan felt a tightness claw at her throat. A veil of darkness had swept over war-torn Bethnal Green that night.

As dawn crept in through the hospital windows, Joan and her two young students were exhausted and sick at heart. Not a drop of water or food had passed their lips in twelve hours, not that she had the stomach for it in any case. At eight o'clock, the junior doctor found herself summoned by a hospital superior.

'You can go now,' he told Joan somewhat starchily. 'Go for twenty-four hours, but you must be back here without fail tomorrow morning at eight o'clock sharp.'

Joan nodded wearily, and made to move off.

'And, Dr Martin . . . Do not breathe a word of this to anyone.'

Sworn to secrecy, Joan issued her grateful thanks to her two student helpers, and stumbled exhausted on to the Hackney Road.

Haunted by the sight of so much death, she began to walk, grateful for the fresh air in her lungs. The East End was coming to life, milkmen and costers (street sellers of fruit and vegetables) trundling their barrows out on the streets, newspaper hawkers shouting the day's headlines. Strangely, there was no mention of any disaster down the Tube.

Her mind felt fractured, images of falling bodies unspooling on a sickening loop, so her feet took over and walked as if of their own accord – and walked. Usually, she would have got the Tube back to her lodgings in West London. This morning, she gave it a wide berth.

Joan got a shock as she saw rushing grey water flowing under Hammersmith Bridge. In a trance, she had walked *all day*, a distance of ten miles from East to West London, to the home of the one woman she could really trust, her mentor, consultant paediatrician Ursula Shelley.

The older woman opened the door and gaped at the sight of the younger doctor, frozen on the doorstep, a pale marble statue of herself.

'Joan, come in, what's happened?'

Through tears, Joan told her the full story. Ursula nodded as she listened.

'This is what we're going to do,' she said, with her usual air of efficiency. 'I'll get my housekeeper to fix you some supper, then you're going to have a bath and go to bed. When you wake up, you will return to hospital and we must never speak of this ever again, understand?'

Behind her, a clock ticked loudly on the mantel. The silence stretched on. Joan nodded. The message was loud and clear. Never question your superiors. Do as you are told. And above all, keep going *whatever* happens.

Ursula wasn't being unkind; she was simply echoing the wartime mantra of survival. If they were to win this war, personal suffering must be sacrificed for the greater good. But that didn't stop the nightmares. After her bath, Joan gratefully clambered into Ursula's spare bed. As she laid her weary head on the starched bed linen, she had a dream so vivid, it wrenched her into consciousness.

Bodies being trampled to death, faces crushed under boots, crumpled limbs . . .

Joan woke gasping for breath. The nightmares were to haunt her for the next seventy-three years.

Babs was waking to a nightmare of a different kind. The past twelve hours had been the strangest of her life. When they had arrived home last night, a policeman neighbour had taken them into his house, and Babs had got the shock of her life when her dad Nick had rushed in – completely unexpectedly, as he was away from home serving with the Navy as a driver. Not only that, but her big tough dad who, like her mum, never usually shed a tear, was weeping and showering her and Jean in kisses and cuddles.

'Why are you crying, Dad?' she had asked in all innocence.

Her mum gave her a slap for the impertinence of the question and packed her off to bed.

This morning, she woke and as she got changed out of her nightie, she looked down in disbelief. One whole side of her body, where she'd been caught in the crush, was covered in a purple and black bruise, mushrooming over the creamy white skin of her torso like an exotic flower. She knew better than to make a fuss. Her mum was already on edge as it was. Instead, she changed into her school clothes and, grabbing a piece of bread and marge, headed to Morpeth Street School. In the classroom, she spotted one empty seat, then another . . .

'There was an accident down the Tube last night,' announced the teacher, Mr Roberts, solemnly. 'If you were in it, you can be excused from school for the day.'

Back at home, Babs' mum was at her new job as a school dinner lady. Jean was at work too, for the Prudential. There was nothing for it but to sit on the doorstep and wait. As she waited, she wondered: what world was it normal to go to school and find half your classmates missing, suffocated to death?

Minksy was also waking to the news that her last-minute decision not to accompany Dolly down the Tube had saved her life. Dolly – real name Doris Warrington – had been crushed to death. She was sixteen.

It took more than sixty police, home guards, rescue services and volunteers to pull corpses and injured people from the top of the staircase. The darkness, the pressure and angle of the bodies made extricating people from the crush extremely slow, difficult work. Horrifyingly, dead and alive were pressed together in a tangled mess of such complexity that it wasn't until three hours later, at 11.40 p.m., that the last casualty was pulled out.

The next morning, a fine ghostly rain shrouded the deserted entrance to Bethnal Green Tube. The steps had been washed down. No bodies remained, only a neat pile of shoes stacked by the entrance, and a broken pram. Sorrow had slid deep beneath the soil.

Over the next hours, the true horror of the accident became shockingly clear. An unimaginable 173 people had lost their lives in the crush – 84 women, 27 men and 62 children.

Children like eight-year-old Iris Clatworthy, two-year-old Pauline Ellam, seven-year-old Roy Leggett, fourteen-month-old John Yewman, and six-year-old Sylvia Geary. The list goes on and on. They are amongst the forgotten victims of the Second World War.

It is by sheer good fortune that Babs and Minksy were not amongst their number, and even greater fortune that courageous Dr Joan was on hand to tend to the dead and injured. The wartime medic found her faith in God tested that night, but her resolve to carry on and help those suffering in the East End strengthened. All the matriarchs suffered deeply as a result of what they witnessed, none more so than Dr Joan. The night she waded through corpses lived on hauntingly in her mind. Then, there was no such thing as counselling, no acknowledgement of what we now call post-traumatic stress disorder, and none of the compensation that today's society would demand. Their suffering was to be endured, silently and alone.

The day after the disaster, a team of men was dispatched to add central handrails to the station staircase. Pressure grew for an enquiry. Home Secretary, Herbert Morrison, appointed the London magistrate, Laurence Rivers Dunne, to conduct the investigations and produce a report. Ignoring pleas for a public enquiry, Morrison stipulated that the investigations should be conducted in private. Controversially, the enquiry report was kept secret until the end of the war. In 1945, the report was released in which Dunne revealed: 'The stairway was converted from a corridor to a charnel house in ten to fifteen seconds.'

The sudden crush of people attempting to get down the stairs to the shelter had been triggered by the unexpected firing of an anti-aircraft rocket from a Z Battery in nearby Victoria Park.

Two years before the tragedy, alterations to the hoarding at the entrance to the station had been recommended by Bethnal Green Borough Council over fears of a collapse under the pressure of so many people. They were rejected by the government-run Regional HQ as a waste of money. What neither the Borough engineer nor the Regional HQ engineer recommended was a central handrail on the staircase, nor did they recommend that the poor lighting on the staircase be improved and the rough concrete steps made even.

This accident, in a bomb-battered area that was only just recovering from the horrors of the Blitz, is Britain's biggest civilian wartime disaster. The death toll was greater than the 1966 landslide disaster at Aberfan and the 1989 Hillsborough stadium tragedy. It seems strange that the Bethnal Green shelter disaster is not better known.

Dr Toby Butler from the University of East London led detailed research into the disaster, producing an oral history book, two audio trails around the memorial in Bethnal Green Gardens and an archive of memories, so that it will never be forgotten.

'The tragedy did not end that night – far from it,' he explains. 'The event inevitably had a dreadful effect on the survivors and witnesses, many of whom suffered long-term trauma as a result of what they experienced that night. Bethnal Green was a close-knit community and almost everyone in the borough knew somebody who was affected by the disaster. I think we owe it to those involved to listen to what they have to tell us and, in so doing, acknowledge something of the psychological burden that has been carried by them for so many years.

'After the disaster, the Government withheld information to prevent news of it reaching the enemy. Survivors were told by officials not to speak about the tragedy for fear of undermining the war effort. The circumstances were so traumatic that some survivors did not speak about it for the rest of their lives. With no counselling and no opportunity to share stories, the memory of the disaster stayed deeply buried in the individual and communal consciousness for decades.'

But thanks to a dedicated team who set up the Stairway to Heaven Memorial Trust charity, an astonishing seventy-five years on from that night, a fitting memorial has finally been unveiled. A beautiful teak roof in the form of an inverted staircase carries the surnames of all the victims, who are also represented by 173 conical light shafts in the roof, through which sunlight can shine.

The survivors cut the ribbon and then the rain came, much as it did that night.

'You can judge a community by how they respond to a tragedy,' said the Mayor of London, Sadiq Khan, to the hundreds of people who turned out to watch the unveiling in December 2017. 'The story of this memorial is an inspiration to the rest of London.'

The circle is now complete. It is testament to the unswerving power of love and loyalty that the memorial is there at all. It took the Trust and the architect over ten years of relentless fundraising and wading through punishing red tape and council bureaucracy to raise the £600,000 to build it. Lesser people would have given up years ago.

Sandra Scotting, the secretary of the Trust, who herself

lost her grandmother, Sarah, and a cousin, Barry, in the disaster, says: 'I owed it to my family to stick with the project, despite all the setbacks we encountered, to ensure this was not the forgotten disaster any more. It has taken longer than expected but has been worth it in the end. The evocative memorial will help to honour all those poor souls for posterity. It has also given closure to everyone affected by the tragedy. I hope my mum can rest in peace now.'

Alf Morris, an eighty-eight-year-old trustee – who was a thirteen-year-old boy when he was wrenched free from the crush of bodies by shelter warden Mrs Chumbley – says: 'I can die happy now that the memorial has been finished. I think I was spared to ensure that my schoolmates that were not so lucky could be honoured.'

He is not the only person there who recalls that night with a vivid intensity. Also present to watch the final unveiling is none other than Dr Joan Martin. Aged 102, this wonderful woman has kept her bond with Bethnal Green and has attended every single one of the annual memorial services. So strong was Joan's sense of duty and instinct to never break her word, she kept her lonely secret for over sixty years. Ursula was the only person she confided in. After that, her lips remained tightly sealed. She did not even tell her parents of the terrible things she witnessed that night.

It's a freezing December day at the memorial unveiling, but Dr Joan is here, braced against the wind and the rain. Nothing would keep her away.

'Yes, I'm still here,' she jokes, when I go to greet her, but then her mood turns sombre.

'The nightmares only stopped last year,' she admits. 'Although seeing the fire at Grenfell Tower triggered the same feelings of helplessness and despair. It was entirely preventable, just as the disaster at Bethnal Green was. I visited the tower, to take some food and clothing, offer what little help I could, and it filled me with sadness. When will authorities learn?'

The image of a 102-year-old wartime doctor wandering once more amongst London's burnt ruins is a powerful one. Joan visited because impoverished North Kensington was her patch as a doctor for many years, a place where she worked tirelessly to dispense health and healing. Witnessing so much death and destruction amongst people she loved was almost unbearable.

'People are so selfish these days, and only think of themselves,' Joan continues. 'We have lost the culture of volunteering. Those that lived through the war understand the need for self-sacrifice and pulling together. How is society organising itself to help weaker members?'

Through campaigning for the memorial, Joan has retained her links with the East End and has nothing but praise for its wartime women.

'Back then, people had such pride in poverty. East End mothers suffered terrible deprivation; they often went without themselves so that their children could eat. They were remarkable in my eyes, so strong, tough and uncomplaining. They would push prams piled high with washing down to the wash house. They were poor but never dirty; to be clean was a mark of pride.'

That's a sentiment Babs – who's also present at the unveiling – agrees with. Blessed with an intelligence and adventurous nature that means she leads a full life in her eighty-sixth year, Babs is still possessed of a quick wit and a bone-dry sense of humour.

'I've only been holding on for this; I can pop off now,' she jokes, shivering in the cold.

Like everyone else involved in the Trust, Babs has worked tirelessly to help raise funds and awareness of the disaster that blighted her and her sister's life, by giving talks and rattling collection tins on rain-soaked high streets.

'My sister, Jean, also never spoke of that night. She was traumatised by it. Later in life, I found out the room at the back of the shelter she went in was full of dead bodies. She hadn't told me. She hadn't wanted to frighten me.'

Babs is a proud mum of two sons and has one grandson, and though she suffers with her heart – the same condition that killed her tough-as-boiled-brisket mum Bobby aged fifty-two – she has a steely inner strength about her. Babs, along with so many other wartime East Enders, would never turn in for the night, without saying: 'Goodnight, God bless. See you in the morning. PG. Please God.'

Let's hope this memorial will see an amelioration to the silent suffering of Babs, Joan, Minksy and everyone else affected by the events of that dark night seventy-five years ago. Because as the Blitz and the disaster down the Tube proved, who knew if they would live to see the dawn of a new day? As we part and she wends her way down the street in Bethnal Green, this stately matriarch who has survived being blown up, machine-gunned and crushed, turns and waves.

'See you soon, Babs,' I call.

'Please God,' she replies.

Sally's Remedy

In the cold winter months, place a warm flannel on the back before dressing and then put on a warm winter vest to keep out the chills.

Sally's Recipe

Do you know you can make a nutritious meal out of a bone? Boil up beef, lamb or chicken bones to make delicious soups. They're packed full of marrow, which is so good for you and contains all the natural antibiotics you'll ever need. Better than modern medicine.

Sally's Pearls of Wisdom

Stay curious. Keep learning. I'm ninety-two and still learning every day.

Mount Terrace by Sally Flood

This small street is fast receding
Growing smaller, day by day
Over years I watch it crumble
Watch the houses swept away,
Streets that share my childhood moments
Saw the war years, heard the bombs
Proudly held itself together
Now prepares itself to die.

Another monster now emerges
Tower blocks that blot the sky
Helicopter on the rooftops
Needs the space above to fly,
The green of years will disappear
Underneath the cars and muck
Canteens block the sky and hide
Sunlight from the garden path.

My twilight years in noise and rubble
Drown the birdsong that I love
London known for exploitation
Sees pollution rise above,
Takes no heed of past mistakes
Or normal humane needs
Only pound signs line the pavement
Privatising rules this way.

So I watch history crumble
My small voice is barely heard,
A local caught with no defences
Politicians' views preferred,
Once again construction gangs
Bulldozers, diggers line the road,
I close my door on this destruction
Peace and progress now explode.

6. Working Life, 1943

The sun was cracking the cobbles on a stifling August day as Minksy made her way along the Cambridge Heath Road wearing her best cream blouse and her last pair of patched silk stockings. The air was sticky-sweet, laced with the threat of a thunderstorm. Ignoring the wolf whistles of a couple of suited spivs, she paused outside Silberston & Sons garment factory and drew in a deep breath. Her mum Hetty's words rang through her mind: *Listen. Learn. And don't be saucy to the older women.*

In her hand, she clutched the letter from the labour exchange and a reference from the school she had attended while evacuated, along with one from the church choirmaster. Up above, the taped-up windows of the firm were flung open in the heat and a George Formby song – quite unlike one the dear old church choirmaster would recognise – belted out.

> *They say there's a troopship just leaving Bombay, bound for*
> *old Blighty shore . . .*
> *F*** 'em all, f*** 'em all, the long and the short and the tall . . .*

Raucous women's voices drifted down to the cobbles below, followed by a gale of filthy laughter. Minksy felt as if she had been preparing for work in a factory all her life, but in that moment she felt terrified. Factory life was in her blood – even now her mum was working up the road in a firm which made bedsprings. But after being evacuated and exposed to another way of life, Minksy was worried she might come over a bit, well, you know . . . posh!

Outside Silberston's, war-weary Bethnal Green was as familiar to her as the back of her hand. Factories sat hugger-mugger with rows of crumbling, grimy terraces, pubs, markets and music halls, all stewing in poverty.

Dig for Victory allotments were popping up in the grounds of old bomb craters, and nippers ran wild in the sealed-off bombsites. The neighbourhood was putting on its best face after the tragedy down the Tube and simply getting on with things.

No one talked about all those deaths, as if they simply hadn't happened. The dark heart of the East End had been concealed in the name of morale.

Minksy glanced up the road in the direction of the Tube and felt the hot red mass of fear as she recalled the putrid smells and sounds of that night, followed by the familiar realisation that she would never see her pal Dolly again.

By rights, Dolly should be standing next to her, also about to start her first day. Working in the rag was a rite of passage, or as many cockney machinists put it, 'the East End's own finishing school', employing girls right out of school aged fourteen, so that their much-needed wage could go straight into their mother's apron. Girls like her, girls like Dolly . . .

Like many other concerns, East End garment factories had been turned over to war work, helping to make and repair Army and Navy uniforms, and by 1943, firms like Silberston's had stopped making dresses and suits for West End stores and were now churning out uniforms in their thousands. The war was now in its fourth year and a new generation of young men was being sent off to fight the enemy. Now it was her turn to step up and do her bit.

Minksy's eyes travelled up the dirty brick wall. The firm

had managed to avoid a direct hit during the Blitz, but even so the building seemed to lurch slightly drunkenly towards the pavement.

'Come on, Minksy Agombar, you silly mare,' she said, blotting her cheeks with a handkerchief and blowing out slowly. 'You can do this.'

The singing and hum of machinery grew louder with every floor and by the time she reached her floor, Minksy's heart was pumping in her chest.

The factory door crashed open and a bulbous woman loomed over her. Her hair was twisted around metal curlers set under a headscarf, and a wrap-around apron seemed scarcely able to contain her breasts.

'What's yer name, love?' she asked out of the corner of her mouth, without dislodging the fag that was glued to her bottom lip.

Minksy panicked. Minksy? Too Russian-sounding. Her real name of Henrietta? Too posh.

'Er . . . Joan,' she blurted. 'Me name's Joan.'

'All right, Joan darlin', well, don't hang around like a bad smell on the landing. Guv'nor's waiting for yer.'

Minksy, or as she now realised she would be known, Joan, was ushered through a glass door on to the factory floor.

Inside, the noise was even louder, and a fug of heat and sticky sweat enveloped her. The room was filled with long wooden benches covered in Singer sewing machines. The heat, like the noise, was something else. A few women had tied rags to the wheels of their machines, but the limp breeze they gave off was about as powerful as a gnat's fart, Minksy thought with a grimace.

Bundles of material flew down from a chute in the ceiling

and the machinists grabbed them, had them unpackaged and were machining them within minutes. Their bodies rocked gently in time to the music that pumped out from the tannoy system as they worked, their hands a blur of seamless activity.

Minksy's head began to spin.

'Blimey, they ain't 'alf quick,' she murmured.

'Why do you think? They're on piecework,' said a throaty voice behind her. She turned to face an older man with a warm, well-lived-in face.

'Hello, Joan,' he grinned, extending a hand. 'I'm Wally Steiner, the guv'nor, and I look after my girls, don'cha worry about that. Work hard and you'll get on all right here, gal. A good day's work for a good day's pay, huh!'

Minksy followed the guv'nor to his office and sat down opposite him, immediately put at ease by his bluff voice and easy manner.

'Come on, *bubbeleh*,' he said to a young Jewish girl in his office, 'get that kettle on and we'll have us a lovely cup of tea.'

Minutes later, a hot, strong cup of tea with sterilised milk was pressed into Minksy's hand and she began to relax.

'No time for proper training here, you'll have to learn on the job and learn fast. You're a fast learner, right, Joan?'

Minksy nodded, her blonde curls bouncing. 'Oh yes, Mr Steiner.'

'Get that hair tied back, Rapunzel. You'll end up scalped if that gets caught in the wheel.'

'Sorry,' she blustered, rummaging around in her bag, 'I've brought me own headscarf.'

'Clever girl, I knew you was a fast learner. Your hours are eight a.m. until six p.m. Thirty minutes for your dinner. I'll give you a pound a week, with the chance of piecework when you're good enough. Wages'll be docked if you're late.' With that, he handed her a card for clocking in and out.

'If the siren goes, we sit it out on the stairs, or if it's too close for comfort, we head down the nearest shelter.'

Minksy closed her eyes, felt her heartbeat quicken and pulse in her ears. In the darkness, the images rushed at her.

Bodies on the pavement. Blood trickling from blue lips . . .

'You still with me, Joan?'

'Sorry, Mr Steiner, yes, yes . . .'

'Good, 'cause I can't be carrying no dead weight, you understand? We're making uniforms for the Army here, and we can't turn 'em out fast enough.'

Minksy nodded as she quickly knotted the headscarf round her head.

'Good, knock back yer tea and off you trot.'

'Can I spend a penny?'

'Up the passage, down the stairs, out in the yard.'

Minksy let herself out of his office, but the guv'nor's voice carried after her.

'Four minutes only.'

'Right-o, guv'nor,' she called, pelting up the passage.

By the end of that hot, sticky morning, Minksy had learnt she was going to have to do more than work out how to keep her toilet breaks to under four minutes if she was going to survive life in the wartime rag trade. The pace was punishing. A strict forelady walked the line, eyeing everyone's work, and a picky passer, whose job it was to check the quality and finish of their work, was never far away.

The more experienced, older machinists worked on an assembly line. Uniforms would come down the line and one woman would sew on the sleeves, then it would be passed to the next to sew on the pockets and so on, until it got to the end of the line as a finished garment.

Minksy was placed with all the other new starters, young giggly girls in the main, on a bench stitching linings. By keeping her wits about her, she began to see the unwritten rules.

Sloppy seams and bad workmanship weren't tolerated, but swearing and singing were. Though Minksy quickly realised singing had less to do with morale and more to do with keeping work momentum up. The more the women sang, the faster they worked.

She also realised there were no end of dodges going on. Minksy saw women smuggling extra bundles under their workstations, and an additional tea break sneaked in when the women in the line in front simultaneously held the wheels of their machines, thereby fusing them.

At this, she thought Wally might blow a gasket.

'Bloomin' fuse box!' he huffed, storming out of his office. 'Have a quick break while we fix it.'

The girl next to Minksy whipped her ciggies out of her bag.

'Don't worry about old Wal. He comes over like he's got the needle, but he's a big teddy bear really.' Her face opened into a bright smile.

'I'm Peggy,' she said, shaking a fag loose and thrusting it at Minksy. 'Fancy a smoke?'

'No, ta, I don't,' Minksy replied.

'You got a fella?'

'No.'

'Blimey, what do you do for fun?' Peggy asked.

'I sing,' Minksy replied.

'Ooh, smashing,' Peggy grinned. 'Now I come to think of

it, I reckon I've seen you and your sisters sing under the arches. Behind the Salmon & Ball?'

'That's right.'

'Got any brothers?'

'One, but he's only ten.'

'Typical. There ain't any men under forty or over sixteen left in Bethnal Green.' Peggy gave a theatrical shudder. 'I'm eighteen and the way this war's going, I'm gonna end up an ageing aunt!'

Glancing about conspiratorially, she leant in closer to Minksy.

'Mind you, I reckon as how I've found a way to meet a fella.'

'How's that?' Minksy asked.

'Keep it under yer hat, like, but I've been sewing these into the linings.' She winked, pulling a small note from her handbag. 'How long before I get a reply, do you think?'

Intrigued by the bold, chatty seamstress, Minksy unfolded the note and read: 'If you're in the mood, write to me, and I'll be in the nude.'

Peggy signed it with a kiss and her address. Minksy gulped.

'Blimey, Peggy! Not that long, I shouldn't wonder.'

'Here, why don't you write one?' she suggested, taking back the note and quickly hiding it away.

'Not as long as I got a hole in my arse,' Minksy shot back.

'Don'cha wanna keep some soldier's pecker up?' Peggy replied, lifting her little finger suggestively and arching one pencilled brow.

Peggy and Minksy looked at each other and burst out laughing. Peggy might have been a bit of a good-time girl with more front than Blackpool, but Minksy instantly warmed to her. Being a machinist was going to be hard work, but she had a feeling she was going to like the banter and camaraderie of factory work. Peggy wasn't Dolly, but her friendship in such a fragile, uncertain world was something bright and beautiful to clutch at. Peggy sensed it too.

'I like you, Joanie. I reckon as how you and me are going to be pals.'

As it turned out, factory work liked her too. As the days unspooled into weeks, Minksy discovered she was a dab hand with a needle and thread. Wally obviously agreed, as he very quickly moved her up to the assembly line with the promise of piecework not far behind.

Not everyone was as thrilled as Minksy with her sudden promotion.

'What's a girl like her doing on the line?' an older married woman by the name of Sandra demanded to know, shooting Minksy a look that could curdle milk.

'Shut your cakehole,' Wally retorted. 'She's got clever hands.'

Torn between the need to impress the guv'nor and heeding her mum's words about not rubbing the older women up the wrong way, Minksy decided to go all out on a charm offensive. On morning tea break one Friday, she sidled up to where Sandra was sitting with her pals, smoking a fag and doing the crossword.

'Five across, ten letters, clue is "intrigues" . . .' Sandra grumbled, chewing on the end of a scrubby pencil. 'Well, it ain't intriguing me, it's giving me the right ache, in fact.'

Minksy leant over the paper.

'Titillates.'

''Ere, she's only right an' all, Sand!' exclaimed her pal. 'Shove up, let her help with the rest.'

Sandra glared at Minksy, a nerve in her jaw jumping.

'You saucing me, girl?'

'No,' Minksy protested. 'I was only trying to help, is all.'

'If I want yer help, I'll ask,' she said slowly, small beady eyes glaring out from the fleshy folds of her face. 'Now hop it.'

Minksy saw the warning signs. The last thing she needed was a clump off the factory matriarch.

'Jealous,' Peggy sniffed, as they sat outside later on dinner break, eating their corned beef and brown sauce sandwiches.

'What of?' Minksy asked, puzzled.

'She's only jibbed 'cause you can sing, you can sew and you're better looking than her,' she said bluntly.

Minksy shook her head, feeling confused. She'd only been trying to get Sandra to like her.

Peggy's whole face suddenly lit up like a sunbeam in the cold concrete stairwell.

'I nearly forgot: I got an answer to one of my notes.'

'You never have, Peg,' Minksy laughed, nearly choking on her corned beef.

'I have an' all,' she said proudly. 'A messenger in the Royal Artillery. He's on leave. We're meeting up the Lyceum later. Hope he's a dish.'

'You know what these soldiers are like. Make sure you keep yer hand on yer ha'penny,' Minksy said, parroting back the warning issued to every young girl. Everyone knew what became of girls who let hands stray too far south and ended up in trouble. Despite having grown up in the pubs and music halls of East London, Minksy had led a sheltered life, with her mum drumming the fear of God into her about hanky panky before marriage.

'He's expecting a full frontal, don't forget,' Minksy went on worriedly.

'Don'cha worry, Joan,' Peggy breezed, standing up and dusting down the crumbs off her skirt. 'I won't let him go below the dotted line.'

Back on the floor, Minksy was surprised to see crossword Sandra sidle up to her. Usually her mouth was puckered like corrugated iron, but now she was actually smiling.

'Minksy, be a doll, would ya, and pop down the shops before the bell goes and get us a rubber mallet? I'd go meself, only I've pulled a hamstring.'

Minksy smiled sweetly, but inside she was seething. Cheek of her! She must think her green as a gardener's thumb!

'Why, course, Sandra. Would you like me to fetch you some pigeon's milk while I'm there?' Her smile slipped. 'Or how about a yard and a half of elbow grease? Or maybe a long weight and some tartan paint?'

The floor fell about, thirty women screeching with laughter, which rattled round the factory.

'She's tumbled you, Sandra. Back at yer with knobs on!'

Minksy might have been the new girl, but she wasn't daft. Ever since her sister Marie had tricked her mate Nellie Richards into queuing up for a penn'orth of trippy hairs and some elephant's milk at the local corner shop, Minksy had vowed not to fall for any pranks.

'That's enough!' sighed Wally, coming out of his office. 'Dinner break's over. Come on, girls, sharp's the word . . . and let's have a song while we're at it.'

'How about Vera Lynn, "White Cliffs of Dover"?' suggested Peggy.

'Or what about "There's a Boy Coming Home on Leave"?' Minksy bantered back, with a wink.

'Shut yer bleedin' trap, saucy cow,' Peggy cackled, flicking an empty bobbin at her.

Soon the room was filled with the humming of machines. Minksy lost herself in the romance of the song.

'There'll be bluebirds . . .'

Soon, all the women on the line were swaying as one, as the melody drifted over the factory floor. Hands steadily fed strips of khaki material through Singers, but hearts were hijacked, dreaming of loved ones.

Minksy's thoughts strayed once more to Dolly. Sixteen years old, full of life and fun. How proud she'd have been to have started work here as a machinist. Minksy was gripped by an awful feeling of guilt. What if she had gone with Dolly down the Tube – maybe she would have been able to prevent her death? Hot, angry tears filled her eyes.

What on earth? Where was the blood coming from? Blinking back tears, she saw thick red oozing from beneath her nail. In her distracted state, she'd driven the sewing machine needle clean through her thumbnail into the soft flesh beneath. She gave a queer little cry at the sight of her thumb, impaled under the needle.

An excited chorus went up.

'Joan's got her thumb under the needle!'

Wally was over in a second. He took one look and, cool as a cucumber, turned and fetched the first-aid kit from his office.

'All right, calm down,' grumbled the elderly Jewish man as he shuffled over, rubbing his lower back, 'it's only a needle.'

As he slowly turned the handle of the wheel to remove the needle from her thumb, Minksy closed her eyes, unable to watch. When she opened them again, Wally was briskly bandaging up her thumb.

'You're lucky,' he muttered. 'The needle came out whole. You ain't a proper machinist—'

'Until you've got your thumb under the needle three times!' chorused the rest of the floor.

Without even realising it, Minksy had passed two machinist rites of passage in one day.

'Right, let's get you up the London!' Wally said.

'I'll be all right, guv'nor,' Minksy replied bravely.

'No, you must get it looked at,' he insisted.

Sandra nodded with grudging respect, and Minksy got the feeling that from then on, they were going to be all right. No one liked a wet blanket. Minksy had just marked herself out as one of them – a proper machinist.

As she clocked off and headed to hospital, Minksy's back was stiff as a board, her thumb was throbbing and every time she closed her eyes, all she could see was flickering needles, but she felt a deep sense of satisfaction as Wally pressed a wage packet into her hand. Out of the twelve shillings she earned, she knew her mum Hetty would take ten and give her back two, and that was a fact of which she was proud. She was paying her way. This job was making a woman of her. But she realised, when it came to womanhood, she still had a lot to learn.

One week later, as the hands on the clock hit 6 p.m., the machines shut down with a shudder, and a carnival atmosphere filled the floor. Talk about eye-opening! Minksy had never seen the like.

Sandra and her pals ripped off the turbans that anchored their metal curlers in place. Hair was plumped. Fresh stockings were slipped on – or in the absence of that, gravy browning applied – rouge rubbed in and the brightest red lipstick Minksy had ever seen was slathered on. All of them swanking about the big dances they were going to, and the fellas they were meeting, including, to Minksy's shock, the married ones!

'Where you meeting your fella, Sand?' a passer by the name of Mavis asked Sandra.

'Round the back of the Regal, Mav,' she replied, as she separated castor-oiled lashes with a needle.

'I thought Sandra was married?' Minksy whispered to Peggy.

'She is,' she replied, as she carefully stuck what looked to Minksy's eyes like the black bit out of a winkle to her cheek as a beauty spot. 'But her old man's away. Trust me, she ain't the only one doing the double shuffle!'

Peggy turned to face her and Minksy had to hand it to her. She really did look smashing. Out of her turban and tunic, and wearing a cherry red dress that showed off her nipped-in waist, she scrubbed up a treat. Her blonde hair fell in soft waves about her face and her full lips were painted a rich ruby red.

'You're gonna stop traffic!'

This seemed to please Peggy, who picked up her handbag and bundled her work uniform into a brown paper bag.

'Wish me luck, Joan! Ooh, nearly forgot.'

Fishing about in her purse she found a bottle of black market Evening in Paris, and dabbed a bit behind each ear and one for luck between her breasts.

'Now, I'm dressed.'

'Peg . . . You sure about this?' Minksy ventured.

'Never surer,' she replied, snapping her purse shut. 'I'm gonna enjoy myself. I could be dead tomorrow. Goodnight, God bless, see you in the morning . . . PG!'

'Please God,' Minksy echoed.

And then Peggy was gone, heels tapping on the scuffed lino as she hurried off to meet her mystery soldier. Pretty soon the floor had emptied, and Minksy was left alone in the darkened factory, the stench of sweet perfume and sweat hanging over her head like a cloud, her ears ringing from the banter and the ticking of the treadle.

Racks of finished Army uniforms hung on a rail, casting shadows on the distempered wall.

In her heart, she knew Peggy was right. If the disaster

down the Tube had taught her anything, it was to cherish and respect each new day. Shivering slightly, Minksy grabbed her bag and clattered down the steps, back home to the warmth of her tiny terrace in Shetland Street. Clutching her wage packet, she felt like she'd finally stepped into her own shoes.

Minksy's entry into wartime working life certainly removed the blinkers, but more importantly, it taught her a valuable trade. In time, not only would she meet a sweetheart to call her own, she'd make it all the way to the top of the tree as one of the East End's most experienced sample makers on thirty quid a week, with a body that seemed moulded to a sewing machine. Over the years Minksy worked for many firms, acquiring new skills with each job, her favourite being alongside Jewish machinist Izzie Cohen, who she credits with teaching her so much. But she would never forget those first few months as a young Singer girl, earning an honest crust. But what of pert Peggy, Minksy's factory pal, whom we last saw tottering off in a cloud of Evening of Paris to meet with the soldier who had responded to her note?

'Blow me if they didn't get married and start a family!' Minksy laughs.

This wartime liaison was a success, but there were many others that didn't make it to the altar and whose stories had sadder endings, mired in scandal and shame. Even so, the 'live for the day' attitude helped to relax the nation's moral code somewhat. As Minksy accurately observed, women were no longer as desperate to 'hold on to their ha'penny' and did indeed 'go below the dotted line'.

During the war, young women workers enjoyed their first taste of money and emancipation. Before, their lives had been mapped out for them, constrained by their class and sex. They were supposed to be compliant, respectable and domesticated. The war destroyed all that, triggering sweeping social change and freeing many from a life of endless drudgery and a cycle of childbirth and housework.

In December 1941, just over six months after the Blitz ended, the National Service Act (No. 2) was passed introducing conscription for women. All unmarried women and childless widows between the ages of twenty and thirty could now be set to work for the wider good of the war effort. And just like Minksy, for many an East End woman, working 'in the rag' lives on in the memory as the happiest days of their lives.

'How I used to love my job as a machinist at the Rego on Bethnal Green Road. It launched me into life,' Pat from Bethnal Green confided in me shortly before her death in September 2016 aged eighty-nine. 'I started work soon as I turned fourteen. I went from being a schoolgirl on the Friday, into the factory on a Monday, and pretty soon I was working forty-eight-hour weeks. We never questioned it. We just did what our mothers told us. It was like a continuation of our education, a finishing school for us East Enders.

'Yes, it was hard work, but was it fun? Cor, not much! Picture forty girls all machining in a line, all of us wearing curlers under our turbans. We sang along to *Music While You Work* on the wireless. My favourite was "Moonlight Serenade" by Glenn Miller.

'On tea break, we'd all stand around giggling, smoking and plucking each other's eyebrows. We might have been on war work but we was kids really.

'I remember a fourteen-year-old girl started her periods at the factory. You never spoke to your mum about that in those days, so she was sent along to the nurse and given a sanitary towel. Unfortunately she wasn't told what to do with it. She told nurse she was bleeding and had a headache. When she came back she was wearing the sanitary towel on her forehead, with the pad looped behind her ears! We fell about. "Wot'cha doing, you daft cow?" "It's for my headache, ain't it?" she replied, mystified.

'Then the bombs started and everything changed. One time I was sitting at my workbench machining, when the entire front of the building blew off and just slid on to the pavement in a great cloud of dust. We were so shocked, we sat staring at the passers-by in the street from behind our machines.

'During the war, you never knew who would be there the next morning. Quite often you'd come in to find empty seats where women had been killed or bombed out. They were very sad times, but despite this, by God, we took the war on!'

'Too right! We went from being mothers and wives to workers and fighters,' agrees ninety-seven-year-old Dolly from Bethnal Green, who was at pains to stress this to me before her death in October 2017. 'It's us women who were the true heroes. It's we who deserved the medals. We toiled while the bombs dropped around us, risking our lives, working and raising our families in a war zone. My friend's brother came home on leave during the Blitz. He couldn't believe it – he couldn't wait to get back into the Army.'

Despite the fear, Dolly says work defined her and gave her a purity of purpose during the war. Clothing was inherently rooted in East End communities, in the way steel was to Sheffield, or coal to Newcastle. For many East End girls, work in the clothing industry either as a court dressmaker, piecework seamstress, milliner, cutter, finisher, passer or presser was already decided upon before they left school. A skill with a needle and thread was bred in the bone for girls who grew up in the shadow of the factories.

'Sewing is in my blood,' Dolly nodded proudly. 'I could always do it. I remember sewing wedding dresses for my dolls when I was a small girl. I had such patience and nimble fingers. Aged fourteen, I went into a Jewish-owned factory sewing dresses. I started just trimming threads, but watched and learnt and quickly worked my way up to assembling whole dresses.

'I started on seven and six a week. I used to give my mum my wage and she would give me back one and six. Out of that, I always bought her a packet of her favourite chocolate brazil nuts each Friday for thruppence a quarter, just because she loved them.

'When war started, I was nineteen, and I got a job sewing Army uniforms at the Rego. All us girls slipped notes into the uniform pockets, or sent the soldiers cigarettes. It was just a bit of a lark, a way of finding a fella. I remember getting a letter back from Jimmy Kray, the twins' uncle. Needless to say, I didn't write back!

'I did loads of jobs after that – making tyres for trucks and in munitions filling bombs and bullets with gunpowder. Let's be clear. The country would have collapsed without us women. I'm proud of the role I played.'

That work ethic was so strongly ingrained in Dolly that she was still working at the age of seventy, making fry-ups for the workers in a café in Walthamstow, East London.

Not all memories of work are wrapped in the warmth of nostalgia or patriotic pride, however.

'I was working as a typist in a City firm during the war, but living in the East End,' recalls ninety-year-old Dee.

'Every time the sirens went off, the boss would make us lug our typewriters down to the basement in case they got damaged during the raid. Great big heavy things they were. I didn't want to get killed because I'd been looking after someone else's office equipment, so one day I stood up to him and refused. "It's their typewriters, not ours," I told the office girls in a great gesture of defiance. The boss sacked me! Still, that experience taught me to stand up for myself in life.'

There were plenty of others whose heart wasn't in their work.

It was mid-morning tea break. Fourteen-year-old Sally's gaze slid out of the factory windows to the occluded skyline beyond. As she sipped her tea, she stared bleakly at the barrage balloons bobbing about in the greasy skies. All the factory chimneys of East London were reaching up to the skies, pumping bilious clouds of noxious fumes into the air. But Sally knew there was a whole wonderful world out there beyond the jumbled rooftops and narrow streets around Brick Lane.

Evacuation had taught her to lift her gaze. By the wide green waters of an estuary in Torquay, Devon, the skies over her head had seemed endless, the world suddenly full of infinite, shimmering possibility.

'Join the Girl Guides,' they said, so she had. 'Come to the country school,' they urged, so she did. 'Try your hand at fishing.' Sally had picked up a rod and was soon plucking perch from the silvery waters.

'Become a teacher . . .'

And here the dream had abruptly ended.

'A teacher!' her mother, Annie, had exclaimed, when she came down from the East End to visit. 'Oh no, no, no . . .

That won't do,' she muttered, casting her eye about suspiciously. 'They're trying to exploit you. You're going to be a machinist.'

Sally was delivered back to the East End so quickly, she sometimes wondered if she hadn't dreamt Devon up. Within days of her arrival back in Bethnal Green, her mother had taken her to a garment factory in the choked heartland of the rag trade, and spoken for her.

'She's good with her hands and she's a fast learner.'

The Jewish guv'nor had looked her up and down. 'And she'll need to be,' he'd muttered, nodding to an enormous roll of khaki.

And so it was that Sally had found herself aged fourteen, not working with words, but machining Army uniforms at Louis London's on weekly wages of ten shillings, just one of millions of girls doing their bit for the war effort.

Come Into the Factories, the cheery propaganda posters beckoned. What a joke! As a poor, working-class Jewish girl raised in the tight-knit streets around Brick Lane, Sally's destiny had always been the factories of the East End.

She measured the milestones of her youth against pockets sewn and hems pressed, watched the years unspool like cotton from a bobbin. Every day rolled out with the same regularity.

Clock in. Join the production line. Sew. Snip. Clock out.

The khaki flowed beneath her eye in a river of brown, passing between deft, nimble fingers. Here a pocket, there a sleeve, until it reached the end of the production line and became the next raw recruit's uniform.

Sally was proud of her job – putting food on her mother's table was a privilege – but sometimes she wondered . . . Was there not more to life than the factories? She and the other machinists were cogs in a relentless war machine.

The thought took hold and, glancing about, she pulled a scrubby pencil from her apron pocket, grabbed a piece of paper that backed the embroidery machine and began to write. Words spilled out like water.

> *Machines crashing! Like flailing whips*
> *Introduction to a man-made hell,*
> *Barely fourteen years old earning a crust,*
> *Outside these walls, London listens for enemy planes . . .*

As Sally scribbled her secret poem, she felt a lightness take hold and the grey factory walls melted away.

> *Louis London was geared to win the war,*
> *Just one tiny cog in a world gone mad,*
> *The sweatshop had nothing on this one-way system*
> *No one stopped or dared to breathe . . .*

'All right, girls, pull out! I said pull out!'

The voice of the factory foreman tore through her thoughts and Sally realised he was nearly upon her. Hastily, she tore up her composition and stuffed it under the bench.

'I said, break time's over, girl. What you doing?'

'Nothing.'

'Good, look lively, these uniforms won't sew themselves.'

Fifty or so Singer sewing machines rumbled into life and the war machine began once more. Poetry would have to wait. Another thirty-five years, in fact. There was a crust to earn. A family to help feed. A war to win.

Girls like Sally, Minksy, Dolly and Pat were cogs in a machine, but they were important nonetheless, clothing the British Army and contributing to the family income.

Actress and *EastEnders* legend Anita Dobson speaks with

nostalgia of a childhood woven through with rich memories of the rag trade.

'Growing up in the East End of London was something to be proud of,' she told me. 'There was never going to be an abundance of money, but there was an overwhelming abundance of love and sense of community. My dad worked for a big firm called Blanes, where he was a dress cutter. He worked long hours, often doing overtime to make a bit extra, and Mum raised me and my sister.'

Like so many others brought up in the East End, Anita was poor, but thanks to the thrift and imagination of her parents, she was never aware of that fact. All the money that came into her house went on the table and on their backs so she and her sister never went hungry.

At school, Anita was nicknamed Chocolate Box by the school nurse because she was always turned out well, and often wore a big bow in her hair. Like most East End mums, Anita's was a gifted seamstress and she ran up her daughters' clothes on her trusty Singer sewing machine.

'I can still remember the pretty outfits Mum would make my sister and I, but the moment that stands out like a beacon was the Red Coat!' Anita laughs. 'It was coming up to Christmas and Mum had been machining like a demon, so that we all looked good for the holiday season. It was my first grown-up coat, because I wanted to look like the women in the Blanes catalogue. Well, when she finished I couldn't believe my eyes. It was red and black, with shiny black buttons. Oh, it was so smart and elegant. I felt like a film star.

'We scoured the Roman Road market for the right pair of shoes, and Mum found a pair of black patent high heels with bows on the front, and a pair of black gloves. When I put it on to show the family, my eyes were shining as I turned away from the mirror to look at them. My dad smiled at my mum, turned to me and said: "Kid, you look a million dollars." So I never felt poor. I always felt like a million dollars.'

In common with so many other East Enders, the soundtrack to Anita's early years was the trusty humming of a Singer sewing machine, which in a sense was as much a weapon during wartime as a gun was.

Of course, it wasn't all sewing and secretarial work. War work pushed women outside the traditional feminine roles and into jobs usually reserved for men. Women were conscripted into jobs in munitions, transport, welding, engineering and the shipyards, to name but a few, and were paid relatively well for their efforts. But in some cases, the boost to their identity, self-esteem and strength was of far greater value.

'The best thing my husband ever did was die,' remarked ninety-one-year-old Sarah from Poplar, with typical East End candour. 'He was a no-good lazy bastard. He was a merchant seaman and didn't treat me so good. I wouldn't have him back for all the tea in China. During the war, I found independence. The men were gone and the women stepped into their place and made a bloody good job of it an' all. I worked as a painter. I painted the sides of giant container boats in dry dock and every inch of Ascot race stand. Every inch! I was a good painter too. A good worker.'

East Ender Sarah, like millions of other wartime women around the country, was proving she was of equal competence to the menfolk and exploding the inequality myth. The efforts of these women were all the more prodigious when you consider how much juggling was required to keep the home running in addition to their duties at work.

'The mothers never stopped! My mum Eva would start

work at three a.m. until five a.m. – then go home to get food ready for our breakfast and prepare a dinner, before going back to work in a wood yard, cutting up large trees,' recalls eighty-year-old Betty from Stepney, before adding proudly: 'Soon as I was old enough I joined her, drove a lorry and a three-gear crane, I did!'

Sarah, Eva and Betty weren't the only ones getting their hands dirty. By 1943, Beatty, who we last saw fighting fascists at the Battle of Cable Street, had gone from beating black-shirts to making bullets. Battling Beatty, like most East Enders of her generation, was parochial. Her world was confined largely to the bustling Jewish quarter around Petticoat Lane. But when a bomb took the roof off her buildings during the Blitz, she had no choice but to move.

'I knew things were bad when I was sitting with my new baby daughter, June, in a shelter beneath our buildings and we heard a tremendous bang. Our buildings had copped it so that sealed it for us. The East End was too dangerous. Me, my mother and sisters, upped sticks and left Whitechapel in search of safety and work.

'First, we went to Oxford and I got a job as a postwoman. Mum would look after June. I used to get up at four a.m. and a W.H. Smith van would give me a lift along Magdalen Bridge.'

Once again, Jewish Beatty and her family experienced the same ugly prejudices that had led her to stand up and be counted against the fascists in 1936.

'The people in Oxford hated us Londoners. "Go Home," they said. Go Home?'

Beatty rolls her eyes at the two words that were the sound-track to her early life.

'So we moved to Leeds, which was much better. I got a

job on war work, making bullets in a factory. I had to use a micrometer. I've always had a clumsy hand, so you can imagine, I was terrified of dropping one of these things or breaking the tool. But despite this, I loved my new life in Leeds. We had a six-room house for one pound a week and more food than in London.

'I've always had to work as my husband was discharged from the Army with pneumonia, no pension or nothing, so I've had to graft. Even after I had two more children, I carried on working. If I didn't work, we didn't eat, and I had three hungry mouths to fill. But at least the Government cottoned on to the fact that women needed help, so they started to open the first nurseries, which really was a help.'

Wartime nurseries were set up by the Ministry of Health in conjunction with the Ministry of Labour and Ministry of Education. The majority were located in close proximity to the factories to make it easy for mothers to drop their children off and pick them up at the end of the day. Children's nurseries popped up in the strangest of places, including Underground shelters. Many favoured the time-honoured reciprocal method of childcare, with neighbours and family taking it in turns to look after each other's kids.

The children of wartime Britain were a different breed to those that exist today. Not only were they forced to grow up quicker, facing dark and harrowing events, but they were also expected to pull their weight and contribute to the war effort, just as their mothers were.

By 1943, the indomitable rent-striking mothers of Quinn Square were out working in the factories. Their sons had hit upon a scheme, which by anyone's standards demonstrates enormous enterprise and flair.

With lots of schools closed down or evacuated, it would

have been easy to get into mischief in the many bombsites that peppered the district. Instead, Frankie, Ronnie, Joey, George and Ken, otherwise known as the self-styled School-boy Gardeners of Russia Lane, borrowed rakes and shovels from George's dad, who owned stables down Russia Lane, and set about transforming a bombsite into a Dig for Victory allotment.

A toxic rubble-and-scree-filled hole in the ground in a bomb-battered slum was hardly the most promising envir-onment in which to grow fruit and veg, not that this deterred Frankie and his pals. Once the Heavy Rescue Service had removed rubble and masonry, the boys used dustbin lids pierced with holes to sift through the earth and get rid of all the glass and shrapnel. George's dad came in handy again, providing them with a ready source of fertilizer in the form of fresh horse manure to dig into the soil.

The Schoolboy Gardeners took their lead from the Bethnal Green Bombed Sites Producers' Association, which saw over 300 adults and children transforming East London bombsites into highly productive allotments. The boys must have used up an awful lot of elbow grease to ready the ground so that it was fertile enough to plant and grow 'Vegetables of National Importance', as the Dig for Victory scheme grandly named them, such as Home Guard potatoes. But, like their mothers before them, they didn't give up and on Thursday, 14 May 1943 at 6 p.m. they proudly invited the neighbour-hood to the opening of their first garden at 57–68 Russia Lane, E2.

Word of how the residents of Bethnal Green were trans-forming the borough's bombsites spread and on 17 June 1943, the Queen even paid a visit. To see the pride and swag-ger on the Schoolboy Gardeners' grubby faces, all scabby knees and patched-up pullovers, is to glimpse back into a childhood that was harder, but infinitely kinder. This must have been a formative experience for this group of boys.

Ron Hilson, eighty-three, remembers his old pals fondly. 'They did a lot of work developing two bombsites in Russia Lane, one for allotments and on the other one they built a push bike race track,' he recalls. 'It was great, we had wonderful times, even when Hitler was dropping bombs on us.'

It is staggering to consider the ways in which women – and as we can now also see, children – were able to step up and contribute like never before, with society adjusting to meet this new work force. Women's employment increased during the war from 5.1 million in 1939, to just over 7.25 million by 1943, as women ventured out of the home and traditional work in domestic service, and into war work in factories.

'The Second World War had a huge impact on women's lives in Britain. Despite the chaos and uncertainty that war brought, women experienced a new-found cultural liberation,' says Jennifer Daley from the Department of War Studies at King's College, London. 'With the vast majority of men gone abroad to fight, British women eagerly stepped up to the challenge of single-handedly running households and businesses. In the absence of men, women executed men's work efficiently and with skill, which created a profound sense of accomplishment.

'When provided with the opportunity to do the work of men, women rose to the occasion. During the war, British women accomplished so much and contributed so greatly to the war, and this encouraged a sense of confidence and pride. When the war ended, women of Britain maintained this new level of confidence and pride, which contributed to the development of equal rights between genders that we enjoy today.'

It is true that some women wanted to explore what they were capable of and contribute towards the war effort, but in reality, for our East End matriarchs, they have always had to work, not because their King and country required it, but because their wage was needed to help keep the family off the breadline.

'My dear mum Sophie held down three jobs,' recalls eighty-seven-year-old Vera from Bethnal Green, who still lives a two-minute walk from the street she was born on in 1929.

'She had to. My dad was bone idle and spent all his wages on beer and bets. She had seven kids and lost goodness knows how many more, but still she kept going. She went off to the city at the crack of dawn to go cleaning, come home and start work in a tailoring factory. Then she'd get back home in the evening and still carry on home-working, sewing into the early hours. I remember once the gaslight was fading so she actually put her chair up on to the table to be closer to the light so she could carry on sewing! Not that it seemed to make much difference, we were still poor.'

To Sophie, life was about survival, and with little support from her husband, it was her phenomenal efforts which kept her seven children fed and clothed.

'I always said to Mum, "Why don't you leave him?" and she always replied, "And where would I go?"'

Sadly, Sophie was right. Between the wars, where would a single mum of seven find board and lodging? Hard work was a currency which ensured her whole family's survival. And her children adored her for it.

'Her wages spread to many mouths. When Dad died no

one gave a jot,' says Vera, 'but when Mum died, I was heart-broken. I'm eighty-seven and I still miss her. She was an angel on earth, a real lady.'

Sophie's efforts were matched in every borough of the East End.

'The biggest thing my mum taught me was how to graft,' insists eighty-one-year-old Glad. 'I was one of six, born into buildings on Poplar High Street. We had nothing, but my mum, Gladys, was a force of nature and could always conjure up a meal out of something. She was tiny – four foot eight inches – and a real character. Looking back, my biggest memory of her is one of intense pride.

'I always knew I had to go to work, and what's more, I wanted to. I wanted to be able to help Mum out. Office work was my first choice, but Mum said, "No, be a machinist, you'll always be able to earn a quid," and she was right.

'I started as a machinist at London's making Army over-coats at fifteen. Nothing beat seeing Mum's face when I handed over my wages.

'I got married at nineteen. Times were hard. My husband got work as a lighterman on the docks, sometimes he got work, other times he didn't. Sadly, he died young and I had to take up three jobs to survive as our two kids grew up. I worked as a machinist, cleaning in an office, and on weekends I did bar work.

'Over the years, I've never stopped. I've run a jellied eel stall outside the Blackwall Tunnel, worked as a telegraphist in Fleet Street, ran a pub in Canning Town and worked as a laboratory assistant in the London Hospital.

'Nobody is ever going to give you anything, are they? So you have to work for it,' Glad says, echoing a sentiment I've heard time and again from the mouths of East End women.

Today, the vibrant, Jewish-run factories of the rag trade where our matriarchs cut their teeth and honed the skills that allowed them to feed their families, are no more. The rich legacy of the clothing trade has gone, migrated out to the suburbs or, worse still, the sweatshops of China. There are no more sewing apprenticeships for school-leavers in the East End now. The Singers are silenced. But the memory of those times lives on in seamstress Sally, whom we last saw scribbling poetry behind her sewing machine during the war.

Fortunately, she did finish that poem, and hundreds more beside. In fact, she went on to become one of the most prolific poets of her generation, performing alongside Benjamin Zephaniah and as one of the renowned Basement Writers. Sally's verse appears in poetry books that are taught in schools and universities around the world. She herself went on to teach poetry and creative writing, ironically joining the very trade her mother prophesied would exploit her. Sally's lived a rich life, and has documented those experiences in poetry.

'I wrote on scraps of paper, in whatever moments I could snatch back from life,' Sally says with a wistful smile, revealing the passion for poetry that lived on in her secret heart. 'I married outside my religion, to a wonderful Irish tailor, raised our seven children and worked as a seamstress, going on to be a skilled embroidery machinist. But I always held on to my love of writing.

'War work taught me to be resilient and to never give up.'

Today, Sally Flood is a ninety-two-year-old force to be reckoned with. She has never left the East End and though the world around her has changed beyond measure, she herself has not. She still continues to write and perform her own poetry, working in her Whitechapel home, a skinny Edwardian terrace situated along a narrow cobbled back road. Her drawers and cupboards are stuffed full of poems and embroidery, the walls smothered with photos of her three grandchildren and five great-grandchildren. A lifetime of love and endeavour sings from the walls.

Little wonder, then, that when that home came under threat in the 1990s, Sally fought tooth and nail to protect it. Developers tried to buy her street to demolish it and encompass it into the neighbouring London Hospital. Sally, her husband and her neighbours formed a committee and lobbied to get a protection order placed on the entire terrace.

Now, her street is Grade II listed and developers can't touch it. Today, the street and its history remain. Sally remains. This is a woman who refused to leave London when the Blitz broke out and worked her way through the war. She's certainly not budging in the face of a greedy developer!

'The whole community drew together and lived as one and it brought out the best in people,' she says of the war. 'We thrived in the East End because we are resourceful, natural-born fighters. We also know the true value of hard work.'

Hard work is drummed into the DNA of our East End matriarchs, with the war adding another layer of danger to the grind, but to a woman it helped define them, and is the key to their longevity.

Jessie's Recipe

Jessie's chocolate cake. Much loved by her ninety-nine – yes, ninety-nine – great-grandchildren.

Jessie's Chocolate Cake

6oz margarine or butter
6oz sugar
5oz flour
1oz cocoa
3 eggs
Gas mark 4 – 35 minutes

Chocolate icing;
3oz icing sugar
1oz cocoa powder
1½oz margarine or butter
2oz caster sugar
2 tablespoons water

Mix margarine or butter and sugar together. Sieve flour and cocoa into a bowl and mix in. Add eggs little by little. Add splash of milk if needed. Put into a greased cake tin and bake.

Now make your icing.

Sift the icing sugar and cocoa powder into a mixing basin. Measure the margarine or butter, sugar and water into a saucepan and set over a low heat. Stir well until the sugar has dissolved and the margarine or butter has melted. Bring it just to the boil, then draw off the heat and pour at once on to the sifted ingredients. Beat with a wooden spoon until the mixture is smooth, then allow to cool, stirring occasionally until the frosting is thick enough to coat the back of a spoon. Spread thickly over the top of your cooled cake and leave to set.

Jessie's Remedy

I used to leave my babies in their prams to cry for a little while outside if they wouldn't settle, never did them any harm.

Jessie's Pearls of Wisdom

Have another cup of tea and get on with it.

7. Birth and Death, 1944

Her face was red with rage, her voice reaching a pitch only the neighbourhood dogs could hear. 'Your father ain't gonna be happy! What the hell were you thinking, girl?'

It was a fair enough question, under the circumstances. Seventeen-year-old Jessie was unmarried and pregnant. In 1944, there was no greater shame. The war was raging, but Jessie knew the hostilities would have nothing on the murders that would break out when her father got home.

Jessie's mum, Elizabeth, and dad, William, were respectable working class. She had been raised to keep her hand on her ha'penny until she had a ring on her finger. But that was before she met Arthur Smith. *Oh, Arthur.* Just the thought of him made her go weak at the knees.

They'd met when she'd got a job in the same rag factory as him in Plaistow, East London. He might have been shorter than her, but what he lacked in size, he made up for in sparkle. On their first date, she'd been late.

'You got one more chance,' he'd said cockily, his eyes twinkling as he pushed back a mop of thick, dark hair. After that, Jessie hadn't been late for any of their dates. There wasn't much to do after dark in the blackout, so they'd made their own entertainment – which was why she was now in this mess.

'I'm sorry, Mum, but I love him,' she protested, eyes filling with tears.

'I'd like to marry your daughter, Sir,' Arthur said bravely to her father later that evening. 'I'll work my socks off to support us.'

'I should bloody well think so,' was the retort.

In October 1944, a scandal was averted when Arthur and Jessie tied the knot at a registry office in Stratford, her four-month baby bump covered by a simple white dress. East London looked as patched up and war-weary as the rest of Britain. Five long years of war had taken their toll. But Arthur and Jessie were the proudest, happiest couple alive. They were young and in love, and nothing else mattered.

There was no money or food for a reception, so they went to the pictures instead. Jessie can't recall what they watched, because they were too busy kissing and cuddling. In the snug, dark warmth of the picture house, cocooned from poverty and the war, she melted into Arthur's arms.

'I don't half fancy you, Mrs Smith,' he whispered in the darkness. 'I can't keep me hands off you.'

'You're not so bad yourself, Mr Smith,' she giggled.

Jessie waited for the romance to fade, as so many people told her it would. But the strange thing was, it didn't. Not after their first daughter, a little girl also called Jessie, screamed her way into the world in March 1945, two months before the war ended in Europe. Nor when their second daughter, a little smasher by the name of Maureen, joined their family sixteen months later. When she gave birth to baby David in September 1947, followed by Brian just over a year later, she was as crazy over her Arthur as the day they had set eyes on each other in the rag factory.

'Blimey, love, I've only got to wink at you to get you in the family way,' Arthur joked, when she gave birth at home to Linda in November 1949, followed by Pamela in February 1951.

'Just as well we like nippers,' she laughed. And she really did. Every child born to her and Arthur was an extension of their love, and their family grew stronger and happier with each perfect baby she delivered.

In 1948, they got a council house, a lovely new build in Dagenham, with, glory of glories, an indoor lav, running water and three whole bedrooms.

'How do you do it, Jessie?' her neighbour May Spratt asked, over their twice-weekly treat, a fag in the kitchen, shortly after she gave birth to their seventh child, Julie, in July 1952. 'All your kiddies are immaculately turned out.'

'Search me.' Jessie shrugged. 'Actually, tea. That's what keeps me going, so be a pal, May, and stick the kettle on!'

Tea definitely helped – there was a never a time Jessie didn't have a huge brown pot covered in a knitted tea cosy on the go – but there was something else she realised as food rationing ground on and on. The war had been horrible, but it hadn't half made her resourceful. She never bought anything that she could make herself, and all her free time was spent sewing and knitting baby clothes. Jessie's hands were in perpetual motion and she could jig a baby on one hip, while stirring a pot or unravelling knitting with the other hand.

Breakfast was an enormous pot of porridge made with water, and tea was bread and jam, or bread and dripping (with yesterday's bread), washed down with a gallon of well-mashed tea. Once a week, Jessie would cook a stew, made of scrag-end meat simmered for hours with a penn'orth of potherbs. She had an alchemist's gift for conjuring up meals from nothing.

When she wasn't cooking, cleaning, darning or wiping noses, Jessie was scrubbing. Cloth baby napkins and Arthur's work clothes would be scrubbed down in the old dolly tub, before being wrung out through a giant mangle.

Arthur did his bit too, and true to the promise he made her father as a seventeen-year-old lad, he did work all the hours God sent, and more besides, even getting a second job as a painter and decorator to support their ever-growing brood.

In July 1954, food rationing finally ended in Britain, but it didn't make much difference in the Smith household, as by the December of the same year, they had another mouth to feed, their eighth child, a little girl called Lesley.

However, that Christmas was Jessie's happiest ever, as their children unwrapped one present each. It wasn't much – just a scooter or a dolly – one toy was all they could afford from the little bit of money they had managed to squirrel away each month from Arthur's wages.

'Where's my Christmas present then?' Arthur murmured in her ear as they snuggled up in bed later that night.

His present came in the form of another son, Michael, born in June 1957, then Peter in November 1959. Arthur took on yet more work to cope with the demands of their large family, but he was always there on a Friday evening for the weekly bath-time fun. Together, they'd drag in the old tin bath from the garden and fill it with warm water in front of the fire, and in they went, two at a time.

'Blimey, this is like a conveyor belt,' Arthur joked, as he struggled to contain a slippery little person, desperate to avoid the weekly wash. It was worth the effort, though. What was better than seeing ten perfect, clean little children snuggled in front of the flickering firelight in their pyjamas and nighties?

As a new decade dawned and the 1960s exploded, Jessie realised that she'd been having babies more or less non-stop for fifteen years. There was no swinging in the Smith household, just scrubbing! The new fashion for beehives and mini-skirts passed Jessie by, especially when she fell pregnant with their eleventh child. Barbara was born as 1961 came to a close.

Package trips to sunny foreign climes like Benidorm were

beginning to open up to curious Brits, but not for the Smiths, where a yearly camping trip to the South Coast was all the household budget could stretch to. Jessie would pack up a bumper stack of Spam sandwiches and off they'd go for a day at the beach. Days out were so much more fun with eleven kids to help bury Dad up to his neck in the sand!

After one lovely day at the beach in Brighton, Arthur flung his arms around his wife and kissed her, his lips tingling with salt.

'I do love you, Jessie,' he whispered. Jessie took in his thick dark hair, now sprinkled with grey and his eyes, baggy with exhaustion. She felt the same as she did all those years back when they'd had their shotgun wedding.

'Smile for the camera, lovebirds,' said a friend, who'd brought down an old Box Brownie. Larking about in front of the pier, Jessie hitched up her skirt and whooped it up for the camera. Arthur grinned. 'And you still got a cracking pair of pins!'

Heading back home to Dagenham, Jessie realised she'd never been so content. They turned down their street in a great belch of petrol fumes, their old car bursting at the seams with sun-kissed kids – no such thing as seat belts in those days.

'Oh Gawd!' the neighbours joked. 'The Smiths are home!'

By 1964, most homes down their street had televisions, but not the Smiths', so they had to make their own entertainment. And so it was that Jessie gave birth to their twelfth, and final, child.

'I think we better make this our last, Jessie,' Arthur said as the familiar contractions began. Though Jessie hated to admit it, she knew he was right. She'd been having babies for nineteen years, after all.

'In that case, do you want to watch him or her being born?' she asked.

When all the rest had been born at home, as was customary with men back then, Arthur had been safely out of sight, leaving it up to the midwife.

'Why not?' he agreed.

A few hours later, he watched, dumbstruck, as Jessie pushed out baby Martin on a warm July evening.

'Good grief!' he exclaimed, mopping his brow in the syrupy heat. 'It's like watching a baby calf being born!'

'Cheeky sod,' she laughed. 'It's definitely our last now!'

With twelve children, their family was finally complete.

Jessie's story paints a mind-boggling yet affectionate picture of how mothers coped with large families in pre-welfare state Britain. And she is by no means alone. Twelve children might sound a lot, when the national average today is 1.81 (according to figures published by the Office for National Statistics in 2016), but back then, big families were the norm and women's approach to childbirth was far more pragmatic.

Supporting, and sometimes unofficially acting in place of the midwife when events moved rapidly, was the local auntie, childbirth being an area where our matriarch truly came into her own.

'Mum was a great Irish character by the name of Kate Fairclough,' seventy-seven-year-old Mary confided in me. 'She was head of a large Irish family who lived in a tenement flat in Matilda House in Wapping, close to the docks, and I don't think there was a birth there she didn't have a hand in. The Burgesses had ten kids, as did the Hughes, the Murphys had seven and the O'Sullivans six. There was always someone going off!

'The cry would go up. "Call the midwife!" and Mum would also be called upon, to sit with the labouring mother and wait with her.

'There was a fashion back in the 1940s for expectant women to drink castor oil to empty the bowels and bring on contractions. I don't know about that, but I know that sometimes Mum would've delivered the baby before the midwife got there. Oh, she loved it. She used to bring home the babies' nappies with their first wee in. "Get that on your mush," she'd say, wiping the nappy over mine and my sisters' faces. "It's the Maiden's First Water." It was supposed to be good for your complexion, but, ooh, I hated it!'

There were many rituals surrounding childbirth back then. Newborn babies were dressed in stiff binders to support their supposedly weak backs, before being encased in long flannel petticoats, which were turned up at the bottom and secured with two safety pins, like a sealed envelope. It wasn't unusual in Wapping to see newborn babies with veils over their faces to keep the flies off. If a baby was restless, it was given a sugar teat to suck, which was made by rolling a piece of slightly damp bread into the size of a marble. This was then coated in sugar, put in a piece of rag and tied with a length of cotton.

In 1940, the year of Mary's birth, Wapping was a tight-knit, village-style community of largely Irish families, made even closer by the bombing. They lived cheek by jowl with the teeming docks and warehouses, in which Mary's father worked, coming home smelling of exotic spices.

It's hard to picture a more atmospheric place. When a thick consumptive fog rolled through the streets, Mary would navigate her way through the pea-souper by feeling the hulking brick walls, listening to the gentle slap of water against the quayside and the ships' mournful foghorns wailing out through the yellow gloom. High brick warehouse walls caked in centuries-old soot surrounded her on all sides, with the odd tantalising glimpse of the rushing river through the dark shoreway passages. And the noise! Ships hooting. Men shouting. Warehouse cranes groaning.

In Matilda House, though, Kate was the heartbeat of her buildings, singing Irish songs with all the other mums as they pegged out their washing in the communal courtyard. It wasn't all domestic duties. Kate was also called upon to ink home-made tattoos for the dockers' wives.

'Could they gossip? Cor, not much,' Mary laughs. 'Mum was a case. Growing up, she had names for us all. My sister Kitty was a "bookworm". My brother Teddy was "Telephone Teddy" 'cause he talked in telephone numbers, always bragging about how much dough he had. Esther was "To the Manor Born", 'cause of her airs and graces. Her beloved son, Artie, was "My Angel". Iris, my other sister, was an "actress" — swanks across the square like she's walking on eggshells.'

'What were you?' I ask.

'I was "Harum-scarum",' Mary answers with a great gravelly laugh, ''cause I never stopped laughing and charfing.' I suspect Mary took after her red-headed Irish nan, Mary Mahoney, who was more than a little harum-scarum herself, especially when she was jailed for nicking a copper's whistle after a pub fight.

This was a dockers' community, which lived almost entirely within itself, so little wonder Kate knew of every birth and death going.

'I was eight when a crippled neighbour called Anna lost her six-year-old daughter, Pat,' Mary recalls. 'Mum insisted we all go and pay our final respects.

'"She won't hurt you, she's dead," she remarked bluntly. Little Pat looked so pretty, laid out in her little white coffin. I didn't fear death after that.'

As she grew old, it would be fair to say, the matriarch of

Matilda House became more than a little obsessed with her own death.

'Oh, the dramas!' Mary exclaims, rolling her eyes. 'By the time she reached eighty-five, Mum moved in next door to me as she was growing frail. She sat me down and told me exactly what I needed to do, once she'd died.

'"Wash me, Mary. Then close my eyes and put two pennies over them. Tie a scarf round my head, knotting it at the top to stop me jaw flopping open. Once the rigor mortis sets in, I'll look a pretty sight in my coffin if you don't! Lay me flat in an open coffin at home for a week. White satin interior only! Then I want Tadman's on Jubilee Street to bury me."'

Kate left nothing to chance, but she was a little premature.

'The dead are calling me!' she cried to Mary one evening. 'Fetch our Kitty, Teddy, Esther, Artie and Iris. I'm gonna die tonight.'

'Oh leave off, Mum,' Mary replied.

'Ooh, you wicked cow,' Kate scolded her youngest daughter.

'Anyway, you can't die tonight. It's Friday! Tadman's are shut until Monday.'

'Oh yeah,' she replied, rallying a little. 'Fetch us a cup of tea then.'

'It was a Tuesday,' Mary confesses. 'I kept her going like that for a good few years!'

Eventually, the matriarch of Matilda House did die in her own bed at her daughter's house, aged ninety-five.

'I carried out Mum's last wishes to the letter,' confirms Mary. 'More than my life's worth not to.'

In wartime East End, death was a part of everyday life, with people far more accepting of their own mortality than we are today. It was the greatest wish of any self-respecting family to give a beloved relative a proper and fitting send-off, with glossy black horses swathed in velvet palls and long black plumes on their heads, to transport the coffin to its final resting place.

Preparations often rivalled those made for marriages and christenings. And like weddings, they were shared community events, with whole streets often clubbing together to provide a funeral wreath. Remember Old Boots in Chapter Two who turned out to play the piano at every neighbourhood funeral – regardless of whether she knew them or not?

Catholic Sister Christine Frost, MBE, of St Matthias Community Centre in Poplar, is eighty years old and a formidable crusading woman. She feels our disconnection to death is to the detriment of society.

'Everything has become professionalised. Words like "health and safety, safeguarding, political correctness".' She shudders. 'We've gone too far. Back then, women delivered their babies in their bedrooms and laid out their dead in the front parlour and, in doing so, made it all the more natural. Nowadays, children aren't even allowed to go to funerals, which stores up a whole heap of psychological trouble for later years.'

Sister Christine first arrived in East London from Limerick via Canada in 1950, vowing to do all she could to keep alive the wartime community spirit of sharing and tolerance.

'I'm not a Bible thumper,' she insists, 'but to me it's best summed up by these verses from Luke 6:37–8: "Do not judge, and you will not be judged. Do not condemn, and you will not be condemned. Forgive, and you will be forgiven. Give, and it will be given to you. A good measure, pressed down, shaken together, and running over, will be poured into your lap. For with the measure you use, it will be measured to you."

'When I got the job here in Poplar, I came with the vision of humanitarian Jean Vanier, who had created a scheme called Homes for Disabled to stop people with disabilities being institutionalised. His belief was that people with disabilities are teachers, rather than burdens bestowed upon families.

'This resonated with me. I wanted to create communities where people weren't isolated and could lead active, meaningful lives. It's so important not to shut away the disabled. After all, we're all disabled in one way or another, are we not?'

Of all the comments made to me in the course of researching this book, I found this question to be the most thought-provoking.

'I have met so many incredible wartime women,' Sister Christine continues, 'so gracious, so humble, so grateful. Women like Martha Massett, who used to sing at the top of her voice drinking a cup of tea with her little finger cocked.

'These women were connected to their communities and families in ways we struggle with now. They had real spunk. They were profoundly respectful towards the church, teachers, police, midwives and doctors. They taught their kids to be respectful too. Nowadays, you have kids telling their parents what to do, and parents holding teachers up against the wall. The matriarch would not have tolerated that.'

Sister Christine's belief is borne out by the following story from a bright-eyed lady by the name of Mitsy from Stepney (not to be confused with Minksy from Bethnal Green).

'Our street in Stepney was a proper community, with proper values,' the fiercely independent eighty-eight-year-old told me. 'The men ruled the roost in the home, but it was the women who ruled the cobbles. We weren't just parented by one woman; all the women down the street took collective responsibility for the nippers. Strayed out of your neighbourhood and were spotted? You'd be packed off home sharpish. Saucy to a neighbour? You'd get a stinging clip round the ear. But it was lovely, because everyone knew where they stood and felt cared for. You belonged.'

Mitsy was at pains to stress to me the fierce sense of belonging and altruism that a childhood in Stepney instilled in her. She grew up watching the Stepney Doorstep Society calmly caring for its own.

'There was a blind woman called Rose who lived alone up our street and all the women would go in daily and keep her house neat as a pin and do her shopping,' she told me. 'An old boy, Jimmy, over the road, had fits all the time, and the women would see to him with no fuss. Then there was warhorse Kate, who looked more like a man than a woman. She was a giant in women's clothing and had a few problems, shall we say, but she was looked out for.'

No one was looked after by the state back then; instead, communities looked after one another and this bred enormous camaraderie and togetherness. Mitsy's street, like the majority of East End streets, shared their pleasures, like weddings, which could go on for weeks, or at least until the beer ran out. Sometimes they'd take the window frame out to get the piano through it and on to the street. All strangers were welcome and everyone from the neighbourhood brought something to the party. What little you had, you contributed.

When Mitsy's cousin Bertie, who lived down the same street as her, married a local girl called Bertha, they celebrated for three weeks. A piano was a treasured musical instrument, and during their wedding at least three were rolled out on to the cobbles, with her mum singing and her dad playing the accordion. The street was alive with music for Bertie and Bertha.

Respect. Tolerance. Pride. Cleanliness. Cherished virtues I have heard time and again as being the bedrock of East End communities.

Woe betide you if you didn't share those values, though.

'Mums were tough back then,' Mitsy added, shaking her head. 'I once saw a woman wrap metal kirby grips round her knuckles, like a DIY knuckle duster, and have a fist fight with another woman.

'I saw razor fights too. Curly Mac, who ran a fruit stall in Watney market, was razored by Mr Brown. Curly had been warned about having loud parties and keeping the local kids up night after night, so he was razored by Mr Brown, who swore his life (vowed vengeance) for good.

'I'm not saying it's right or wrong, it's just the way it was. Women were tough back then, because they had to be. Above all, though, the mums down my street raised their kids with love and discipline. That's why most East End kids were so clever. They were either streetwise or book-wise, with sharp, enquiring minds. Vibrant, caring communities turn out vibrant, caring children.'

Shall we return now to Jessie Smith, who we opened this chapter with? Fast-forward a few years, and her family is somewhat larger. Today, she is the head of an enormous clan with, wait for it, 44 grandchildren, 99 great-grandchildren and 20 great-great-grandchildren! So many, in fact, her family have made her a spreadsheet so she can keep track. The papers dubbed her Supergran in July 2017, when her 163-strong brood threw her a surprise ninetieth birthday.

Camera crews from around the world beat a path to her door to interview this mighty matriarch, but Jessie is an unassuming, humble woman and declined. Fortunately, she did open the door to her Dagenham home to me. She answers pushing a blinged-up, diamanté-encrusted Zimmer frame and wearing an enormous sparkly necklace.

'I bought it down the market,' she confides. 'Jewellery's my little indulgence these days, now I got a bit more money.'

I hand her a box of chocolate biscuits I've bought as a gift and she quickly squirrels them away in the cupboard.

'Ooh, smashing,' she grins, a wide smile blossoming across her face. 'I'm hiding these otherwise the family'll be through 'em in a flash.'

We share a pot of tea – Jessie's tea drinking is legendary – and, as we flick through photo albums, I marvel at her hands, parchment-thin but soft and smooth.

'I must've washed thousands of cloth nappies over the years, but I've got terrible arthritis nowadays. I still managed to crochet all my grandkids' blankets, forty-four of them,' she says proudly.

We pause on a glorious photo of her and Arthur, taken that day when they larked about in front of Brighton Pier as young parents. Despite its seaside sauce, it has such an innocent quality. You can almost smell the chip fat and candyfloss.

'Look at me flashing my knickers!' she laughs. 'I was a caution back then.'

Arthur died in 1995, aged sixty-nine.

'I still can't believe he's gone,' Jessie whispers disbelievingly. 'We were so in love. We never went to bed without a kiss and a cuddle on the settee.'

After her surprise party, Jessie got home and said goodnight to Arthur as she does every night.

'Ninety!' she whispered, touching his face, cool behind the glass. 'What about that then?'

She closed her eyes and heard his throaty voice in her ear. 'Well done, old girl.'

Jessie's life has been a phenomenal achievement and a masterclass in making do. She is the mother of all matriarchs, running a happy, love-filled home on a shoestring, calmly going about her domestic duties against a backdrop of cataclysmic world events.

'I've no complaints,' she shrugs, ruminating over her epic child-rearing journey.

There is circularity to Jessie birthing her first child as the war entered its final turbulent months. But before Allied victory in Europe, Hitler had one final act of revenge in store. And for our Gladys, still recovering from the Blitz, a new peril was about to strike from the skies above.

Vi's Recipe

School dinners were mine and my brothers' main meal of the day, so I look back on them with real affection. It was always a good day when you got roast meat of some variety, with roast potatoes and a thick gravy, followed by a syrupy sponge pudding. I still can't stand stews. They remind me of the food we had to eat growing up. Take me to a carvery for a roast beef, Yorkshire puddings and all the trimmings any day.

Vi's Remedy

Mum used to rinse my hair in vinegar to get it really clean.

Vi's Pearls of Wisdom

Oh, Mum had hundreds of these, but her favourites were: 'God pays debts without money' and 'God knows who needs it', if her eagle eye spotted some money on the pavement. If I had a penny for every time she said to me and my brothers, 'Stop acting the goat'!

8. The Last Year of War, 1944–45

Eleven a.m. Sunday, 18 June 1944. The neighbourhood was alive with word of a new bomb, which had landed at 10 a.m. that morning. Flying shrapnel from the anti-aircraft guns had injured a man, but amazingly, no one had been killed.

'Sounds like a one-off,' declared Gladys' mum, Mary. 'Be a good girl and take your sisters out for some fresh air.'

Twelve-year-old Gladys did as she was told, bumping the pram containing her two younger sisters down the concrete steps and out into a drowsy Sunday morning. She had just taken the turning into Marsham Street, when a strange spluttering sound broke open the still summer air.

Gladys stopped. Listened. She stared up at the sky, then back to the faces of her two sisters in their pram. No siren had gone off.

What should she do?

In wartime, the smallest action had a consequence. Her mind flashed alarmingly back to the Blitz. It had been three and a half years since she'd seen her best friend's body carried past her, encased in a cardboard coffin.

The noise grew more persistent. The green leaves on the tree trembled. The sound rose up from the bowels of the earth, growing from a dull throbbing to a full-throttle staccato. A feeling, primal in its intensity, gripped her. Palms slippery with sweat, she gripped the handles of the pram and took off, her skinny white legs pumping in the direction of whatever looked like safety.

Spotting an alcove in the side of Westminster Hospital

nurses' home, Gladys managed to push the pram inside to safety and wedged herself in next to it. Gazing up, her blue eyes widened in horror. *God in heaven, what was it?*

A huge black rocket was heading unswervingly in their direction. Heart punching in her chest, she squeezed her eyes shut.

Please don't let the babies be killed.

A tremendous noise rose up over the neighbourhood. The pom-pom guns started firing, the siren wailed . . . But over it all, the continual *putt-putt* of whatever that thing was bored through her brain like a speedway motorbike.

A dark shadow engulfed the pram. Silence. The engine had cut out.

Where is it? she wondered, sticking her head out of the alcove for a closer look. The rocket was slicing through the skies towards them.

Fear crashed over her, her blood roaring through her ears. Helpless tears streamed down her cheeks.

Please God, don't let it be us . . .

She closed her eyes, but when she opened them again, she could see the rocket lurching, changing course. All of a sudden, it nosedived with terrifying speed straight into the Wellington Barracks, home to the Regiment of Guards. A thick, choking cloud of smoke mushroomed into the sky. The noise and debris was out of this world, but Gladys wasn't hanging around to see who'd copped it. Pushing the pram out of the alcove, she turned and ran like a bat out of hell in the direction of home.

Sunday, 18 June 1944 was not Gladys' or her sisters' day to die. That was, however, the fate of 121 civilians and soldiers who had congregated in the Guards' Chapel on Birdcage Walk SW1 to worship, but never left. The choir had just started the sung Eucharist when the concrete roof caved in. The entire congregation, including the officiating chaplain, several senior British Army officers and a US Army colonel, were flattened by several tons of concrete. The ten-foot-high pile of rubble included the remnants of over 2,000 small memorial plaques, dedicated to the service of Guardsmen since 1660.

Gladys did not know it then, but she and her sisters had just avoided being hit by a pilotless rocket. Over time, they became known as buzz bombs or doodlebugs because of the strange buzzing noise they made. Their official name, by which they were known to the German scientists who developed them, was *Vergeltungswaffen 1*, meaning 'revenge weapons'. For short, V-1s.

Three years after the terror of the Blitz, Britons were finally daring to dream that an end to the war was in sight. News of the D-Day landings on 6 June 1944 had been greeted with jubilation, and a cautious hope prevailed. The Germans were being pushed back by the combined might of the Allied forces. Victory in Europe at long last seemed a tantalising possibility.

Hitler, however, had other ideas. His scientists had developed a top-secret *wunderwaffe* – 'miracle weapon'. The age of missile warfare was about to begin, and what Gladys witnessed that dark Sunday morning was the most serious V-1 rocket attack of the war. The mouth-parching fear she experienced remains indelibly inked in her brain seventy-four years on, and with good reason.

All our matriarchs were in peril as this new form of terror weapon rained from the skies. Five days earlier, on 13 June, Minksy had watched, dumbstruck, as a peculiar black object with its tail on fire had sailed over the roof of number 11 Shetland Street, before crashing into a railway bridge over Grove Road, Bethnal Green, killing six, including an eight-month-old baby boy. She hadn't known it then, but this was the first recorded V-1 strike in London. Over the next two and a half months, V-1s were to kill and wound a total of 22,892 civilians.

Beatty, back from Leeds where she had been working in munitions, was visiting her old pal, Ginnie – with whom she had stood shoulder-to-shoulder at the Battle of Cable Street – when the pair found themselves facing fresh danger. As a shadow of death passed over their heads, they clung in terror to a shop doorway in Petticoat Lane. The ground beneath their feet trembled like an earthquake as it exploded.

Girl Walker, whom we last met clawing her way out of an Anderson shelter after being buried alive for three days, blanches at the memory of these rockets.

'Some pals of mine, twins, were missing for days. They were finally discovered dead on the roof of a church in Duckett Street. They had been blown up there when a rocket dropped nearby.

'It was just terrible when the engine cut out and they began to fall. I got used to running at high speed.'

In fact, all the women I interviewed for this book cite these missiles as, psychologically, the most disturbing aspect of the war, in particular the dreadful loaded seconds between the engine cutting out and its descent to earth.

But worse was to come on 10 November 1944. In the grip of a ferociously cold winter, Churchill admitted that Britain was under attack by the new long-range V-2 rockets. Hitler had saved the worst till last. No effective defence against the V-2 could be found for, unlike its predecessor, it arrived unseen and unheard, delivering over a ton of high explosive at a speed of 3,500 feet per second.

And for Babs, still recovering from narrowly avoiding being crushed to death on the steps down to Bethnal Green Underground, it came like a thunderbolt from the blue.

*

'Bet you haven't got one of these,' Babs boasted to her school pals at Morpeth Street School as the bell sounded for the end of class and they trooped into the playground.

'Ooh, you jammy so-and-so!' her pal said, green with envy.

Babs felt like the bee's knees. Thirteen years old and she had just been entrusted with her own front-door key. She wore it round her neck on a piece of string like a precious pearl.

With her mum working as a school dinner lady, her big sister Jean employed at the Prudential, and her dad serving with the Admiralty, Babs had finally become a latchkey kid.

Babs fingered it proudly as she walked into the turning to Old Ford Road, but as she approached their house, she stopped in her tracks.

What the . . . ?

Her front door was gone. Blasted clean off its hinges, it was strewn up the passage.

Babs started to laugh. If she didn't, she might just cry.

'Well, if that doesn't put a tin lid on it!' she declared to no one, staring at her now redundant key.

Poor old house! It was missing a roof from an earlier blast and had a great length of tarpaulin stretched over it to keep out the rain. Now it was minus a front door. Still, at least they had a home, and for that, Babs was grateful. So many houses were missing from the street after the Blitz that Old Ford Road looked like a smile with missing teeth. Turned out a rocket had dropped nearby and the reverberations had rippled across the neighbourhood.

Some weeks later, she was sitting at her desk in class, trying her hardest to master the finer points of algebra, when suddenly an almighty crash rang out through the classroom. A bitter, choking dust rained down on the pupils.

For a second, there was a perfect silence. The odour of

chalk dust and red-hot metal bloomed through the classroom. Then pandemonium broke out.

'Calm down! Calm down!' shouted Mr Davies, appealing for quiet over the hubbub. 'I must have quiet.'

Everybody was staring up at the gaping hole in the ceiling, but not Babs.

Her attention was caught elsewhere.

'Sir?' she said slowly. 'Sir, why's Roy got red on his head?'

The lad Babs sat next to, Roy, was sprawled across his desk, his bright white-blonde hair slowly turning a dark shade of crimson.

'Roy! Roy!' shrieked Mr Davies, his face blanching of colour.

But his cries could not reach him. Roy was dead, killed at his school desk by a chunk of masonry that had fallen from the ceiling when a V-2 rocket dropped nearby.

For the second time in this miserable, never-ending conflict, the headmaster sent Babs home early. The next day, another boy was sitting in Roy's seat. How many more of her friends needed to die, thirteen-year-old Babs wondered, before this war ended?

Babs had no choice but to keep quiet and carry on, her suffering to be endured silently and stoically. Children were paying a heavy price for this war. Predictably, the East End had the dubious honour of receiving both the first V-1 strike and the last V-2 strike in London. V-2 rocket troops were almost cornered, but they managed to fire off one last rocket, which landed in a place called Hughes Mansions in Vallance Road, Bethnal Green. The residents of the so-called mansions were readying themselves for work and school when the rocket hit at 7.21 a.m. on 27 March 1945, claiming yet another 134 East Enders' lives.

How much more could the East End endure in this war before the lights finally came back on?

The month after the Hughes Mansions disaster, in April 1945, shockwaves rolled through the country when films were shown in cinemas of British troops liberating German concentration camps, such as Bergen-Belsen and Auschwitz-Birkenau, revealing the full horrors of the Holocaust.

'Anti-Semitism is as rife now as it's ever been,' insists 100-year-old Beatty, who has lived through two world wars. 'I turn on the news and there it is again. Hatred, racism and a lack of tolerance. I've seen it all before,' she sighs.

Before the war, Beatty risked everything to fight fascists at the Battle of Cable Street. And now, as the war comes to a close, we can see clearly why she took to the streets in 1936 to protest.

On 7 May 1945, the German High Command surrendered. The war in Europe was at an end.

Hermann Goering, whose Luftwaffe failed to kill our matriarchs, was later sentenced to death by hanging, but committed suicide in October 1946 by taking a cyanide capsule the night before his sentence was due to be carried out.

Nazism and fascism devotee Unity Mitford, who was chased by Beatty through Hyde Park, attempted suicide when war was declared by shooting herself in the head. She failed, but in 1948, she succumbed to meningitis, thought to have been caused by an infection in her old bullet wound.

William Joyce, whose transmissions as Lord Haw-Haw enraged our matriarch Gladys, was captured and sentenced to death for treason.

Oswald Mosley, whose notorious march Beatty successfully helped to stop, attempted a political comeback after the war, but failed – again.

On 30 April 1945, Adolf Hitler and his wife of one day, Eva Braun, killed themselves in his secret bunker in Berlin.

Back in the East End of London, the skies fluttered with a sea of red, white and blue as jubilant cockneys thronged their beloved streets. On VE day, Tuesday, 8 May 1945, each of our matriarchs celebrated in her own way.

In Bethnal Green, Minksy, by now a ravishing eighteen-year-old, did what she did best – put on the glamour and kicked up her heels.

'I was footloose and fancy-free, so I went up West, didn't I?' she exclaims. 'Oh, you should've seen us! Me and my sisters all dolled up to the nines in our pencil skirts and satin shirts. Wiggling along Piccadilly, bold as you like, with our hair up like dollops of grapes on our heads. Everywhere we went, people calling us the Andrews Sisters, begging us for kisses.

'The streets were going mad with joy, strangers embracing and kissing, dancing in the fountains at Trafalgar Square, conga lines up the street. We were euphoric. The war was over.' Seventy-three years on, she struggles to contain the emotion in her voice. 'I danced and sang all day until my feet ached and my voice was raw. I felt like my life could now begin.'

In Stepney, though, twelve-year-old Girl Walker felt like her life was over. Being locked in a cupboard when she was evacuated and buried alive during the Blitz, to say nothing of the shocking deaths of her pals in a rocket attack . . . All that she could deal with, but finding her family torn apart was a bitter pill to swallow.

'Nothing was the same after the war,' she laments. 'My mum and dad split up. Both had taken other lovers during the war. Mum moved out to live with Old Boots, and they came to an agreement that Dad fed me and Mum clothed me. Come to think of it, I can't remember any of my friends having a mum and dad together after the war. How many men came home from the war to a little bastard? It wasn't a happy time.'

The heart and soul went out of Flamborough Street, and Girl Walker was no longer the ruler of her own Stepney kingdom. She would have to figure out a new identity for herself.

Back in Bethnal Green, it was a new beginning for Babs too. Now fourteen, she had left Morpeth Street School, something her classmate Roy never had the opportunity to do, and had begun an apprenticeship at smart court dressmakers Auerbach & Steinitz at 296 Regent Street.

Babs had wanted to be a nurse, but her mum Bobby had other ideas.

'I'm not having my Babsy do that! It's dressmaking or upholstery for you,' she had declared. Babs had known better than to argue.

The week before VE day, Babs had been getting ready to go to Girl Guides when her mother shrieked up the stairs. 'That bleedin' Hitler's killed himself! I think the war's over.'

When Babs returned from Guides, she was stunned to see all the lights of the house blazing and an enormous Union Jack hanging proudly from the front of the battered old home.

The lights were coming back on all over the East End.

A wiggle further west, we find Beatty, now a twenty-eight-year-old mum of one girl, with a second on the way. She has moved back from Leeds and is living in a tiny City of London Corporation flat down Stoney Lane, after her flat in Brunswick Buildings got bombed. Her handsome Irish husband, John, has been demobbed, and together they sell handbags on a stall down Petticoat Lane.

Being pregnant, Beatty saw VE day as a well-earned opportunity to put her feet up. The next morning, it was with a weary sense of relief that she looked out upon the bomb-shattered East End. As a member of the Labour party, who were about to sweep into power, she, like the rest of the country, wanted to forget about the war and begin instead to *Face the Future*, as the party manifesto urged. She hoped that future could include a welfare state to support the poorest members of society, decent housing, jobs and a safe world for her children to grow up in.

Only Dr Joan bucked the trend. By VE day, she was forging a new life for herself in Australia. After a hasty wartime marriage, her husband, a naval commander, wanted her by his side in Melbourne. When she managed to get herself a job in Sydney, her husband told her he would not allow it: he did not want a professional wife, but a naval one. Sadly, upon arrival in Australia, Joan realised she could no more be a trophy wife than she could fly to the moon. She left him and, after a successful few months as a GP in Sydney, smuggled herself out as a ship's doctor onboard a cargo ship bound for England. On her travels back across the equator, she weathered ferocious storms, nursed broken limbs and burns, and tended to a nasty case of VD amongst the crew. Dr Joan was back in business.

Excitement. Relief. Exhaustion. Stability. Adventure. Independence. Hope . . .

Each story provides a snapshot of the prevailing mood as each woman attempted to pick up the threads of her life. After a long five years and eight months, the war was over. Blackout blinds were torn down with relish. Church bells at

St Mary-le-Bow Church in Cheapside (which, it is said, a true cockney must be born within the sound of) rang out again over the East End. The bunks in the underground community of Bethnal Green Tube were taken apart, the stage where Minksy sang, dismantled.

Down in Vicky Park, the barbed wire and the Z Battery, which fired the rocket whose blood-curdling noise triggered the deadly stampede down the Tube, had been removed and the park was once more filled with dappled sunshine and shrieks of laughter. The gentle creak and splash of oars lapped at the boating lake. Except beneath the surface on the dark, murky bottom, God knows what wartime secrets lurked.

Life as our matriarchs knew it was packed up and put in a metaphorical box under the bed marked *Wartime. Do Not Open!*

Bombsites all through the East End were already sprouting drifts of purple buddleia and willow herb, helping to hide the scars of war with cool verdure. There was a bleak kind of beauty to be found in these desolate places.

To our matriarchs, they were reminders of all they had endured. No weeds could cover the memories they carried in their hearts and minds, of burning buildings, children tumbling to their deaths, of suffocation, mutilation and suffering. The dead whispered from their concrete tombs.

To the young kids of the East End, however, it was just known as *the debris*, a place to build camps, play cowboys and Indians, and allow their imaginations to roam free.

Vi from Bethnal Green has vivid memories of playing in one, and her return to the East End when war ended was a rude awakening.

'I was two and a half when the bombs started, so I was

evacuated to Cambridgeshire, away from my older brother, Ronnie, and Mum, Leah. It was glorious. I lived with an elderly widow who doted on me. I had my own bedroom overlooking lush green fields, slept on snowy-white sheets, ate fresh food, went to the village school and roamed the countryside. The lady who I was billeted with wanted to adopt me, but Mum wanted me home, so back to London it was.

'Talk about a shock! In my absence, I'd lost my cockney accent and Mum had gained another child, my little brother, Johnny. I looked at these two boys, Ronnie and Johnny, with their grubby faces, and grimaced.

'"Who are those filthy boys?" I asked Mum.

'"Cheeky cow!" she shrieked. "They're your brothers!"'

Vi's new home was a far cry from her countryside idyll.

'Mum had been bombed out twice in the war, and was now living in a tenement building called Cavendish Dwellings in Clerkenwell,' Vi explains.

A darker, more forbidding place you'd be hard pressed to find. Let us walk with nine-year-old Vi now as she enters her new home for the first time.

'The rooms were under a stairwell so no natural light got in. It was dark and dank,' she shudders. 'There was a small room with a double bed and a chest of drawers. That led into the kitchen, which had a single bed in it. That, in turn, led on to the scullery with a copper. Then you reached my tiny room, with barely space for a single bed. It looked out past a rickety iron fire escape into a dark, narrow yard where everyone slung their rubbish.

'It stunk and it was running alive with rats. I used to see them bounding along the back wall, the size of cats. Poor Mum. I could tell how miserable it made her to bring her daughter back to such a rotten hovel, but she had no other choice. She didn't have a pot . . . I cried myself to sleep every night for a year, but silently so Mum wouldn't hear.'

The living conditions in Cavendish Dwellings sound very similar to those described in the Preface in Quinn Square in 1938, except that this was the late 1940s. The slums that hadn't been destroyed by Hitler were much the same as they had been before. Post-war, everything had changed, and yet nothing had changed.

Vi sighs as she recalls the moment she realised her childhood was over, aged just nine.

'Mum did her best, but we were desperately poor. All that mattered was earning enough to pay the rent and keep a roof over our head,' she recalls. 'She worked full-time as a machinist, then when she got home, she would bring extra work with her and stay up until late doing her second job. I'd stay up and help her to sew linings into men's trousers. Life was a grind, and there was never enough coal for the fire or food for the pot, just scrag ends of meat that Mum cooked up into a watery stew once a week.'

Vi was rapidly learning that when it came to domestic duties, it was a woman's world.

'While Mum was at work, after school on a Friday, I would do the housework, and on Saturday, I'd go shopping, not that we had much money for anything beyond a loaf of bread,' she sighs. 'My brothers and I would go for second helpings of school dinners, which, looking back, saved us from starvation.

'Eventually, I said to Mum, "I've got two brothers with arms and legs, why can't they help?"

'"You're right," she replied, and from then on, Ronnie and Johnny were roped in to help.'

It was Vi's closeness to her siblings that provided some light relief from the poverty trap.

'Between where we lived and St Paul's Cathedral, the streets were filled with empty bombed buildings,' Vi recalls.

The raging infernos of Sunday, 29 December 1940, which we learnt about in Chapter Three on the Blitz, were responsible for these wastelands.

To Vi and her brothers, though, they were playgrounds, rich with opportunity.

'We couldn't believe it when we found a big white rabbit in a deserted building!' she laughs. 'We took him home and named him Jiminy Cricket. I adored that rabbit, and for months, I fed him every last scrap of food I could find.

'Then, at Christmas, he went missing. Turned out Mum had taken him to the butcher's, where she'd had him slaughtered. She served Jiminy up for Christmas lunch. She hadn't meant to be cruel, just practical, but I sobbed all through Christmas Day.

'Every single thing my mum did was for us kids,' Vi says protectively of her darkly comic memory. 'We were the most important things in her life.'

You might be wondering where Vi's dad was in all this. Vi was about fourteen when she began to realise her family was not quite like others.

'I've got a friend round and she suddenly asks, "Where does your dad sleep?"'

It was an innocent question, but it revealed a secret her mother could no longer hide from Vi and her brothers. Vi's father visited every week, but never stayed, on account of already having another family. A legitimate one.

'Gradually, Mum admitted that our dad was married to

another woman with four kids,' Vi says. 'My brothers and I were what was then commonly referred to as bar stewards!'

Post-war, Leah was a woman with the worries of the world on her shoulders, a ravaged single mum to three kids. It probably wasn't how she envisaged her life ending up when she stepped into the Blind Beggar pub in Whitechapel as a vibrant twenty-four-year-old woman, and caught the eye of an apprentice bricklayer.

'Dad spotted Mum and her mate, Lilly, singing round the piano, and he went on the charm offensive,' Vi explains. 'I can see why Mum fell for him, mind you. He was so good-looking you wouldn't believe, like a matinee screen idol with his pencil moustache and chiselled cheekbones.

'He wooed Mum, telling her that, though he loved her, he couldn't leave his wife as she was Catholic.'

Leah could perhaps have walked away, created another life for herself, beyond that of 'the other woman'. But then she found she was pregnant with Vi's brother and her fate was sealed.

'Mum bought herself a wedding ring, but people knew, and the stigma of her pregnancy out of wedlock coloured everything,' Vi explains. 'She was turned out of jobs, out of lodgings, all because she was a single mum.

'It sounds strange now in today's society, but back then, she was the lowest of the low, nothing but a "tart" to most in the community.'

But Leah had her dignity and a deep pride that meant she never asked Vi's father for a penny in support.

'Despite everything, she truly loved him,' says Vi. 'He was her god. I remember him coming round once a week and she would say to me, "Make sure you change the tablecloth and fetch Daddy a sandwich." She wanted everything just right for him.

'Dad was a keen fisherman, which gave him the perfect excuse to be away from home at weekends. We used to go with him on fishing trips, and share a picnic on the riverbank. To the outside eye, we must have looked like the perfect 1950s family.'

Did his wife have any clue that her husband had three more children and a secret life with another woman? Of that, Vi is unsure, but she is certain that her mother never wanted that life for her.

'As I grew older and began to get boyfriends, Mum was more honest with me,' Vi tells me. 'She used to say, "I love your father, but it's not the life I wanted. I want more for you."'

Despite the loneliness of her situation, Vi insists her mother never once felt sorry for herself, despite over forty years of being relegated to the sidelines. Vi's father died in 1968, aged sixty-five.

'Mum was broken-hearted, and do you want to know the saddest thing? Obviously we couldn't go to his funeral. But we did,' Vi says.

'We crouched behind a bush in the graveyard and watched from afar as his body was lowered into the ground, surrounded by his legitimate family.'

Meanwhile, his illegitimate family said their silent good-byes, hidden in the shadows.

For grafter Leah, it was a poignant end to a life spent hiding and concealing the truth from society's judgemental eyes. It sounds like something from a film, but to Vi it was heartbreaking and left an enormous impression.

'I vowed to have my independence, and have no man lord it over me.'

Single-mum Leah died in 1987 aged eighty-two in a bedsit, history's forgotten heroine. She lived through two world wars, got bombed out twice, raised three children on her own, with absolutely no help, and was a man's secret for over forty years.

'How easy would it have been to have given me up to that woman who I was evacuated with?' reflects Vi. 'But she didn't. I always knew, no matter how desperate things got, that I was loved.'

Today, Vi is an exuberant eighty-year-old. Having freed herself from a bad marriage, she now lives happily alone in a cheerful flat, whose windows look out over Columbia Road Flower Market and the city beyond. Her walls are painted ruby red.

'Because I can and I don't have to please anyone,' she smiles, casting her eye over her vibrant interior, though you can't help but think Vi's rich palette of colour comes from growing up in a drab post-war tenement.

She's forever busy, organising bingo and day trips for the older folk at the Sundial Centre in Bethnal Green, and is never without a smile on her face, despite – or maybe because of – her desperate start in life.

Leah's peacetime was as rocky as wartime, with arguably little in the way of romance. But for many of her fellow East Enders, romance was very high up on the agenda, now that war was finally over.

Part of their acclimatisation to peacetime meant accepting that a new way of life beckoned. What the dingy, drab and threadbare streets needed now was an injection of glamour and escapism . . .

Dr Joan's Remedy

A cup of coffee every day saw me through the Blitz and many long working days.

Dr Joan's Pearls of Wisdom

Keep a stiff upper lip and do your duty.

9. Post-War Wedding Bells

Staring down the barrel of Ronnie Kray – or was it Reggie? She could never tell them apart – was an unnerving experience, but Girl Walker had her orders. Sticking out her chin, she met his gaze unflinchingly.

'I've been told to deliver this message directly to our Georgie.'

Ronnie, or Reggie, stared at her for what felt like a very long time, before lifting her clean off her feet and depositing her on the pavement.

'Saucy little f***er!' he said, shaking his head and laughing. A second later, the door to the Black Boy pub on the Mile End Road slammed shut in her face. Through the opaque glass doors, Girl Walker could make out the outline of men in suits, smoke, the rumble of deep cockney voices. This was a world completely off limits to women.

Sighing, she turned back down the shabby road, full of boarded-up buildings and corrugated iron, and ducked down into a rabbit warren of dark Stepney streets. In her butcher's shop, her mum Alice's face was a picture when Girl Walker recounted the story.

'You'd answer the devil back, you would,' she scolded, as she wiped down the counter. 'Anyway, never mind all that, when you gonna meet a nice man and settle down, Babe?'

It was a good question. The war was over. The rest of her family had moved on. Her older sister, Laura, hadn't even returned from where she'd been working in the Land Army, opting to stay instead in rural Lincolnshire.

Her cousin George, to whom she'd been trying to pass a

message from her dad, had certainly moved on. No longer just the Stepney Steamroller, he was now the British amateur light-heavyweight champion, making waves of his own in the East End, with his new friends the Kray twins and notorious gangland boss Billy Hill.

Post-war East End was a very different place. No longer content with getting by, everyone – or so it felt to Girl Walker – was trying to better themselves.

Now they had been released from military prison, the Kray twins were on the up. The young bloods were fast becoming the rulers of the East End underworld from their new base, the Regal, a billiard hall on the Mile End Road. They used the streets, clubs and pubs of their turf as a tribal proving ground. Girl Walker knew none of this, of course – to her they just seemed like decent blokes who looked after the old women in the area.

Married women were out of the factories and back in the homes, their newfound independence vanished. The streets were filling with prams, and each week it felt like someone else she knew was getting married. Girl Walker's nan, Old Boots, could hardly keep up with all the weddings!

Little did Girl Walker know, however, that even as she was sparring with the Kray twins, a new life was on the horizon for her as well.

Minksy had heard a new firm in Hackney was hiring machinists and on good wages too. She and her mate, Betty, fancied their chances. They'd been laid off from their last firm and needed work. But almost as soon as they stepped into the guv'nor's office, they realised some jobs just weren't worth any amount of money.

'Hello darlins', said Reggie Kray, perched on the edge of

the desk, wearing a sharp double-breasted suit and knotted tie. The old guv'nor stood stricken in the corner of the office.

Reggie's gaze slithered up and down Minksy.

'You start Monday!'

'Er, right . . . Ta, Reg . . .' mumbled Minksy, backing out the office with a fixed grin.

'Not bleedin' likely, pal,' she muttered under her breath as she and Betty clattered back down the steps as fast as their feet would take them.

Taking the turning into Pritchard's Road, where her family now lived above a greengrocer's, Minksy heard a deep male voice.

'Hello, Curly!'

Not another bloody upstart. Turning to give him a piece of her mind, she felt the breath leave her body.

Sat up high on his horse-drawn coal cart was the most handsome man she had ever seen. His tar-black hair, so dark it was almost blue in places, was slicked back with pomade and glistened in the morning sun.

'For you,' he grinned, tossing her an apple.

'What's that for?'

''Cause I wanna keep you sweet,' he replied teasingly, his smile deliciously bright against his soot-blackened face.

'I'm sweet enough as it is,' Minksy bantered, rolling the apple between her palms with a coy look on her face.

As the man jumped down on to the pavement beside her, Minksy became aware of the sheer physicality of him. Her senses thrilled. The heady scent of him – coal and tobacco, mixed with something richer and earthier, the warmth coming from his skin.

'I can see that, Curly.'

'You can call me Minksy.'

'Very well. And you can call me Joe.'

The air between them shimmered.

Joe Keeper worked on his family's coal round, Keeper & Co. 'One of the biggest coal rounds in the East End,' as he told her proudly.

Hoisting a one-hundredweight sack of coal on his back like it was a feather, he turned and swaggered backwards up the pavement.

'I've seen you about, I think you're smashing,' he grinned. 'How about coming to the pictures with me, Curly?'

Minksy hesitated. There was nothing she'd love more.

'I-I can't,' she sighed, handing him back the apple. 'I ain't got nothing to wear.' With that, she turned and ran up the stairs to her flat.

The next day, she heard the rhythmic clopping of horse's hooves, followed by the soft thud of feet landing on the pavement. She parted the nets. There he was again, clutching an orange in one hand and a bag in the other. Minksy pelted down the stairs two at a time, but opened the door as cool as a cucumber.

'Blimey. You don't give up easy, do you?' she grinned nonchalantly.

'Will this do?' he asked, and from the bag he pulled a pale-blue woman's suit with smart lapels and a white blouse. 'I thought it would go nicely with your eyes. So now will you come out with me tonight?'

Minksy's jaw couldn't get any lower. Stunned, she reached out, letting the cool, silky material slide through her fingertips. Her eyes met Joe's. His horse, Trigger, blew out gently through velvety nostrils, as if urging her to answer. Joe stared at her intently, his dark eyes gleaming in the pearlised light of dusk.

'I got this for your mum,' Joe added, pulling a bag of coal

off the back of the cart. 'Gotta keep her sweet too, if I want to win you round.'

Truth be told, he had won her round from the moment she set eyes on him. Minksy can't recall what they watched at the pictures that night, but from that moment forth, life took on a dazzling new intensity. Joe the handsome coal man had swept her off her feet, and all the fear of the war years, the grind, and the memories of that dark night down the Tube, lifted.

One evening, soon after their first date, they were sitting outside in the yard, the comforting, primitive sounds of a blacksmith's hammering drifting over the back wall from the forge, when Joe sank down on to one knee.

'Marry me?' he asked hopefully, dark eyes shining like wet paint.

'Oh, shut up,' she laughed nervously. 'You're only making out.'

'No, I mean it. I-I love you.'

'Oh!' she blustered. 'In that case, ask me again.'

So he did.

Outside, the evening sky over the gas works blushed pink. Minksy closed her eyes, felt his warm mouth on hers, his strong hands encircling her waist, and, for the first time since the war, she felt such sweet joy.

Joe and Minksy married not long after in bomb-shattered St Andrew's Church in Bethnal Green, and the whole neighbourhood turned out to wish them well.

Twenty-year-old Minksy looked like she'd stepped off the silver screen, picture-perfect and petite in cream lace, her tiny twenty-two-inch waist cinched in and her white-blonde curly hair scooped high on her head.

The reception was modest, a few sausage rolls in a chilly church hall, and, as for a honeymoon, who had the money for that? Minksy was back to work on the Monday as a seamstress, not at the Krays' new firm in Hackney, but at Bartman & Co. in Bethnal Green. Joe returned to his coal round. The new marital home was a room in his mother's house in Cranberry Street until they had enough for a place of their own, but none of that mattered. They were head over heels in love and utterly devoted to one another, a devotion that would see them through fifty years of marriage.

Girl Walker's winter wedding to Jimmy 'Wag' in neighbouring Stepney was not going quite as smoothly. She and her father had got as far as the church door of St Dunstan's when the vicar headed them off.

'I'm so sorry, Marie, but I can't marry you and Jimmy,' he apologised, arms flapping over his cassock.

'W-what? Why not?' she exclaimed.

'You didn't have your banns read in Limehouse,' he explained.

'But I've lived in Stepney all my life,' she protested.

'They've changed it all now. E1, E2 . . .' Girl Walker drifted off as he launched into a lengthy explanation about the changing of postal codes.

'The only way is if you get up to St Paul's Cathedral and get a special licence,' he concluded, 'but you'll have to go this instant.'

'Leave it with me,' said Jimmy, taking off his jacket and tie, and thrusting them at her. Then he was gone, vanished into the diaphanous winter light.

Clutching her bouquet, Girl Walker stared disbelievingly at the stunned faces of her mum, dad, sisters and bridesmaids as the groom legged it. Only Old Boots seemed unfazed, raking about in her bag for her snuff.

'Well, no good wasting a morning,' said her bridesmaid

Sheila breezily. 'I'm going down Chrisp Street.' She kicked off her bridesmaid shoes, changed into a sensible black pair and headed off in the direction of the market.

'That's a good idea,' agreed some of the congregation, who were by now filing out the church. Even the chimney sweep, paid to stand outside the church for good luck, nipped off for a cup of tea and a fag.

'It's an omen,' muttered Nanny Walker, folding her arms disapprovingly behind the vicar and sniffing dramatically. 'You oughtn't to marry him.'

'Don't create, Nan,' Girl Walker warned.

'I'm going back home to check the buffet hasn't gone cold,' muttered Jimmy's mum, who had prepared a lovely spread of mashed potato and boiled ham for the wedding breakfast.

'Nothing for it,' said Girl Walker's mum. 'We may as well go home too and have a cup of tea while we wait.'

It wasn't the best of starts. Girl Walker knew that, when it came to Jimmy 'Wag', her family wasn't exactly head over heels about the union. Her mum hadn't said it in so many words, but she could tell they thought she was marrying beneath her.

When it came to the working class, there were different levels. The Walkers were respectable. So far as Girl Walker could tell, her family was in a different class because they had sheets on their beds; Wag's family used coats. The Walkers had a Sunday roast; when she'd first met Wag's family, they were tucking into a sheep's head.

Truth be told, she was herself a bit wary of Jimmy's parents, who came from a Romany gypsy family. His dad was a bare-knuckle boxer with a face like a bag of spanners, and his mum was rumoured to be a mind-reader and a witch.

But you can't choose who you fall in love with, and Girl Walker had fallen hook, line and sinker for Jimmy, with his elfin features and his crooked smile. She didn't really know what he did for a living, beyond a bit of this and a bit of that, but he had all the charm and plenty of sauce to match her own.

On their first date, the cheeky swine had taken her to the Troxy down Commercial Road and nicked her leather gloves at the end of the night.

'I'll give 'em back when I see you again,' he'd promised.

'Who says I'm gonna see you again!' she'd exclaimed.

'You will,' he'd grinned cockily, sauntering off.

There was something chemical between the two of them, a reaction that sent a thrill inching up her spine whenever she saw his cocky gait strutting up the road. Jimmy walked like he owned the neighbourhood. She knew marriage to him would not be straightforward, but it would never be dull. What she hadn't predicted was that the drama would start the moment she tried to walk up the aisle.

An hour or so later, they were assembled back at the church, a breathless Jimmy clutching a piece of paper. The vicar read it and his face fell.

'I'm so sorry, the priest at St Paul's has forgotten to sign it twice.'

'Oh bleedin' hell!' snapped Alice, then, remembering herself, she added, 'Excuse me, Father.'

Off Jimmy went again.

By now, the congregation was getting restless, tired and hungry, the bridesmaids were fighting and Sheila was still down the market. They were supposed to marry at 2 p.m., and now it was well past 4. As the shy winter sun began to melt into the gloaming, the vicar glanced nervously at his watch.

'I have to marry you before six p.m., I'm afraid,' he explained. 'We are cutting things very fine.'

A young Dot Smee, who lied about her age to get into the Land Army and was promptly sent back to a factory in the East End, just as the Blitz broke out.

Joan Martin as a young doctor on a drive to immunise babies and eradicate unnecessary childhood diseases.

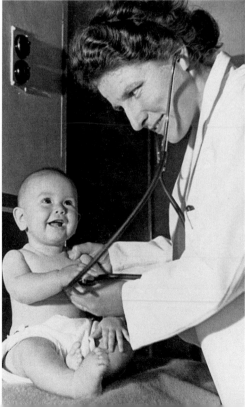

Minksy Keeper, the songbird from
Bethnal Green.

Minksy (far right) with her sister
Marie (middle) and friend Kathy
(left), Bethnal Green's answer to the
Andrews Sisters.

Minksy doing what she loves best, singing. She learnt her trade in the East End's crowded wartime shelters.

Minksy on the day of her wedding
to handsome coal delivery driver
Joe Keeper in 1947.

Minksy in pearls with
her daughter Lesley.

Seamstress Sally Flood from Whitechapel honed her sewing skills in the wartime rag trade.

Parents of twelve! Love and passion burned bright at the centre of Jessie and Arthur Smith's marriage. Here they are larking about in front of Brighton Pier as young parents.

Just married… in the nick of time. Girl Walker on the arm of her new husband, Jimmy.
She had to sprint up the aisle to make it in time.

Pat Spicer looked like a screen siren when she married barber Bill Spicer in 1948.

Lusciously beautiful Renee Stack, married on a shoestring, looking like a star on her wedding day when she married handsome war-hero Brian Stack in 1948.

From top to bottom, left to right: Girl Walker; Minksy with her wedding photo; Dr Joan Martin aged 101 taken July 2017; Jessie Smith; Babs with Doreen Golding, the Pearly Queen; Gladys, Blitz survivor; Cable Street ladies, left to right: Millie, Beatty and Marie.

'An omen,' Nanny Walker muttered again through pursed lips.

'I'll go and check the buffet hasn't dried out completely,' scowled her future mother-in-law. And then under her breath, 'What a carry-on!'

Getting back into her wedding car, Girl Walker looked down at her wilting bouquet and fought off angry tears.

'Here you go, Babe,' smiled her mum sympathetically, handing her a drawstring bag. 'I was going to save this for after, but I think you might need all the luck you can get now. Soap, so you can stay clean; a piece of coal, so you always have warmth; and salt, so that you always have food in your marriage.'

She was touched at the old East End tradition, but right now, she'd settle for a husband.

'He's back!' called her dad excitedly at 5.45 p.m.

'Got it!' yelled Jimmy triumphantly holding up a piece of paper as he sprinted past the car and into the church.

'Hurry,' said the vicar, wildly gesturing from the church door, 'we're running out of time.'

'Look lively,' said her dad, leaping from the car.

'I'm going as fast as I can,' Girl Walker panted, lifting her dress and bundling out the car, straight into a filthy puddle.

'My shoes!' she wailed, staring down at the stain of filthy water seeping into the white satin. 'They're ruined.'

'Never mind that,' said her dad, grabbing her arm and unceremoniously yanking her towards the church door. Sheila, now back from the market, and still wearing black shoes with her pale-blue bridesmaid's dress, ran behind trying to grab her train. Girl Walker actually ran up the aisle, and she and Jimmy were married with just minutes to spare.

Looking back on the photos, which had to be taken inside the church as the light had gone, she could see that the only people smiling were her and Jimmy. Everyone else was staring straight ahead with a face like thunder.

Marry in haste, repent at leisure, or so the old saying goes, and six weeks after the nippy nuptials, Girl Walker had decided she'd had enough of married life.

What did a wife get out of it? Cooking, cleaning, scrubbing and sex. And to make matters worse, it turned out the rumours were true: her mother-in-law was a witch!

As with all young newly-weds in the East End, their married life began in the parental home. From the moment Girl Walker had moved out of Flamborough Street and in with Jimmy and his family in Beaumont Square, her mother-in-law had her beady eye on her, even checking the bed sheets the morning after the wedding night, to ensure her new daughter-in-law was no trollop.

Fortunately, Girl Walker hadn't had to resort to pricking her finger and letting the blood drip on the sheets like some naughty girls in the district, but her gypsy mother-in-law did have an uncanny knack of reading her mind.

It was a dull Sunday morning with the rain hammering fists on the window when she finally flipped. Jimmy was out having a drink with his dad at the pub, so it was just the two of them preparing a Sunday dinner.

'My Jimmy don't like his potatoes cut so small,' her mother-in-law remarked sourly. 'And while you're at it, you ain't cleaned his boots properly.'

Rotten old cow, Girl Walker thought.

'I am not a rotten old cow,' Jimmy's mum said indignantly, whirling round and glaring at her.

How on earth . . . ? Girl Walker fled from the house in tears, straight back home to Flamborough Street.

'It's not for me!' she wailed, bursting into the kitchen. 'I don't want to be married any more!'

'Well now, that's tough,' said her dad, gently grabbing her by the scruff of the neck and marching her back to her new home, ''cause you're married now. You've made your bed, now you gotta lie in it.' Slinking up the stairs, she made a vow never to look her mother-in-law in the eye again.

Over time, Girl Walker gradually adapted to marriage, but it was impossible to navigate the unwritten rules of being a wife and living with a domineering mother-in-law, who was determined to let her know that she was trespassing on her domain.

Could the woman ever have a row! One evening, Girl Walker only just managed to duck in time as she hurled a teapot at Jimmy's father's head. When an indignant Girl Walker later told Old Boots, she howled with laughter.

But worse than flying teapots and words hurled in anger, were the words that weren't said. Growing up in the East End, there were certain topics that you just didn't discuss and, despite her street smarts, like so many of her generation, Girl Walker was surprisingly ignorant about the facts of life.

'You're pregnant,' announced her doctor, two months after she was married.

'I can't have fallen,' she protested. 'My Jimmy withdraws.'

'What do they teach you children?' the doctor sighed, shaking his head. 'For that's all you are – children.'

Her ignorance continued unchecked. As her pregnancy developed, she genuinely thought the brown vertical line her doctor called the linea nigra, which ran from underneath her belly button to the top of her pubic bone, would magically part and out would pop baby. Childbirth therefore came as something of a shock. Afterwards, holding her new baby daughter, Carol, her hair plastered to her head with sweat, feeling like she'd been run over by a truck, she frowned deeply.

'What's wrong, dear?' asked the midwife.

'I-I didn't know where babies came from,' she mumbled.

The midwife sighed, and wearily pulled the curtain round the bed.

'Listen, darlin',' she said, 'didn't it occur to you that it's got to come out the same place it went in?'

But the new mum just stared ahead in shock. It is a universal truth that once you've given birth, you will never view life in quite the same way again, and so it was for Girl Walker.

'Don't you have a mother or sisters who could've set you straight?' the midwife asked.

'I got a mum, three sisters and two nans!' Girl Walker exclaimed. 'They never said a word.'

Patiently, the midwife spent some time explaining the facts of life and, when she was finished, Girl Walker was flabbergasted. How had she reached twenty without knowing all that?

Soon after, her older sister Winnie, herself a mother, got a proper cleaning when she visited.

'Why didn't you tell me?' she demanded.

'Well, no one told me,' Winnie huffed defensively.

Back in Beaumont Square, her mother-in-law insisted she spend six weeks staying in, before she underwent the ancient ritual of being churched in the Lady Chapel at St Dunstan's. The custom of blessing a woman after childbirth recalls the Purification of the Blessed Virgin Mary and was commonplace in Girl Walker's East End. The ceremonial rite was performed in order to restore purity and wash away the sins of making the baby.

Marriage and childbirth sloughed away the last of Girl

Walker's naivety and, from then on, she grew her mother's thick skin. She had to.

Girl Walker and Jimmy's marriage had its up and downs and its downs and ups. At parties and socials, he was charm itself, but when he'd been on the drink he could start a row with King Kong. The mornings after were the worst. One morning, while she was cooking a fry-up in a big heavy pan, Jimmy was needling her incessantly. Girl Walker saw red and smacked him round the head with the frying pan.

'He's dead!' shrieked Jimmy's pal Peter as they stared at him, spark out on the floor, the remains of the fry-up spattered up the walls.

'I'll do more than kill him in a moment,' muttered Girl Walker.

When he blearily came round, he grinned at her.

'Now you've got to clear all that off the wall!'

'He was a tormenting sod, but I loved him, and even after years of marriage and three kids, I still got a thrill when I saw him walking down the road,' Girl Walker recalls.

Like many of her generation, she found that as soon as she had a ring on her finger, she was expected to be under the thumb.

'When a man gives you a child, they think they own you, but no one owns me,' insists the inimitable cockney, who still marches to the beat of her own drum. 'I told him I was going off to work one day to earn a quid, but instead I got the ferry to France to watch the horse racing with some of the boys I was working with down the betting shop. I nearly died that evening when I was sitting with my old man watching the telly and there it was on the box.'

For all the turbulence of their marriage, love and passion

pulsed firmly at its heart, and Girl Walker was at her husband's side in 1984 when he drew his last breath aged just fifty-four.

Her story, and Minksy's, illustrate the desire to settle down and embrace married life after the war, but also the naivety of their generation, raising their babies in the ashes of post-war Britain.

The Labour landslide victory in the General Election of 1945 paved the way for new reforms to improve the country's health, welfare and education. Based on the proposals in the 1942 Beveridge Report, the National Health Service was introduced in 1948, giving free healthcare to all. Family planning clinics were set up, but when Minksy married in 1947, and Girl Walker in 1952, they were still in their infancy, and so the women were largely reliant on old wives' tales and the 'Vatican Roulette' withdrawal technique.

In the immediate years after the war, not just in the East End but all over Britain, there was a desperate desire for a return to so-called normality. Everything was back in its supposedly rightful place, and women were encouraged to embrace their traditional feminine roles. But after finding their purpose, could women return to the people they had been before, and was the husband who came home the same man who'd marched off to war? In some cases, evidentially not. The war had placed unprecedented strain on traditional family life, and by 1947 the divorce figures had nearly doubled in just two years.

Despite this, in the East End, there was a tangible sense of a desire for escapism and glamour, and weddings gave women the perfect opportunity to indulge in both.

'There was so much poverty in those days, we all craved glamour, our chance to feel like a star for the day and chase away the dark clouds of post-war London,' sighs eighty-eight-year-old Pat from Bethnal Green.

Pat was working as an apprentice court dressmaker for West End department store Bourne & Hollingsworth, when she met and married the man of her dreams, gent's barber, Bill.

In her wedding portrait, Pat gazes out like a serene starlet. Like Minksy, with her twenty-two-inch waist and perfect poise, she could have stepped straight out of a motion picture. And yet, her portrait wasn't taken in Hollywood, but in impoverished post-war Whitechapel in 1948.

Pat employed the services of legendary Jewish East End photographer Boris Bennett, whose Whitechapel studio was the place to go for stylish weddings. Boris was famous for bringing a touch of Hollywood style to a wedding shoot. Using exquisitely painted backdrops on wheels and sumptuous lighting, he could transform the most ordinary-looking bride into a sophisticated showstopper.

A canny marketing man, before anyone really knew what marketing meant, he even employed a uniformed commissionaire to meet and greet the newly-weds. His weddings created quite the buzz in the district. Eager onlookers would gather outside his studio on the Whitechapel Road to catch a glimpse of the bride, including dressmakers who would wait, sketchbooks in hand.

'We went for the complete set, nine framed photos and a book at sixteen guineas. It was expensive but I had to have it and my family had saved for my wedding for years,' says Pat. 'Boris was charming and helped me to look stunning. We posed against a beautiful cream archway with dreamy lighting. He arranged extra tulle around the bottom of my dress and taught us how to pose.'

No matter that outside the door of the studio, just yards

from Pat and Bill, snaked a smoke-choked Whitechapel High Street. For a brief time, Pat was in Hollywood. Boris' exquisite portraits shine with a deep pride, for he understood what all East Enders knew back then – there was no shame in being poor.

All these years on, Pat's eyes still sparkle at the memory, and though her wedding was seventy years ago, she has no problems recalling in exact detail the dress she wore that day.

'I wore a white satin gown with a sweetheart neckline with an inlet of lace, cathedral sleeves with a loop on the finger, twenty-two satin buttons on the back to match my waist-size, a fluted train and a lovers' knot embroidered into the veil,' she recalls. 'Local dressmaker Hetty Dipple made it and we had four fittings in her front parlour. Hetty sewed a strand of her hair into the seam, her signature finish.' (A trick legendary East End born designer, Alexander McQueen, used to employ many years after Hetty Dipple.)

Half an hour after posing for her wedding portrait, Pat was back at her mother-in-law's tumbledown terrace in Bethnal Green, East London, clambering over a Salvation Army trestle table for a wedding breakfast of mashed potato, cold roast beef and beetroot, followed by Thursday to Monday in Canvey Island.

'All top show, nothing underneath!' laughs Pat.

Pat's heart-warming story shows the dichotomy between hardship and high glamour that was so prevalent during the grinding poverty of the post-war years. To own a beautiful wedding portrait, in a time when few people owned a camera, much less a selfie-stick, was a symbol of hope.

Pat is not alone in her vivid recollections of those halcyon days.

'It was 1945. He walked right over to me at a dance and said: "I'm going to marry you!" I'd never set eyes on him before!' recalls ninety-one-year-old Renee from Stepney, with a great hoot of laughter.

Brian was a handsome Errol Flynn lookalike, who was just back from serving with the 7th Armoured Division as one of Montgomery's brave 'desert rats'. The dashing demobbed soldier swept eighteen-year-old shop girl Renee off her feet.

Renee's strict Jewish mother was less impressed. 'Wait and see what he makes of himself first,' was her sage advice.

Brian knuckled down to civilian life and spent three years learning Hebrew so he could convert to Judaism in order to marry Renee. At her wedding ceremony at Newbury Park Synagogue in 1948, Renee was so lusciously beautiful, she could easily have passed for Rita Hayworth.

'We had no money, so Brian borrowed a suit and my friend Edie, who worked as a sample machinist, made me my beautiful pale-blue silk crêpe wedding dress. I said to her: "But I've no money to pay you!" "It's a wedding gift," she insisted. That's the way people were back then, helping each other out. I did my own hair and make-up, and the whole family chipped in to pay for the wedding portrait. We married on a shoestring, but I was the happiest girl alive, just twenty-one years old and with so much hope for the future.'

In common with Minksy and Girl Walker, Pat and Renee enjoyed long and fruitful marriages. Notions of romance and glamour might have got these East End brides up the aisle, but it was hard work, commitment and sacrifice that made their unions last the distance.

'Back then, the wedding day itself wasn't so important; it

was the rest of our married lives that meant something,' Pat concludes. 'We never gave up on a marriage. No matter how tough things got, there was nothing that couldn't be talked out.'

The face of Girl Walker, Minksy, Pat and Renee's vibrant East End has changed beyond measure.

Talented seamstress Hetty Dipple, who made exquisite wedding gowns to rival any couturier, is long gone. Boris Bennett's photography studio, where Pat rose above poverty and felt like a Hollywood star for the day, is an Indian take-away. All of the husbands mentioned in this chapter have passed away. Only the women remain. And their memories, of course. Their post-war love stories are testament to a shared survival, and a love of humanity.

But not all stories ended at the altar. Others found their wartime experience had moulded them into someone who could *never* be tied to a man.

Her hasty wartime marriage and rapid departure from Australia had proven one thing to Dr Joan. She was not cut out to be a wife. The war had given her something of an epiphany.

'After all that I witnessed, I vowed not to squander my parents' sacrifices by getting married again,' Joan told me when I went to interview her in her neat and cosy London flat, where she still lived independently at the age of 102. 'I chose instead to devote my life to duty and service. Like so many women, I blossomed during the war and became aware of what I was capable of. I realised I owed it to my parents to work as hard as I possibly could to improve the lives of those that needed it most.'

Joan was resplendent in a vibrant green dress she made herself from Ghanaian fabric that was a gift from a friend, and chunky wooden beads. It's not the outfit you expect a woman born in 1915 to be wearing, but Joan spent her life challenging convention and stereotype.

It was a stiflingly hot day, but Joan was as cool as a cucumber. Her pale eyes gleamed with the shrewd intelligence of one who has been on this planet for over 100 years. The century has not left her bruised or battered, nor hollowed from love and loss. Rather it seems to have made her playful, ebullient even.

'That's the problem with women today,' she told me. 'They labour under the illusion that they can have it all. I sacrificed a personal life to become a doctor. I never dreamt I could marry and have a career. It was one or the other.

'Somewhere along the line, you have to make a choice. I had a marriage to medicine and it made me who I am.'

Joan did not let her parents' sacrifices go in vain. Her achievement in being one of a handful of women to complete her training as a doctor in wartime was just the beginning. After the war, Joan became a doctor, not ambitious to get to the top of her profession, but absolutely dedicated to serving those that needed her care most.

She was given responsibility for the health of disabled children in the Royal Borough of Kensington, a job she found she had a natural flair for. The 1950s saw a big drive to immunise children against polio, and after losing her childhood friend to this disease, she worked relentlessly to ensure all children under her watch avoided contracting an unnecessary illness.

Despite its royal postcode, in the 1950s, much as it docs today, Kensington contained areas of desperate poverty, sitting cheek by jowl with wealth and privilege. Joan made it her business to go into the slums and get families rehoused, and to fight for improvements in the living standards of the poor.

Like Dr Goldie in Chapter Three, Dr Joan was not a woman who worked nine to five. Instead, she was constantly searching for ways in which she could improve the health and happiness of her patients.

In 1955, Joan formed a free swimming club called the Kensington Emperors. It was a revelation. She realised swimming would be excellent therapy for people with disabilities: because the body is lighter in water, it is easier to move. Joan didn't just give disabled children access to a nice hobby. She set them free.

'The look on their faces when they see that they are weightless, just like anyone else, it was enormously rewarding,' Joan reflected.

She never turned anyone away and soon the club was teaching children with learning difficulties, as well as physical disabilities.

Over the years, as news of what her club was achieving spread, Joan met with Prince Charles and the Queen Mother, and talked to them about her work. But it was her brush with Princess Diana at a pool in Westminster that impressed her the most.

'I was sitting with the princess on the side watching the children swim, but she insisted on going right down to the pit that surrounded the pool, so she could speak with them,' she recalled. 'It wasn't the cleanest place, but she didn't care. She sat the children on her knee and was perfectly at home with them, whatever their disability. She understood.'

Dr Joan lectured on the benefits of swimming for the disabled all around the world, from Brazil and Australia to

Greece and Switzerland, and helped train swimming instructors in the Halliwick technique.

In 1963, she also spent a year in southern Africa working for the Girl Guides, to teach African Guide officials how they could become independent of any help from white South African officials.

With apartheid so entrenched, the Africans were amazed at a white woman coming to work and live with them. But travelling gruelling distances in searing heat to the territories, and surviving off one small meal a day and scant sleep, was nothing new to Dr Joan. Her work in the Blitz had been the perfect training ground.

In Africa, she befriended many fascinating people, most notably Seretse Khama, who became the first president of Botswana, and whose marriage to a white woman by the name of Ruth Williams breached South Africa's strict laws forbidding mixed-race marriages. Dr Joan taught their children essential Guide skills, such as knotting, and in turn she learnt much from the couple's dignity and strength.

Here, too, she also had the opportunity to try exciting pursuits, like rock climbing and trekking in Swaziland. Whether it was visiting a leper colony or dining with African royalty, Dr Joan grasped every experience that came her way, always staying open-minded to opportunity. Joan may have closed the door on a husband and hearth, but opened another one into a world rich with adventure.

Would she have had such life-altering experiences had she stayed married? Looking back on a long and challenging career, Dr Joan has never once regretted her decision not to settle down. As she talked of the many friends she has met along the way from all around the globe, it's obvious that, although she never had her own children, she was never short of familial love.

When Joan turned 100, a party was thrown in her honour and it was jam-packed with people from all walks of life, including many whom Joan referred to as surrogate daughters.

At 102, she was still a force to be reckoned with, but her most obvious trait, aside from a no-nonsense approach to life, was one of utter humility and selflessness. Like many of her generation, born before the advent of the welfare state, she believed we have a duty of care to help those less fortunate. With Joan and her remarkable generation, it was never a case of *I*, but always *we*. And we have all reaped the benefits of their wartime sacrifices.

Along the way, her dogged work and unswerving faith have rightly earned Dr Joan prestigious accolades, and she was appointed MBE in 1985, and received the Mayor's Award in 2004, and the St Mellitus Medal from the Bishop of Kensington in 2007. But of all the people she met in her century of life, Joan saved her highest praise for the wartime mothers of the East End.

'They were remarkable, tough women who suffered great deprivation, but always put their children first, often going hungry themselves so that they might eat,' she told me.

'I saw such terrible suffering in the East End. Malnourished children with rickets, covered in scabies and bug bites. The kids would come in and, when given a drink of milk, would ask politely: "Where can I drink to?" They were stunned to hear they could have a whole glass. It was those strong mothers who raised polite children in the teeth of such poverty who deserve the medals.'

What was supposed to be a quick interview so as not to

tire out Dr Joan lasted well over two hours. Outside, the setting sun rimmed the clouds a blazing gold. It was time to leave her in peace and say my goodbyes to this magnificent woman. But Joan had one last thing to say. Her eyes shone with a fierce determination as she leant forward to share this with me: 'In World War Two, it was women who saved the day.'

I am so thankful I met Dr Joan Martin MBE at the eleventh hour. Six months after I interviewed Joan and just four weeks after the unveiling of the Bethnal Green Memorial, she died in her own home in January 2018 with friends at her side. She was 102.

I have never seen a church packed solid with so many people from all walks of life as there were at Joan's funeral, all bound by a deep respect and love for her. Sunlight flooded the church of St Mary Abbots in Kensington as the Right Reverend Michael Colclough, former Bishop of Kensington, the same man who had given Joan the St Mellitus medal, read the eulogy.

'How do you go about summing up a life lived full to overflowing?' he puzzled.

Looking back on Joan's remarkable, convention-defying achievements, I would say it is near on impossible.

Rest in peace, Joan.

Polly's Recipe

Oxtail Stew and Dumplings

Ask your local butcher to chop up an oxtail for you and get a couple of decent-sized pieces. Put the meat into a large pot of water, along with two Oxo cubes, a handful of split peas, a handful of pearl barley, a couple of carrots, a couple of potatoes, a pinch of pepper and an onion. Simmer for three hours.

Twenty minutes before the cooking time is up, mix together in a bowl 8oz self-raising flour, 4oz beef suet, half a teaspoon of mustard powder and a pinch of pepper and a tablespoon of water. Mix it together until it forms a dough-like consistency, adding more water if necessary. Scoop out a large tablespoon of the mixture and form it into round balls. Pop your dumplings on top of your stew, put the lid on and steam them for twenty minutes. Add a good grating of pepper and dig in.

Polly's Remedy

Camphorated oil (Vicks is the same thing) rubbed on the chest and soles of the feet is the way to keep fit and healthy.

Polly's Pearls of Wisdom

You're not a victim.

10. Abortion, 1959

Seven-year-old Denise peeped through the gap in the doorway, into the darkened kitchen. An oxtail bubbled away on the stove, billowing clouds of meaty steam that hung like a thick curtain in the kitchen.

Through the haze, she could make out her mum, Polly, huddled head-to-head over the table top with Mrs Bryant.

'I don't know what to do, Pol,' Mrs Bryant wept, twisting the hem of her apron between her fingers. 'I hope you don't mind me turning to you.'

'Go on . . .' her mum urged.

Denise held her breath. She'd get the mother of all clumps if she was caught earwigging, but she sensed whatever it was Mrs B was about to reveal was worth the risk.

'It's the old man . . . He won't leave me alone.' She trumpeted into a large handkerchief and shook her head.

'Night after bleedin' night he wants it, and I can't have any more kids. I got enough mouths to feed.' She hesitated. 'W-will you have word with your Frankie?'

Polly nodded sagely, her eyes as dark as midnight as she closed her hand softly over Mrs Bryant's.

'You leave it with me, dearie. It'll get sorted.'

Mrs Bryant's shoulders slumped in relief.

'Ta, Pol. I'm ever so grateful.'

Pushing back her chair, Mrs Bryant reached for her string bag and rose from the scrubbed table.

'Better go, the little bleeders will be shouting for their dinner. Cheerio.'

'Ta-ta, love,' Polly replied.

Mrs Bryant turned and suddenly loomed towards the kitchen door. Denise scarpered, feet scrabbling on the lino as she bolted up the steps and outside on to Dugden Terrace. A great pack of her sisters and crowds of neighbourhood kids were playing hide and seek amongst the gravestones in the churchyard directly opposite their Victorian terraced home. This was their favourite place to play, that and the bombsite on the end of the terrace that got flattened during the Blitz.

As she joined in, Denise wondered what it was old Mrs Bryant had been referring to. What was it her husband was wanting 'night after bleedin' night' and what did it have to do with her mum?

An hour later, she heard the sound of the sash window frame scraping up, followed by the mouth-watering smell of oxtail stew.

'Dinner!' Polly bellowed into the brackish air.

The Barrett girls didn't need telling twice. Denise and her six sisters belted up the passage, all flailing arms, elbows and scabby knees.

'Wash yer hands,' Polly ordered, as they charged into the kitchen en masse.

The sight of the sisters tucking into their dinner was a thing to behold. Denise was the youngest of seven girls, a birth order which, for some, might have brought on an inferiority complex. Not for tomboy Denise, though, who was as tough as any boy down her turning.

Polly waited until everyone was sat round the table, tongues hanging out their mouths, before dishing up the oxtail from an enormous pan. It had been simmering for so long, the meat slid off the bone, plopping into the thick, unctuous gravy. The meat was served up in huge, steaming ladle loads, the gravy laced with veg, pearl barley and split peas, with a couple of dumplings made with suet and plenty of mustard powder dolloped on top for good measure. It was a meal cooked with love.

'Go on then,' Polly grinned proudly, wiping her hands on her apron and stepping back. 'Wot'cha waiting for? Get stuck in!'

Minutes later, the sound of slurping and scraping cutlery filled the room. Polly was a mean cook, able to rustle up a melt-in-the-mouth stew out of any old scrag end of meat. Her chunky chips done in the frying pan with lard were famous down Dugden Terrace.

But Denise's mum was also well known in the neighbourhood for other skills beyond her cooking.

Polly was just stacking the plates in the scullery when the door swung open and Denise's dad walked in. Frankie Barrett was a skinny man, not much further through than a coat hanger, with thick frame glasses that amplified two piercing blue eyes. In fact, to look at him, you'd never guess . . .

'Hello, my darlin',' he grinned, pulling his voluptuous wife into his wiry arms and kissing her warmly on the mouth, while slipping what looked like a bundle of notes into her apron pocket.

'Sit down and I'll sort your dinner, love,' Polly smiled, her eyes dizzy with love as she poured her husband a cup of his favourite Camp coffee and set it before him.

'Now you lot, scarper. I need to talk to your father. Don't come back before the hour is over.'

The Barrett girls scrambled off outside, grateful to get another hour of playtime. All except for poke-nose Denise, who couldn't stand secrets. Silently, she waited until her sisters had vanished, before taking up her usual spot outside the door. Her parents' voices were muffled but she could make out snippets.

'I need you to go and have a word . . . But the old man'll cut up rough . . .' Then came her mother, anger icing her voice. 'Make sure you do, otherwise I'll go round there myself with two bricks and a mallet!'

There wasn't a single moment of revelation when Denise learnt that her father was an enforcer for a villain and her mother was the street auntie. Rather, there was a gradual dawning, with moments like these forming an instinctive understanding of the pivotal role her mum and dad played in the neighbourhood. Together, they made a formidable team. Other areas had police, neighbourhood watch, Citizens Advice Bureau, a nurse, midwife and funeral directors. Dugden Terrace had Polly and Frankie, a husband-and-wife team whose word was law and whose execution of it ensured everything was kept running smoothly.

By day, Frankie was in a marching band called the Merry Music Makers, who performed outside the Palladium. He'd even had tea recently with the Lord Mayor. But by night, at work, he used his hands for other purposes. Likewise, Polly wasn't above using her fists to get the results she wanted, but usually only on men, and only when they deserved it. They might have been tough, but so was their neighbourhood. Polly and Frankie were old school, using the working-class code of a quiet word and, if that didn't work, a fist in the face, a boot in the kneecap, or in Polly's case, a brick in the balls.

Born in 1903 in sleepy Barnstaple in Devon, Polly saw marriage to a boxer at the age of seventeen as a way out, but when he started bringing his work home with him, she left him, getting herself a job in the mortuary of a TB hospital. It was her job to lay out the bodies of the dead. She learnt the hard way that if you didn't burp the bodies before you plugged all their holes, the dead had an unnerving habit of suddenly sitting up ramrod straight on the mortuary slab. Laying out corpses may have been a grisly way to earn a living, but it was better than being in a violent marriage, and it helped Polly to hone the skills she would need in later life.

A marriage to Frankie, on Bonfire Night 1940, freed her from the mortuary and she began her new life in earnest. In London, Polly swung from the grave, back to the cradle. If there was one thing Polly loved, it was babies.

'He's only gotta hang his trousers on the bedpost and I'm caught,' she joked. But Polly stopped after birthing her seventh daughter and became the street childminder instead, a job which cemented her role as the matriarch of Dugden Terrace.

Denise was proud that her mother was the go-to woman, respected, liked and feared in equal measure. Naturally, she wanted to emulate her. The next day, playing marbles out on the street, she saw the local troublemaker, Georgie.

'Give us them marbles!' he ordered.

'Or what?' she challenged.

'Or else is what!'

She stared up at him without blinking. Her dad's voice echoed through her mind: If someone throws a punch at you and you see an opening, you take it. If you can't punch, and they're a boy, kick 'em in the nuts. When they're on the floor, step on their throat.

But then another voice chimed over his.

'Do one!' Denise chirruped. 'Or I'll hit yer with two bricks and a mallet.'

The words sounded strange coming from the mouth of a dumpy seven-year-old girl with a blonde pudding-basin haircut, but it seemed to have the desired effect as Georgie slunk off, scowling. A shadow fell over the pavement.

'Denise, get inside now.'

'M-mum . . .'

'You crafty little bastard, you've been earwigging, ain'cha?'

It was pointless trying to deny it.

Denise rose, bracing herself for the clump that would surely follow, but they were interrupted by the rent man, his satchel slung over one shoulder, fag glued to his bottom lip. He nodded at Polly before knocking on the next door.

'She can't pay, you know,' Polly remarked, folding her arms over her faded wrap-around apron and leaning against the door frame. 'Her husband's out of work.'

'I'll give her two weeks to pay, and if she can't cough up then, she's out on her ear.'

'How's she gonna do that then?' Polly demanded to know, as she uncrossed her arms and began walking down the steps with a face that could stop a funeral. The rent collector took a step back, his Adam's apple bobbing up and down his throat nervously.

'Makes no sense, pal,' Polly went on. 'If she can't pay you now, she won't be able to pay in two weeks, will she? Make it more affordable and she'll pay you back in smaller amounts.'

'R-rules is rules,' stuttered the mealy-mouthed rent man as the shadow of the apron-clad matriarch swallowed him. 'I need paying.'

Denise could see her mum's dander was up as she poked him hard in the chest.

'And she's got kiddies what need feeding. Tell you what, I'll have a word with my old man when he comes home.'

The rent man turned a deathly white, his mouth as tight as a clam.

'It's all right, Pol. I'm sure we can all come to some sort of agreement.'

'Good.' She sniffed and, dusting down her hands, she marched back up the steps.

Growing up, Denise often wondered why her mum put herself out for the women of the street, fighting their corner and intervening in any domestic dispute. It's not as if she ever got paid for it. A grateful Mrs Bryant, whose husband had been persuaded that abstinence was next to godliness, repaid Polly with a bit of shopping and twenty Craven 'A' cigarettes.

Another incident helped to shed some light on why. One afternoon, Polly and her girls were walking into their turning when the door to number 18 flew open and a flash of fur flew past. A mangy-looking cat struck the door frame before landing on the pavement beside them, its eye gashed and bleeding.

'Mum!' Denise gaped. 'That fella just kicked his cat!'

Polly's mouth tightened to a thin white line, and she blew angrily out of both nostrils.

'Oi!' she yelled at the open door. 'Get out here!'

Polly already had it in for the young man who lived at number 18, whom she suspected of running a knocking shop. Denise didn't fancy his chances much.

A youngish bloke emerged from the dark passage and stood before her, swaying on the pavement. He'd obviously been on the drink all day and Denise instinctively nestled into her mum's dress skirts.

'That's no way to treat an animal,' Polly said icily.

'It's a stray, it came and pissed in my house,' he snapped. 'Besides, what's it gotta do with you?'

'I'll tell you what it's gotta do with me, mate,' she replied, cracking her knuckles.

Wham! She knocked him out cold on the pavement with one punch.

From then on, Denise understood. If there was one thing her mum couldn't stand, it was a bully. Life was hard enough in the grime and poverty of working-class London. By using an iron fist in a velvet glove, Polly always championed the underdog (or stray cat) and defended the weak.

As her childhood rolled out on Dugden Terrace, Denise realised it was also a love of her community that drove Polly. Despite rationing, there was always plenty of food in their cupboard and coal for the fire, thanks to the black market, and Polly made sure no one on the street went without.

If a labouring woman couldn't afford to call out a midwife or doctor, Polly would jump in and help to deliver the baby. She'd had at least two of Denise's sisters at home on her own, cutting the cord herself. Conversely, thanks to her time in the TB hospital, Polly knew her way around a dead body, and many was the time she was called upon to lay out the street's dead.

When a terrible flu swept the neighbourhood one winter, taking with it the elderly and four babies, it was Polly who solemnly laid them out, wrapping the babies up like little dollies in a drawer until the undertaker came.

Birth and death were a normal part of life in Dugden Terrace, and Polly did not believe in shielding her daughters from the realities of both, or from her ferocious work ethic.

Every morning at 6 a.m. before school, Denise would be up with her sisters, cleaning out the grate, making tea for her mum, going down to the baker's to fetch the fresh bread (and on special occasions, apple doughnuts), making sure to be back in time to scrub three flights of stairs with hot water and carbolic.

Once a week, the outside steps leading up to the front

door needed a good scrub. And it had to be done just so, or God help you! The top three had a good coating of Cardinal Red Tile Polish until they shone as red as the front door, and the rest needed scrubbing with a pummel stone to a snowy white. Even the best rug which got laid out on the lino whenever they had visitors had a regular beating. While Denise attacked the indoor steps, her mum would already be hard at work, washing nappies and readying herself for the stream of young kids that would be dropped off into her care.

'Got to stay clean,' her mum would say, as she hauled out the tin bath every Friday and washed her girls with carbolic soap. Once she'd vigorously towelled them down, she'd rub warm camphorated oil on their feet and back, followed by a good dose of castor oil and syrup of figs. Denise could tell the days of the week by the smells. Friday was fish; Sunday, roasting dinners; and Monday was Daz – wash day.

Cleanliness was a mark of pride to Polly Barrett, her way of saying they weren't lazy or dirty. Good hygiene was a virtue she upheld rigorously, as was her daughters' attendance at church three times on a Sunday.

But there was fun to be found too. Sunday afternoons, Polly and Frankie would head to the local, returning with half the pub and crates of beer for an impromptu knees-up. Drums, accordions, trumpets . . . Frankie and his musical pals filled their terrace with song and laughter. As the Black and Tan beer, and gin and lemons flowed, the armchairs would be scraped back and Frankie would grow sentimental, the heart-melting lyrics to Nelson Eddy's 'Rose Marie' pouring honey through their home. Halcyon days.

But the main fun was to be found outside. Cowboys and Indians in the churchyard . . . Jumping from the top floor of the burnt-out terrace to a strategically placed mattress in the garden below . . . Nicking the empty pop bottles from the back yard of the Crown and returning them at the bar to coin a cheeky thruppence . . .

As the daughter of the local auntie, Denise felt invincible. But as she grew up, certain things began to puzzle her.

Denise must have been seven or eight when she returned from school and walked into the front room to find a young woman on the settee. She was as pale as death itself, groaning softly to herself with her knees drawn up into her chest. Suddenly, she rose, and as she did so, a great torrent of blood gushed from between her legs, splattering on to the lino. Denise stood wide-eyed with horror as Polly leapt to her side. Once the woman had been cleaned up and sent to bed, Polly set to work scrubbing the blood off the floor.

'W-what's wrong with her, Mum?' Denise stammered. Polly looked up from her scrubbing, her dark eyes fathomless through the steam.

'She's got her monthlies.'

The metallic smell of blood mingled with carbolic was making Denise gag.

'I-I don't want to have that,' she shrieked. 'I'll kill myself if that's what it's like.'

Polly rose stiffly to her feet and sighed deeply as she wrung out the blood-stained cloth.

'Go and sit in the kitchen, girl. It's time we had a little talk.'

In the kitchen, Polly made tea and sat down heavily opposite her.

'When you get older, you'll grow titties, then all the boys'll start to chase you. They'll want to get in your drawers.'

Denise recoiled. An image of Georgie rolling over the mattress at the bombsite flashed through her mind.

'I don't want boys in my drawers!'

'And that's why you must say no,' Polly insisted, sparking up a Craven 'A' and inhaling deeply as she drummed her message out on the table top. 'Always. Say. No.'

Denise's brain ached. 'Is that what happened to that girl? She didn't say no?'

Polly hesitated, then blew out the smoke on a sigh.

'Sort of. She was in . . . in, er . . .' She paused, her hands fluttering over her belly, '. . . trouble.'

'Trouble,' Denise repeated, her blue eyes as wide as pebbles.

Bluish cigarette smoke curled around her mother's face, obscuring it so that she couldn't read her expression.

'That's right,' she said eventually, her voice brittle. 'In the finish, nature decided to get rid of the baby, and sometimes, you have to help nature out.'

'Right,' Denise mumbled. She was confused, but gradually, as she grew older and her awareness of such matters grew, things became clearer. She came home one evening early to find her mum vigorously scrubbing the kitchen table with her beloved carbolic.

'H-have you been helping someone out in trouble, Mum?' she asked, hesitantly.

Polly patted the kitchen chair and lowered her voice.

'I have, darlin'. Remember I told you Mother Nature sometimes needs a helping hand?'

Denise nodded.

'There's a girl here, she's resting upstairs. She was in that sort of trouble. Her father would've killed her, so I helped her out.'

'Could no one else help her?'

'Who?' Polly replied hotly. 'God? He ain't going to help, is he? Without me to turn to, she'd have nowhere to go. Her life'd be over. Finished . . .' She broke off, and turned angrily towards the window, staring out as a gritty dusk cloaked the graveyard.

From somewhere outside, Denise heard the distant cries of a rag and boner, leaves hitting the windowpane and a children's skipping rhyme echoing up Dugden Terrace. Inside, the silence stretched on . . .

Polly finally turned, her voice soft and low, her face veiled in the gauzy twilight.

'What I tell you, stays strictly between you and me. Our secret. What goes on inside the house, stays inside the house.' She mashed out her cigarette. 'Understood?'

Denise nodded emphatically to show she understood, and inside she felt a warm glow of importance. She had been entrusted with her mother's secrets. She was no longer on the outside, listening in.

'Good girl.'

Over time, Denise gained an understanding of the way Polly the abortionist operated. She only ever helped girls up to a certain stage. Her chosen method was a crochet hook. She used the kitchen table, laying down a rubber sheet. If the pregnancy had been advanced enough and the foetus intact, Polly would wash it and bury it in the churchyard opposite: 'In consecrated ground,' she told Denise, with a brutal logic.

As her mother's secret unfurled, Denise looked upon her with new eyes, marvelling at the dichotomy of her mother, the local childminder, also acting as the local abortionist. Over the years, dozens of girls in the same predicament traipsed through their doors, pale-faced and terrified. With abortion strictly illegal and birth control inadequate, it was a wonder there weren't more.

Polly was a paradox. A woman of faith, married to an enforcer; a woman who nurtured new life, but was equally competent in ending it. Perhaps it was because she understood the devastation of the scandal, and that it was always the woman's to bear. Polly hated inequality and never turned away a woman in need – including the local prostitutes, whose children she helped care for. Polly couldn't stand the Maltese gangsters who ran the clubs and brothels along the next street to theirs, but sadly her influence didn't extend to them.

It might sound strange, but Denise could see her mum felt a sense of obligation to these young girls, who, when all was said and done, had committed no crime, just made a mistake, but were forced to sneak about like criminals. Did money change hands? Of that, she was unsure, but she is certain of the gratitude her mother received. Many of the girls returned, bearing tins of sweets and chocolates. One even extended an invite to her wedding in later years.

Of course, Denise does not know about those abortions her mother performed that did not end well, and how many girls she helped who were left sterile or suffered devastating infections, which could have led to their death.

Denise often wondered whether her father knew about his wife's forbidden services. She could only assume so. The love and respect between them ran deep and they had no secrets. There was nothing the pair didn't talk out, usually over a drink at the local pub and, even when a distraught Polly realised she'd hadn't posted their pools ticket and their numbers had come up, Frankie remained sanguine.

'Never mind, darlin',' he'd soothed, drawing his wife into his arms. 'What we ain't got, we won't miss.'

When he died of lung cancer, aged sixty-three, one dark

Halloween in 1962, he was missed. Terribly. Polly, the respected matriarch, wept bitter tears at his graveside, resplendent in a fur coat bought for her by her husband in happier times. Denise sensed it was the end of an era. Together, Polly and Frankie were unstoppable, the enforcer and the matriarch.

Polly was nothing if not resilient, though, and in time she would find a third husband to take on her and her seven kids, a trumpet player by the name of Danny. But the life seemed to go out of her after Frankie's death. Without him, she had lost her purpose and became bitter, spending her Sunday afternoons feeding coins into their new telly and watching Liberace, glassy-eyed with grief.

Soon after her father's death, Denise found herself staring out of her bedroom window at the graveyard opposite. A wild white moon rode high in the night sky. Wind moaned and creaked through the tops of the yew trees and beneath the silent, dark earth lay the hidden bodies. Tombstones of the legitimate dead like her father, side by side with the bodies of the unwanted. So many foetuses, buried by her mother's hand, far from society's judgemental eyes. But never forgotten. Never forgotten.

A shifting bank of cloud shrouded the moon and the graveyard was enveloped in a thick velvet blanket of darkness. Denise got into bed and pulled the coverlet over her head, babies' cries echoing through her mind. As her mother grew old, she wondered if she heard them too.

Fearsome Polly died in 2002, well into her nineties and, for obvious reasons, her name, her husband's and that of her daughter have been concealed to protect their identities. It might be easy to frown upon Polly's actions, but there is no doubt that if she hadn't provided those services to the women of her neighbourhood, risking her liberty to do so, there would undoubtedly be another who would have.

Back in the 1940s and 1950s, birth control was hard to come by and unreliable. The Family Planning Association was formed in 1939, but it wasn't until the 1950s that FPA clinics began to offer advice on how not to get pregnant, but these services were only available to married women and you had to produce a wedding certificate to be seen. It wasn't until the very late 1960s, to the early 1970s, that family planning clinics really became accessible to all women.

Abortion was illegal. Anyone caught performing it ran the risk of a lengthy prison sentence and public condemnation. Yet for unmarried mothers, the stigma of illegitimate pregnancies meant social and economic disaster. Many girls would have been turned out on the street and their reputation would never recover. This is hard to comprehend now.

During the war, as we have seen in Chapter Six with Minksy's pal Peggy personifying the seize-the-day atmosphere, out-of-wedlock sex was no longer taboo and imminent danger acted as a powerful aphrodisiac. The arrival of two million American GIs to Britain in 1942, to say nothing of Canadian, Polish and Australian soldiers, added to the potent mix.

Consequently, the number of illegitimate births in England and Wales jumped from 24,540 in 1939, to 35,164 in 1942. Incidences of venereal disease also shot up, rising by 70 per cent.

The Abortion Act, a ground-breaking piece of legislation that allowed doctors in Great Britain to perform abortions lawfully so long as certain conditions were met, wasn't passed until 1967. Until then, women were forced to fall back on what are almost always referred to in the media as 'risky back-street abortions'.

Many East End wartime women talk in dark mutters of unwanted babies at the bottom of Victoria Park boating lake, and of infamous abortionist, hat-pin Bella and her big black bag.

But as Polly's story proves, abortionists weren't always shadowy, unknown figures. Many, like the character in the Mike Leigh film on post-war abortionist Vera Drake, were middle-aged women with a hidden existence. And for working-class women, it wasn't always a case of a young woman pregnant after a tryst with a glamorous American soldier. It was often women like Mrs Bryant, who already had too many children to feed and clothe, and for whom another baby would be an unbearable strain.

During the war and post-war years, it was often women like Polly who offered the women of their neighbourhood an alternative, and her daughter says she did it for no other reason than she felt it was part of her role as 'auntie'.

Another woman fulfilling that role next to the docks in Deptford was Mrs Dudgeon, an Irish matriarch, fondly remembered for the starched apron that was always wrapped around her stout frame, and her long grey hair, which she wore scraped back into a tight bun.

'Our street was run on reciprocal favours by aunties. Mum would say, "Go to your Aunt Lills or Aunt Kits, while I go to work,"' recalls eighty-year-old Betty, who was born in Stepney in 1937 and still lives near there today. 'They'd look after you, and the next day Mum would take them down their dinner or scrub their steps. She couldn't afford to pay them, you see.'

Chief amongst the aunties in Betty's street was Mrs Dudgeon, a mother of seven, childminder and all-round 'go-to' woman.

'She was midwife, nurse, social worker, hairdresser, funeral director, all rolled into one. She fulfilled a need in our society. People couldn't afford any of the above professionals, so she was the trusted woman.'

According to Betty, the range of duties this elderly Irish matriarch and her husband, Eric, performed was staggering.

'She would deliver the babies, cutting the cord with a sterilized razor blade, then she'd wrap the baby in a white boiled man's shirt as a blanket. She laid out the dead. Eric even used to bite the tails off puppies with his teeth when people couldn't afford the vet's fee to have them docked. Honestly!' She laughs when my eyebrows shoot up.

'When the really poor people of the neighbourhood couldn't afford a proper funeral, another local man by the name of Bill would deck his coal cart out really smart and take the body to church. His daughter, Joan, had Down's Syndrome and she would spend hours covering the coffin in beautiful paper flowers and grooming the horse so it would look smart.

'That might sound shabby to some, but it's impossible to overstate the poverty where I lived. Down our street, people were poor. Really poor. There was no welfare state to fall back on. Eric, Bill and Mrs Dudgeon gave people back their pride.'

Poverty breeds resourcefulness, as this story about Betty's dad, Albert, an Air Raid Warden, shows.

'Dad was a loveable character,' Betty chuckles. 'At Christmas, there was no money for presents for any of the neighbourhood kids, so he used to gather eight of us from the street together and take us all to the local pub. We all had to stand outside and wait for his signal. When it came, we started singing carols.

'Inside the pub, Dad would say, "Hark at those poor kids, singing their hearts out for a few coppers." Then he'd suggest a whip-round and go round with his hat. He'd always have a pint in every pub, before we went on to the next. We did the same thing at every pub. By the end of the night, we all had to help Dad home because he was absolutely drunk. Mum would go mad, but he always gave every penny he collected to the kids of the street so they got Christmas presents.'

Down Betty's street, which backed on to the Surrey Docks, generosity often came from unusual places.

'I was seven when an enormous pig and a giant black bag were thrown over our back wall, landing with a thud on the chicken shed. I ran inside and excitedly told Mum. "That's it, you're for it now!" she fumed. "I'm going to tell your father about your lying when he gets home."

'But when Dad got home, sure enough, he found a fully gutted pig, treated and all ready for the pot, on top of the shed. The bag contained sweets, chocolate, chewing gum, stockings and all the luxury items currently on ration. Turned out a Sikh sailor, who Dad had met at the pub and brought home for a cup of tea, had decided to repay Dad's hospitality by liberating a few items from the docks. Typical of Dad, he cut up the pork, divided the sweets and shared it with all our neighbours.'

Betty's mum, Eva, wasn't lacking in the personality stakes either.

'Oh dear me, she had a voice like a foghorn!' Betty laughs, dabbing her eye with a handkerchief. 'When she used to call me in for my tea – "Elizabethhhhhhh!" – it used to roll up Yeoman Street like thunder. All the mums down the street were the same.

'Mr White who ran the corner shop even arranged a competition one year just to see which mum had the loudest voice. All the mums of Yeoman Street stood on one side of London Bridge and had to sing or shout, and the winner was whoever's voice Mr White could hear loudest standing on the other side of the bridge.'

History doesn't recount who won Yeoman Street's Mouthiest Mum competition, but what a glorious image is conjured up by a dozen apron-clad matriarchs bellowing for dear life over London Bridge!

There's no doubt that characters like Albert, Eva and Eric made the war bearable for those living in the close dockside community of Deptford, but it's Mrs Dudgeon who was perhaps most influential in matters of birth, death and family planning.

'She was also the local abortionist,' confides Betty, dropping her voice as we talk in a crowded community centre coffee morning. 'I don't know where or how, I just know girls went to her. One day someone reported her, and the police arrested her. They let her go without charge and after that, turned a blind eye to it. Rather her than someone else.

'Mrs Dudgeon did what she could to try and help girls to prevent pregnancy, though. She used to melt down antiseptic soap, like Wright's Coal Tar, to liquid and fill up lots of thimbles with it. It would harden and set in the thimble. Girls would insert the DIY pessary into their vaginas and it was hoped that would kill the sperm.'

During the Blitz, Albert was patrolling the streets outside, but inside the shelters, the inimitable Mrs Dudgeon reigned supreme.

'She used to help look after all the children in the shelter,' Betty recalls. 'Once the babies were asleep, she'd say to all the mums and dads: "You go down the Plough and have a drink. Just come back if a raid starts." She ran that shelter, making sandwiches for all. Everyone looked to her.

'Her methods might have been rough and ready, but she had a kind heart. I think she died soon after the war. Her kind will never be replaced. Communities could never have functioned without the likes of Mrs Dudgeon. She gave me a stinging slap once when I gave her sauce. "Good," said my mum when I complained to her!'

It's interesting to note how, after her initial arrest, the police ignored Mrs Dudgeon's activities. Perhaps they were sympathetic, or perhaps there was insufficient evidence to prosecute.

'Abortionists like Polly and Mrs Dudgeon acted out of a strong sense of female solidarity and compassion. They were not in it for the money,' insists Dilys Cossey, OBE.

Dilys was the secretary of the Abortion Law Reform Association (ALRA), who successfully campaigned for the 1967 Abortion Act, which celebrated its fiftieth anniversary last year. She has spent her working life championing birth control, abortion and reproductive rights, as well as defending the Abortion Act she and her colleagues worked day and night to get through Parliament.

Of all the magnificent women featured in this book, Dilys has had possibly the greatest impact on the lives of the women reading it. If you have had a free, safe and legal abortion, or walked into your GP practice and come out with a free prescription for the Pill, then you have women like Dilys and her campaigning colleagues to thank for it.

'Before the Act, a clandestine subculture existed in working-class communities,' says Dilys. 'The addresses of women like Polly (sometimes referred to as Knitting Needle

Noras) were known by most women along their street. They provided low-cost (five to fifteen pounds) and sometimes free abortions, usually by injecting soapy water into the uterus with a Higginson syringe or by using a rubber tube. Far from being shadowy back-street figures, they were well known and trusted by their communities, and often, very good at what they did.

'Women were desperate when they knocked on their door. They might have already tried one of the methods believed back then to terminate a pregnancy – like gin and a hot bath, or tablets bought from the chemist with oblique names like Occasional Tablets for Ladies. All of these remedies were total con tricks.

'In sexual health terms, the 1950s, when I was growing up, were the Dark Ages. Contraception was patchy, and many relied on sheaths, some of which were washable, sold by certain chemists or barbers. There was also the diaphragm, only available for married women from the Family Planning Association (FPA) or local authority clinics, a pessary, or simply the withdrawal technique, often referred to as Vatican Roulette.

'It's no surprise that abortionists were an essential part of society, but things could and did go wrong. Friday nights on the wards of hospitals were often filled with women bleeding from abortions that had gone wrong, and of course the abortionists themselves ran the risk of arrest and imprisonment.

'In a study published in 1963, psychiatric social worker Moya Woodside interviewed forty-four abortionists imprisoned in Holloway Prison. She found that, except in a few cases, financial gain was not the main motive. Three-quarters gave their religion as Church of England, and five were Catholic. They were often working-class mothers and grandmothers, acting out of a sense of compassion and feminine solidarity.'

Dilys never set out to be a campaigner. In her twenties, she answered an advert in the *New Statesman* for a part-time secretary for the Abortion Law Reform Association, earning £2 a week, working from home. She was motivated by a strong sense of injustice that women faced such a life-changing risk, simply by having sexual intercourse, and therefore were not in control of their own bodies.

'As ALRA secretary, it was my contact details which were published in the phone book, and I got a lot of calls from women seeking abortions. There was no type – the women were of all ages and classes – but what bound them all was a primal urge to have an abortion. I began to see it was actually a deep love of children that motivated most women to seek that abortion.'

What followed was an intense four-year campaign to reform the abortion law (1964–8) resulting in the 1967 Abortion Act, an all-absorbing period, which awakened in Dilys a lifelong interest in the workings of Westminster. This steely woman worked long days and nights alongside campaigners like Diane Munday and Madeleine Simms. This was all done in the days before social media. There were no faxes, photocopiers, internet, emails or mobile phones to assist, just hard graft and the personal touch.

Their punishing workload paid off and women have lived with the gift of choice ever since.

'The past fifty years have been dedicated to defence of the Abortion Act,' says Dilys. 'But we should not stand still and be content with just defending. I am a firm believer in the importance of challenging. In the light of the experience built up over the past half-century in providing accessible abortion services, particularly the advent of medical abortion, I welcome warmly and support the campaign now to decriminalise abortion.'

The days of gin and hot baths are now thankfully consigned to the past, just as women like Polly and Mrs Dudgeon belong to another age. A harder, more brutal time, where the repercussions of giving in to desire, or simply making a mistake, meant ordinary, law-abiding women were treated like criminals. But Dilys believes we can still learn from these unflinching matriarchs.

'Polly and Mrs Dudgeon had real common sense and practicality,' she says. 'They saw life for what it was, not how they would like it to be.'

There are no reliable statistics for how many women sought out an abortion during the war and post-war years, but we do know abortion was the leading cause of maternal mortality in England and Wales. The risks for all concerned were high, which makes you wonder why women like Polly, a mother to seven, did it.

'My mum believed it was her responsibility to help women who needed it,' insists Denise. 'Today, help is institutionalised, with women going to their doctor, birth control clinics, social worker, midwives, or a women's refuge for help in dealing with marital problems, poverty, unwanted pregnancy or a violent partner. Back then, there were women like my mum to step in and intervene as the go-to woman.

'I'm not saying what she did was right or wrong, simply that it was needed. God knows she had her faults – she could be an absolute bastard to put it bluntly, a real git, if you got on the wrong side of her – but she did what she had to do. She taught me how to stand on my own two feet and be strong, and for that I'm grateful.'

Fifteen years on from her mother's death, Denise and I meet outside a Tube station, and she takes me on a tour of her old neighbourhood. The autumn sun is bright, whipping cotton-wool clouds across the rooftops.

I try to get a sense of her community and her mum's place in it all, but discover Denise's once vibrant neighbourhood has been buried under a landslide of gentrification. The baker's on the corner, where Denise fetched warm apple doughnuts, is now a café serving expensive lattes. The butcher's, the baker's, the wet fish shop . . . all gone. The old corner shop, which Denise says sold everything from tights to brooms, paraffin and biscuits, is now a Farrow & Ball outlet, selling pots of paint at £25 a pop.

Denise pauses outside a terraced house, painted in the aforementioned Farrow & Ball, which is probably worth well over a million pounds. 'That used to be a knocking shop,' she sniffs. 'All these shops, and nothing actually sells anything you need.'

Denise is no longer a kid with a pudding bowl haircut, but a grandmother, a matriarch now in her own right, who over the years, has helped to bring up children with learning difficulties and worked in some of the East End's roughest pubs as a troubleshooter.

You don't want to mess with Denise; she is not a woman to be trifled with.

'I can hold my own,' she confirms with a glint in her eye. 'I got that from Mum. "You're not a victim," she used to say to me. "I didn't go through hell to give birth to you for some man to batter you."'

Denise has enormous strength of character and robust working-class pride. She is also ferociously funny.

'Cor, he's got a face that could stop a funeral,' she mutters as we pass a grumpy-looking man. 'Funky fafas,' she adds, gesturing to some bearded trendies.

But she is kind too. The values of sharing are embedded within her, a throwback to her childhood. I give her a bunch of sunflowers to say thank-you for being interviewed, and she promptly gives them away to a little old lady who looks as if she has the worries of the world on her shoulders.

'Here you go, darlin',' she says cheerfully. The lady's face melts from surprise to pleasure.

'I hope you don't mind,' Denise says as we continue walking. 'But she needed them more than me.'

It strikes me that although the physical topography of her streets has changed since the war and post-war years, the people born and raised within it, have not.

We reach Dugden Terrace, and Denise stops, her bright blue eyes greedily scanning the length of the street, going back and forth between the past and the present.

'That's where I used to leap out the top-floor windows of the bombed house,' she says, gesturing to a block of flats. 'All along this street we played knock down ginger, tying a piece of string from one knocker to another, then knocking on both doors at the same time.' She pauses as if overwhelmed by memories, takes a deep breath and begins again.

'I don't envy kids today. They don't have the freedom we had growing up. No one is trusted to run their own lives any more. All these so-called learned people, who make and enforce laws affecting women and families, get right up my bugle. They're out of touch with reality,' Denise scoffs.

We walk in the direction of her old home and I half hope that an apron-clad Polly will wrench open the sash window and, with a voice like a klaxon, call us in for oxtail stew and dumplings. But the past is a locked door. And then we come to the church graveyard, opposite her house. Here, Denise stills and suddenly the past rises up and grabs us both by the throat. Under the rank earth of an untended border, in the shadow of an overgrown ancient grave, lie the unmarked graves.

'There's a babby there ...' Denise murmurs, her voice thickening as she points behind a bush. 'Another babby there ... one there ...'

A deep air of melancholy seeps over the graveyard as what she is saying sinks in.

Foetuses, folded in the shadows, a painful reminder of the shameful secrets of our not-so-distant past, a time when life presented women with impossible choices.

Doreen's Recipe

It's got to be fresh beigels, spread with proper butter, filled with smoked salmon, and served with pickled cucumbers.

Doreen's Remedy

The best remedy is a reason to live. Join a local group, volunteer, find a reason to leave the house every single day. Once you've made a commitment to someone or something, it's harder to stay in and wallow.

Pearls of Wisdom from a Pearly Queen

You have a duty to give back to your community.

11. Slum Clearance and New Beginnings, 1967

Doreen turned her pram into Newnham Street and was overcome by sadness. There Hettie was, in her usual spot, settled down on her haunches outside number 17, scrubbing her step so vigorously her whole body shook.

With her round little body all wrapped up in a starched apron, bright blue eyes and rough, chapped hands, Doreen's mother-in-law could have been any one of a hundred Jewish widows in Whitechapel. But she wasn't. She was Hettie Roundstein, a four-foot-eight force of nature.

To anyone else, Hettie's life would have felt like one long round of drudgery: cooking dinners, scrubbing steps, running sheets through a mangle in the yard . . . But to Hettie, it was a glorious life.

Kith and kin were never far away. Her youngest son, Martin, was Doreen's husband, and they and their three children lived in the rooms upstairs. Year round, Hettie made dinner for her brother – known to all as Uncle Nibby – whose wife Katie owned a clothes shop down Brick Lane called Rosenberg's, where once a year, Hettie was treated to a new winter coat in return.

Hettie visited Petticoat Lane and Hessel Street Market, where she'd pick her live chicken from Robotkin Kosher Butcher, who'd have it slaughtered, plucked and ready to collect by the time she'd finished the rest of her shopping. There was a bakehouse a few minutes' walk away, where she could take her cholent on a Friday, a traditional Jewish one-pot dish of meat and vegetables slow cooked overnight, and they'd have it bubbling and ready to collect on the Sabbath. Everything Hettie needed was right here on her snowy white doorstep.

Except now it was under threat.

'Oh hello, Doreen,' Hettie said when she spotted her daughter-in-law. 'Go on inside, love. Soon as I've got me nets down, I'll fix you a nice cup of tea and you can tell me how you got on. Leave the baby to sleep out here.'

'You and your nets,' Doreen chuckled, parking the great big pram outside and putting the brake on. 'They're more down than they're up!'

Hettie shrugged in that way that only an older Jewish woman can.

'What, and have someone accuse me of dirty nets?'

Besides, it was Monday – wash day. Everything got piled into the copper, then scrubbed to within an inch of its life. Once the nets were boiling away and tea was made, Doreen and Hettie sat down. Even in a moment of rest, Hettie insisted on peeling potatoes as they chatted. She always kept a bowl of ready-peeled potatoes permanently in a bowl of salted water to make chips with, just in case anyone popped in that needed feeding.

'How do you get on, love?' she asked.

Doreen grimaced.

'Ooh, it was horrible, Mum,' she sighed. 'Prostitutes and drunks everywhere.' Her lips tightened to a thin white line. 'I'm not living down Cable Street and that's that. I'm telling them it's a no-no. They're giving it some flannel about getting offered three places only and then we're off the housing list. But I'll keep on fighting them until they come up with somewhere else. If I've got to uproot my family, it's going to be for a better life.'

'So you think they're serious, we really do have to move?' Hettie asked, looking up worriedly from her peeling.

'I'm afraid so. Slum clearance, they're calling it.'

Hettie sighed and her face crumpled into a spiderweb of fine lines.

'Slum! Well, that's a fine thing to be calling it. It . . . It's not a slum, it's my home.'

Hettie looked around the spotless scullery that led off the kitchen of her Victorian terraced home as if seeing it for the first time. Everything in those rooms could have been replicated in a thousand other East End houses. The ubiquitous butler's sink, the black-leaded range, even though she had a new-fangled gas stove, and meat safe that served all Hettie's culinary needs. Then there was the sacred front room, saved for high days and holidays . . . No one dared venture into that room without Hettie's permission.

'It's a bit creaky round the edges, like me, but it survived the war, didn't it?' she went on. 'What do they want to go and pull down a perfectly good house for? And what about my plum tree in the yard?'

There was nothing that Doreen could say. From the moment the letter had landed on the mat from the Greater London Council (GLC) informing them that Newnham Street had been designated for redevelopment in the next round of slum clearance, she had known the fate of the old house had been sealed.

Like it or not, they were moving out, and the bulldozers were moving in. That bulldozer now presented a bigger threat to Hettie's way of life than Hitler's Luftwaffe ever had.

Doreen took her tea and went outside to check on her one-year-old daughter, Sheree, fast asleep. As the sun sank over the slate rooftops, streaking the smoky skies a vermilion pink, Doreen felt a storm of emotions.

The old smoke-blackened street looked the same. Babies asleep in prams. Kids playing on the bombsite next door. Every door partially open to let air up the passage . . . On the corner huddled a group of apron-clad women, gossiping voices carrying on the breeze. Could these women talk, and how!

If it's not my bunions it's my back . . . I never go anywhere else for a perm . . . Do you like it? . . . I got it down Brick Lane . . . Oh, you should have seen the bride . . . Terrible shame, her whole family moved to Gants Hill . . .

The women of Whitechapel, merrily jawing away. Newnham Street was like a theatre in which the small domestic details of life played out. But world events had also left their mark. The street had watched silently as death and destruction had crept up its cobbles.

Chairman of the Whitechapel Vigilance Committee, Albert Bachert, had plotted the capture of Jack the Ripper from number 13 Newnham Street in 1888. The Germans then did their level best to wipe it off the map in both world wars, and the surrounding labyrinth of streets had been the cradle of so many struggles for justice and better conditions.

Throughout it all, the ancient Whitechapel street had remained. Hettie Roundstein had remained. How ironic that now, with the war over, it was a council surveyor with a theodolite who had issued its death warrant. The question was, would Hettie survive being uprooted from all she knew?

Doreen gazed up the street, a smile playing on her lips as a troop of kids charged across the debris, caught up as the stars of their own action adventure film. Sitting in doorways in straight-backed chairs, the watchful eyes of older women followed them, net curtains dancing in the breeze.

As lovely and familiar as this old street was, Doreen wanted more for her three kids than a scrubby patch of debris to play on. She craved green fields, recreation grounds, a garden, fresh unpolluted air, indoor plumbing . . . But mainly, she wanted the chance to give her kids a better future. Simone, eight, Jonathan, five, and baby Sheree were the first generation to be born into a welfare state world.

Times were changing, horizons widening. Recently, they'd got a fridge, and the whole street had turned out to take a look. It had given Doreen a taste for the good life, and now she had her eye on a new maisonette in Wanstead, out in the smart new suburbs of Redbridge. But at a weekly rent of £7.50, it was out of their price range, even with the heating and rates included. Wanstead really was the business. Rumour had it the Peanut King himself, Percy Dalton, had a big flashy house down there. Still, she could dream, couldn't she?

'Cable Street indeed,' she tutted, picking up the baby and heading inside.

Later that evening, when Martin got home from his job as a television engineer for a telly rental firm, he was obviously feeling full of himself.

'I'm not moving to Cable Street!' Doreen announced, before he'd even got his coat off.

'You don't have to, love. I've got it sussed,' he replied excitedly. 'I sweet-talked the wages clerk. If I work all the hours God sends, she'll tally up the total and put the overtime down in the basic so it looks better. Better get her a box of chocolates, mind.'

'But I thought we had to have two guarantors who are house owners to vouch for us?'

'Sorted. Aunt Mabel and Uncle Alf have agreed.'

'Do you really think we can do it, Martin?'

'There won't be much of my wages left after we've paid the rent, but we know why we're doing it, don't we, Doreen?'

'Come here,' she grinned, grabbing his face and planting a big smacker on his lips. 'I love you, Mr Roundstein.'

'About that,' he replied thoughtfully, 'we might have to change our name to Rend. You know, anglicise it, if we want to fit in.'

Later, as she bathed the kids in the old butler's sink, Doreen ran through the move in her mind. Her great-grandparents – Jewish refugees by the name of Jacobovitch – had fled persecution in Poland sometime in the nineteenth century, with nothing but the clothes on their back, and a needle and thread.

In Whitechapel, her grandmother and mother had sweated in the rag trade. She'd had a father who worked all the hours as a cutter until he was run over and killed at the age of thirty-seven. Life was fragile, hard and short.

She'd miss the hustle and bustle of Hessel Street Market, and the old men in black hats with world stories etched on their faces. Was there anywhere quite like the vibrancy of the Jewish East End, where everybody knew your mother, grandmother and, likely as not, your great-grandmother? But she owed her kids more than a sub-divided portion of a damp terraced house built in the last century. If that meant upping sticks and changing their name, then so be it. After all, it was only what her people had been doing for centuries.

There were hoops to jump through, of course. The new block of flats in the estate they had their eye on didn't want council tenants – who they felt might lower the tone of the area. Upper income bracket only, respectable working class was what the newly flourishing suburbs demanded. That didn't faze Doreen, though. She could deal with the toffee-nosed snobs.

'I understand why you're going, but I'm stopping here in the East End,' said Hettie, when they broke the news to her. 'You won't get kosher butchers in Wanstead.'

'I know, Mum, but we've made our minds up, it's something we've got to do for the kids,' Martin said gently. 'And I've still got to travel into town for work so I'll come in every day for my lunch.'

At this, Hettie softened. She couldn't stay angry with her youngest son for long.

'I'm proud of you, son,' she said, hugging him fiercely and blinking back tears. He towered over his tiny mum, but he was and always would be her baby.

Leaving Newnham Street was every bit as emotional as they thought it would be. Every last stick of furniture was packed up in Martin's work van and the family car – a second-hand Ford held together with string, which Doreen had nicknamed the Flintstones Special.

Hettie clung to the door frame as she watched her family pack up their lives, her brown eyes fearful of the cataclysmic change ahead.

'Don't worry, Mum,' Martin said, bending down to kiss her on the forehead. 'I'll be back in a few days once we're sorted, then I'll get you moved.'

'What about my furniture, son?' she asked worriedly.

'I'll see to it all, Mum,' he soothed. 'I'll even get the lino down and have it looking lovely for you.'

Hettie's new flat in neighbouring Bethnal Green was

ready, but she was hanging on to her terrace to the bitter end. Most of Newnham Street's occupants had already gone, relocated to new lives in the suburbs. Only Hettie remained . . . Hettie and her plum tree, both of whom were about to have their roots wrenched from Whitechapel soil.

Hettie put on a brave face as they left, smothering her grandkids in kisses and waving furiously as the old Ford bumped up the cobbles, groaning at the seams with kids and luggage. It was the end of an era, Doreen thought as they turned on to Whitechapel High Street. As they drove, she printed a mental map in her mind of the familiar social squash of people, of pubs on every corner, street markets, music halls, picture houses and synagogues, sheets flapping in thousands of identical back yards, aunties watching from doorways . . .

Life was about to change.

As the newly renamed Rend family drove along the Eastern Avenue, the narrow grey time-slip streets gave way to manicured gardens and smart semis surrounded by privet. Even the sky seemed bigger. By the time they pulled up in front of their new maisonette in Wanstead, Doreen's stomach was doing flip-flops.

'Look at you all,' she scolded, as Martin began unpacking the boxes from the boot. All three of the kids – and Martin – were covered in angry red spots. 'You could have chosen a better week to come down with chickenpox! What'll the new neighbours think? You go and play while we unpack,' she said, shooing Simone and Jonathan outside. Her nerves melted when she saw inside their new home.

'Oh look, Martin!' she exclaimed, unable to contain her excitement as she ran her hands over the sparkling Formica kitchen units. Everything fitted together and was the same colour. There was even – and here her heart soared – a down-stairs loo *as well* as one in the bathroom! Two loos! No more freezing your bum off in winter nipping to the outdoor lav like they'd had to in Newnham Street.

'Smart or what! I can't believe this is all really ours.'

'Believe it, love,' Martin grinned, bounding into the bath-room and turning on the taps in the indoor bath. 'How about that! The kids have never even seen an indoor bath.'

It was unimagined luxury with all the mod cons.

However, when trying to better yourself, Doreen dis-covered, there was always someone who imagined they were better than you.

'Are those your children?' asked a querulous voice from the doorway.

'Oh hello,' said Doreen warmly, extending her hand towards the woman, 'we just moved in. Mr and Mrs Rend. Pleased to meet you.'

'I see,' sniffed her new neighbour, staring at her hand in disdain. 'Well, I don't know where you come from, Mrs Rend, but one of your children is playing in a cardboard box sitting in the chute.'

She said the words 'where you come from' as if someone had just waved a rancid kipper under her nose. Martin sup-pressed a laugh as she marched off.

'What have we let ourselves in for?' Doreen groaned, clutching the door frame. She'd had warmer welcomes in a mortuary!

In time, the kids got over the chickenpox, the neighbour came down off her high horse, and Martin and Doreen set-tled into a comfortable new life in the suburbs. They both had to graft to afford it, but neither were strangers to hard work. Martin quit the telly rental game and instead did the 'knowledge', becoming the proud owner of a London black taxi badge. Doreen did her bit, getting a job at the local bingo club, managing it by night, and cleaning it by day.

The only person who couldn't adapt to her new environment was dear old Hettie. The shock of her upheaval from Newnham Street was simply too much, and on the day of her move she had a heart attack. She survived, but was never the same again. The move to Bethnal Green was only a short one from Whitechapel, but in emotional milestones, it was a step too far.

Hettie's generation was parochial, with each East End borough and, more specifically, each turning, village-like in its community. Who did she know in Bethnal Green?

Her new-build flat was warm, secure and easy to keep clean. But it didn't have a place for her to sit and natter with the neighbours. Or a plum tree in the yard. It wasn't *her* neighbourhood, *her* people, *her* community, and she felt its loss like a grief. Hettie's history. Hettie's memories. Hettie's past. All of it, swept away by the raging torrent of change.

In time, the small Jewish shops that sold the essentials of life, kosher poultry, beigels and salt beef, would vanish too. There was no one left to sell to any more. Whitechapel as Hettie knew it had its artery slit by the planner's knife. Her heart broke.

And so we wave goodbye to the Stepney Doorstep Society as stories like Hettie's were replicated all over the East End in ill-conceived post-war slum clearance schemes. By the 1960s, young people had energy and a thirst for change. However, what worked for the robust younger generation, keen to do right by their kids, proved to be an ill fit for older residents.

Slum clearance rubbed out the sight of all those apron-clad

matriarchs shelling peas into their laps as they called out to neighbours across the street, bulldozing clean through centuries of doorstep living.

The council had the right intentions in rehousing families in new flats, but in building high-rise boxes that stretched up into the sky, they decimated communities in one fell swoop, ripping out their heart and soul.

Doors and windows with sturdy locks no longer opened out on to lively streets and communal courtyards, but on to concrete stairwells and empty sky. These doors didn't welcome people in, but kept people out. You have to wonder how many portions of chips Hettie cooked up for impromptu visitors after she moved away from Newnham Street and into her new secure flat.

The Greater London Plan, as it was known, was introduced by London County Council, the forerunner of Greater London Council, which took over in 1965 and supervised Hettie's move.

Meanwhile, Doreen and her family were by no means alone in their exodus from the East End. Many young newly-weds were relocating in new towns like Basildon, Harlow and Dagenham.

The village-like atmosphere of the East End was eroded by post-war depopulation. Before the Second World War, in 1939, there were 419,000 people living in Tower Hamlets, according to the Office for National Statistics. (In 1965 the Borough of Tower Hamlets was formed from the merger of former Metropolitan Boroughs Stepney, Poplar and Bethnal Green.) By 1988, there were just 159,000. That's 260,000 people vanished from the East End in just under fifty years. The impact of World War Two triggered the decline, but post-war suburbanisation fuelled it. And these statistics don't touch on the human stories, and the heartbreak these moves caused to women like Hettie.

A look at a sociological classic, *Family and Kinship in East London* by Michael Young and Peter Willmott illustrates the bond between mothers and their daughters, and how tightly their lives were intertwined. In 1957, Young and Willmott found that more than two out of every three people in Bethnal Green (the area they chose to study) had their parents living within two or three miles of them. Doreen, Girl Walker and Minksy bucked the trend by moving in with their husband's parents. The research found that the majority of young couples either lived with or nearby the wife's parents, making Bethnal Green a matrilocal society, with the mother placed firmly head and centre.

The sense of belonging that people from Bethnal Green got from knowing and being known by so many of their fellow residents is something which Bethnal Greeners prized. Remember Dr Joan's assertion that all of Bethnal Green was profoundly affected by the deaths down the Tube in 1943, because 'everyone knew everyone'?

The book also highlighted the solidarity that was enjoyed by extended families, but then destroyed by post-war migration to the suburbs. The authors concluded that migration out of the East End meant kith and kin were scattered, with relatives no longer enjoying the intimacies of daily life. Neighbours were strangers, and people began to keep themselves to themselves.

A lack of pubs and shops in suburban estates – in Bethnal Green in 1957 there was one pub for every 400 people, and one shop for every 44 (or one for every 14 households) – contributed to the severing of daily contact, with TV sets taking the place of family get-togethers.

Kate Gavron, who co-authored *The New East End: Kinship, Race and Conflict* with Michael Young and Geoff Dench, which revisited the areas Young described in his original study, says:

'This chapter not only brings back the world described in *Family and Kinship in East London* by Michael Young and Peter Willmott, but it also evokes Bethnal Green in the early 1990s when I was interviewing residents with Michael Young. I met Leah several times, a woman similar to Hettie. She was an elderly Jewish woman, born in about 1905, who had lived through the war and seen most of the Jews leave Bethnal Green. Her sister had moved to Southend-on-Sea. The kosher butchers had disappeared and she now bought her chickens from the halal butchers who had replaced them.'

By the time Kate and Michael Young returned in the early 1990s to Greenleigh, the outer London new town to which so many Bethnal Greeners moved, they discovered a close and settled community.

'Their children didn't live as close to them as Hettie's had done,' says Kate, 'but modern communications and widespread car ownership meant that contacts remained strong. Ironically, the problem the local authority had in Greenleigh was that elderly couples and widowed singles were still living in the "family" houses urgently needed by young families, but they were resistant to moving because of the closeness of their local community. As ever, housing shortage is a serious political problem but also as ever, as Martin and Doreen found, if you live in a new place for long enough, it becomes home.'

Housing remains the most pressing issue facing the East End, as it was at the very start of this book. In the twentieth century the biggest threat to the landscape of the East End was the Luftwaffe and overzealous council planners. Today, it comes from a more creeping, insidious source – commercial housing developers, who have their eye on every unlisted and much-loved East End building, with a view to turning it into a millionaire's crash pad. These are beautiful, historic buildings, grand matriarchs in their own right, with as much character as Minksy or Girl Walker.

Take the Queen Elizabeth Hospital for Children in the Hackney Road, where Dr Joan worked with such diligence and care to lay out so many poor souls on the night of the Tube disaster. It held a deeply poignant place, not just in Joan's heart, but also to generations of East Enders, who saw the elegant hospital as part of their shared heritage, an institution which had been saving and enriching lives since 1871. Sadly, there was no CPR for this grand old lady of medicine. It was sold off for luxury housing.

It's one sad story in a long list, which includes the historic Charlotte de Rothschild Dwellings dating back to 1887 – and Gardiner's Corner in Aldgate. Beatty scarcely recognises the place where she and thousands of others stood up to Mosley's fascists. It's now a vast luxury development.

What the Luftwaffe didn't flatten during the war, developers are now working hard to. At the time of writing, London councils had just granted property developers planning permission to build more than 26,000 luxury flats in the capital priced at more than one million pounds each, fuelling anger that councils are prioritising the needs of the super-rich over those of average working Londoners. Understandably, there is bewilderment over the gentrification. And there is anger: 'This country is run by greedy ponces!' spits eighty-five-year-old Phoebe.

We last met Phoebe, whose family fought for the right to occupy Bethnal Green Tube, in Chapter Four, during the

Blitz. Seventy-eight years on, she is stunned by what has become of the East End she and her people fought tooth and nail to protect, her emotions vacillating between sorrow and outrage.

'These politicians and councillors don't live in our world,' she says, drumming her finger down on the table top. 'They ain't got a clue. There is so much greed and hatred now. It's all me, me, me . . . But I still cling to the old East End ways. I visit a club weekly where we dress up smart, bring food and share whatever we have.'

Phoebe is not the only one determined to cherish the past. The East End has guardians, like the East End Preservation Society, formed by 'The Gentle Author', who writes the daily blog Spitalfields Life, and supported by historian and broadcaster Dan Cruickshank and Will Palin – the former secretary of SAVE Britain's Heritage. To say nothing of formidable women like campaigning Sister Christine Frost, whom we last met in Chapter Seven and who is now on a mission to protect communities and fight the developers.

Speaking from St Matthias Community Centre, once a Christian church built in 1654 by the East India Company, she told me: 'The project "Poplar, Past, Present and Future" was developed to raise the profile of the area and to generate awareness in the rich history of this amazing place. There is a great sense of community in the area, which we do not want to lose to the developers.

'We have lived through all the upheaval and regeneration of the London Dockland Development Corporation in the 1980s.

'Poplar ward lost five hundred council homes to make way for the DLR and the Limehouse Link. None of these were replaced, and now in 2018 we are campaigning with the new regime to get five hundred new council rate rent properties, like for like.

'All the new housing going up is beyond the means of people around here, and rents are going up too. People can look across and see homes where people have millions to spend, while they can't afford basic heating.

'Gentrification is now a very real threat. None of us will be able to afford to live in the area soon. Old Poplar is disappearing.'

In Sister Christine's opinion, it's this ever-widening gap between rich and poor that is responsible for most of society's problems. In August 2014, she hit the headlines when she was dubbed the Brave Nun (a term she hates!) for taking down an Islamic black flag from the gates of the Will Crooks housing estate. The press were fascinated by why a diminutive, lone eighty-year-old would risk tackling such a sensitive issue.

Tower Hamlets now has the highest percentage of Muslims in England. The deprivation in which they live, Sister Christine feels, holds the key to why so many young men are vulnerable to radicalisation.

'The lack of housing provision amounts to a kind of social cleansing,' she insists. 'I want the wealthy millionaires who live in Canary Wharf to come over here and help young people, get them into training. Make that an attractive alternative for them. We must find a way to bring people together, like they did in the war.'

Sister Christine is a woman who never ever gives up. She is not one to sit idle. When not tirelessly working in the community, she can be found at council meetings tearing into smooth-talking councillors and developers, demanding to know where their 500 missing homes are.

'Houses are homes,' she tells me. 'And neighbourhoods need to be shaped by our vision of community, not simply by the market. The human spirit needs more than cement, asphalt and metal to blossom, nurturing compassion, care and fun.'

A sliver of mischief flashes over her face. 'After all, if you push out all the working people, who's going to wipe the millionaire's bum when the millionaire is too frail to do it himself?' she observes wryly.

But beneath the humour, there is truth. What will London look like in ten years' time, when there might be no more affordable housing left?

'Your old wartime East End matriarch would not have stood for this,' Sister Christine insists. 'She and her sisters would have been marching on the Mayor's office and running those developers out of town.'

She's right. As we have already seen, solidarity and collective force is what won the day at the Battle of Cable Street in 1936, the Quinn Square rent strikes in 1938, and the Battle of the Underground in 1940, to say nothing of countless more struggles in the East End's long history.

But fighters take many forms, and in the interests of equality, let me introduce you to the Geezers of Bow . . .

'Come on, everybody, shove up and let the lady in!' bellowed chief Geezer Ray Gipson when I went to meet this men-only Age UK supported group in Bow. Ray offers me a sausage roll with one hand, and a naked calendar featuring the Geezers with the other. It's a hell of an introduction, and I quickly realise this group of perky pensioners are redefining what it means to grow old. Here, there is no one shuffling around in a flat cap, staring morosely into a pint.

I nearly choke on my sausage roll as I leaf through the calendar. There's Mr January, aka retired chauffeur Doug, eighty-three, having a cheeky game of naked darts. February is seventy-three-year-old former HGV driver Brian, with his particulars hidden behind a shove ha'penny board, and the merry month of March sees former strongman and postie John, eighty-six, hiding his dangly bits behind the dominoes.

It's all tongue in cheek, but there is an important reason behind it. The Geezers want to raise awareness of the increasing isolation of elderly people as more pubs close their doors. The calendar is part of a wider campaign they've called 'Where's My Boozer Gone?'

The Geezers calculate they have lost a staggering ninety-two pubs in their local community of Bow alone.

'Time was where you knew everybody, but that's all changed,' laments Ray. 'The pubs have all been turned into posh flats. This is our heritage we're fighting to protect. Pubs used to be at the heart of the community, with one on every street corner, a place where men used to get suited and booted in their best rig-out and go for a beer or two on a Sunday. You always knew everyone in there. It was smashing.

'But it's not just about the booze,' he continues. 'We're losing our heritage – the architecture, the traditional games and sports played in pubs, and the local history that has been passed down through the generations.'

Retired Liberal Democrat councillor and former lorry driver Ray is seventy-seven, and helped form the Geezers in St Paul's Church in Bow in 2007, after research by Age Concern in Tower Hamlets revealed that few men were turning up to their day centres.

Today, they have around twenty eclectic Geezers, who meet weekly and enjoy trips out and banter over a beer or two. I suspect their jawing might rival their female equivalent, the Bow Belles, but they are far from just a talking club.

'People just seem to let men grow old and senile. We like to get out and about,' grins Ray. 'And we ain't interested in bingo or line dancing!'

They recently joined the Bethnal Green Weightlifting Club, and have been recruited to promote a well-known men's grooming brand. These aren't your typical OAPs. Who else has beer brewed in their name? Their boundless energy has attracted artists, who come to paint them, and academics, who study them.

As well as their campaign to save the British boozer, they've won a Green Energy Award for their work with the University of East London on renewable energy projects, which included making a turbine-driven sign for an Age UK roof that lit up the words *Geezer Power*.

They are also dedicated to going into schools, sports and youth clubs (dressed, I hasten to add) to spend time getting to know young people that some older people might fear.

'It's about bridging the gap between young and old so none of us feel estranged from our communities or lonely,' Ray explains. 'We have former boxers, butchers, truckers, builders and undertakers in our group. We have stories to tell, and the younger lads are surprised how much they enjoy listening.'

Ray and his Geezers are an incredible example of how a vibrant community group can thrive, using lessons of the past to shape the future. There should be a Geezers club in every town.

Where does Ray get his fighting spirit and enterprise from? The women of his family, of course.

'Could my Aunt Nell have a fight!' Ray laughs. 'She was a five-foot-nothing beanpole, but she ran the show down her street in Bow, a right "macher" as we say. It's a Yiddish word, meaning the Boss or Big Shot, a wheeler-dealer and a mediator. She had six kids and her husband worked away as a lorry driver, so she had to be the boss. There was no flies on Aunt Nell. She'd get a set of saucepans off the tallyman and, half an hour later, be flogging them down the street for twice the price. She also loved a pub crawl, did Aunt Nell.'

How proud Aunt Nell would be now to see her nephew protecting the heritage of the East End and keeping the spirit of the streets alive.

There is a shared human truth that binds all these stories and proves that houses, streets and neighbourhoods are more than bricks and mortar. They are not to be measured in square footage and real estate value. They are charged emotional spaces, which contain valuable memories and even more valuable people. People like Hettie and Doreen. Though she might have migrated out of the East End, Doreen never really left it behind. In fact, some might say, she is now the cultural face of the East End.

I get the Central Line out to Wanstead to meet her on a bitingly cold winter morning, taking the same route she took as a young mother back in 1967.

Today, Doreen is seventy-seven and still living in the same maisonette she and her husband sacrificed so much for. Tragically, Martin met the same fate as her father, dying at the age of thirty-seven, just seven years after they left the East End and three months before their son's Bar Mitzvah.

'I couldn't believe it when history repeated itself,' Doreen says, shaking her head. 'And after we worked so hard to move to our forever home! It was awful having to tell Hettie that she had outlived her youngest son. She was living in a care home in Gants Hill by then, after losing her leg to an infection.

'She was devastated but, to her credit, when I remarried a taxi driver called Larry, Hettie treated him like family and called him her son-in-law. That's the way she was, so strong and loving.'

Doreen herself had much of her mother-in-law's strength, refusing to crumble after being widowed so young.

'I was a mother. I had no choice but to get on with it,' she says with an emotional smile. 'No good churning it all up with counselling and such like. It wouldn't have changed anything. I had my photos to remind me – I still do, in fact.'

We turn to look at a wall of her immaculately tidy lounge, and our eyes fall upon photo after photo. The room is smothered with memories, and aside from Martin, Hettie and Larry, it's like a who's who of royalty and fame.

Doreen shaking hands with Prince Charles . . . being cuddled by Frank Bruno . . . handing the Queen Mother a present on her 101st birthday, rubbing shoulders with Elton John in *Hello* magazine and stepping out proudly at Danny Boyle's Olympic opening ceremony . . .

And there she is laughing with Holly Willoughby and Phillip Schofield, Sir Ian McKellen, Sir Paul McCartney . . . The list goes on.

The phone rings and interrupts us.

'Excuse me, dear,' she mouths as she picks it up.

'Will I be in a music video with Paloma Faith?'

She looks at me and shrugs her shoulders, before returning to the call.

'Will they send a taxi? I'll let you know, dear. All right, ta-ta.'

Doreen's used to this, you see. After all, she is royalty in her own way. East End royalty. She's the Pearly Queen for Bow Bells and Old Kent Road.

The conversation continues over a pub lunch down the George and by the time we've finished, it's all arranged. In return for a donation to charity, a taxi is collecting her tomorrow and taking her to Shoreditch for filming with Paloma. But Doreen doesn't do all this for fame or celebrity. She does it because women like Hettie and her own mum, Minnie, instilled in her the need to have a social conscience.

'We have a duty to help others,' she says.

The Pearly Kings and Queens Society gives its support for free to any charity that needs it, and has a rich history that stretches back to nineteenth-century Victorian London. Identifiable by their iconic outfits, each Pearly wears a suit or dress smothered in hundreds of mother-of-pearl buttons, all sewn on by hand and often handed down from generation to generation. To see a glittering Pearly against the drab London streets is to see the sun emerge after the rain.

The very first Pearly King was Henry Croft, an orphan and street sweeper. In the mid- to late-1870s, he completely covered his suit in mother-of-pearl buttons, creating the first Pearly 'smother' suit. Henry was inspired and then helped by London's costermongers – market and street traders like Babs' mum Bobby, who sold produce from a cart or stall in the street. They were said to have sewn mother-of-pearl buttons on to their clothes to distinguish themselves, and cried their wares with great verve and swagger.

Today, about thirty 'royal families' – one for each London borough – are still active and, over the years, they've raised millions for charity.

So how does one enter Pearly royalty? Just like the more

traditional Royals, Pearly titles are passed down through families. On special occasions, individuals with a strong commitment to charity work may be invited to hold a title.

'So how did you become a Pearly Queen?' I ask Doreen, knowing she isn't related to one.

'I slept with a Pearly King!' she flashes back, with a cheeky grin. 'No, I'm only joking! When I used to visit Hettie in her care home, I got very friendly with the Pearly Queen of Redbridge, Peggy, who came to the home to entertain Hettie and the old folk. Me and my second husband Larry used to help her unload her equipment. One day she asked us to be her "pride" or her helpers.'

Doreen and Larry threw themselves into the role, rattling collecting tins in the rain for hours at a time, always with a bright smile fixed on their faces, and quickly proved they had the extrovert yet dedicated personality required to join the alternative royal family. They were crowned King and Queen of Old Kent Road, in honour of Larry's South London roots.

After Larry's death, Doreen was invited by the King of Bow Bells to become his pride and be the Queen of Bow Bells, a title she duly accepted, but insisted on keeping the Old Kent Road title out of respect to her late husband. And so, the twice-widowed grandmother reinvented herself once more and launched herself into her new life with flamboyant gusto.

Doreen's schedule is punishing, but she is nothing if not tireless in her pursuit of charity. Consider too that a fully pearled 'smother suit' can weigh anything up to thirty kilograms!

'I was six foot when I started,' jokes the four-foot-eleven Queen. Nothing slows this woman down.

'What you going to do?' she shrugs. 'Sit in and become housebound? It would be easy enough to stay in, in the safety

and warmth of my home, but no matter how tired I am, I'm
out doing my charity work.

'Besides, I'm a Pearly!' she adds proudly. 'I made a commitment to give back to the community and I'm not going to
let them down.'

Her tenacity hasn't gone unnoticed. Last year, Doreen was
awarded a British Empire Medal as part of the other Queen's
Birthday Honours. It's a fitting end to an epic story that has
spanned seven decades and began in the humble streets of
Whitechapel. There is a sweet circularity to Doreen leaving the
East End in the 1960s in search of a better life for her kids, only
to return years later and be crowned the Queen of Bow Bells.

Sadly, Hettie was not around to see her daughter-in-law
crowned and honoured. She died in 1986 at the ripe old age
of eighty-six, but she is ever present. Her warm blue eyes and
gentle smile gaze down from a photo on the wall, outshining
all the celebrities she's surrounded by, and you get the sense
that Hettie is at the heart of everything Doreen does.

'Hettie, like all the women of her generation, was always
doing things for others,' concludes Doreen, her eyes shining
with nostalgic affection. 'She lived through poverty and two
world wars, outlived her youngest son, and yet never stopped
giving back. Her life was a continual fight, from the cradle to
the grave. She was a warrior in a wrap-over apron.'

She sighs deeply.

'It's a breed you won't get again.'

Doreen, Hettie, Julia, Beatty, Millie, Marie, Renee, Babs,
Bobby, Girl Walker, Alice, Minksy, Mrs Chumbley, Dr Joan,
Dr Goldie, Kay, Pat, Gladys, Sally, Jessie, Sister Christine, Polly,
Denise, Mrs Dudgeon, Betty, Kate, Mitsy, Phoebe, Leah, Vi,
Old Boots, Sophie, Vera, Kathy, Dot, Dolly, Flo, Aunt Nell,
Mary and all the other redoubtable working women whose

names have been left out of the history books, are all part of a forgotten army. Chief females who were the backbone of their tight-knit matriarchies and who, in the absence of the welfare state, used an unwritten code of honour that included brute force, love, hope, humour, imagination, solidarity and resilience to keep their families fed and their communities safe. Their achievements are heroic and worthy of recording.

I recently heard this saying: *You die twice. Once when your heart stops beating and again when your name is spoken for the last time.*

Hettie Roundstein. Alice Walker. Bobby Clark. Let's keep their names, and *all* the long-forgotten women of wartime Britain, on our lips. Start a conversation with your family about the life of your mother, your grandmother, your great-grandmother. Let's keep the past alive.

Behind every great man, is a great woman, so says the old adage. But for all the magnificent women featured in this book, I think perhaps there is a more significant saying: *Behind every great woman, is an even greater woman.*

Postscript: Can History Unlock the Secrets of a Long Life?

Our five central matriarchs, Dr Joan, Babs, Minksy, Girl Walker and Beatty, have a combined age of 463. How have they done it?

There is much to be gained from looking at their lifestyles. They have lived on rations for the greater part of their lives, rarely snacked or overeaten, walked everywhere and worked since the age of fourteen.

But I think the clue lies elsewhere, in something more nuanced than a simple distillation of diet and exercise. All these women were born into and raised in tight-knit communities. They all have a strong sense of their place within that community and its hierarchy. With the exception of Dr Joan, they are all matriarchal heads of close families.

Whenever I visit, the rich tapestries of photos that smother the walls of their homes strike me. Sons or daughters are always just popping in. Even when family are not close by, friends are, and in the absence of them, they go and seek new friendship groups or activities they enjoy. They attend community clubs for the elderly at least once a week, and if there's nothing else on, they will seek their own entertainment. As I'm writing this, Girl Walker is probably sneaking on to the back of a tour, and Minksy is singing her lungs out somewhere.

Not one of them is afraid to walk the streets of their East End, despite the sweeping changes that have taken place in the area. Loneliness is not an emotion they are accustomed to feeling.

Caroline Abrahams, Charity Director of Age UK, said: 'At Age UK, our mission has always been to encourage people to think differently about getting older and to challenge the negative stereotypes about ageing which can be all too pervasive. Older people have a wealth of knowledge, experience and skills, and play incredibly valuable roles in families, communities and society as a whole. Our ageing population is undoubtedly a cause for celebration – it's incredible that so many people are living so much longer – but this inevitably brings with it a range of challenges. There is an increasing need to support people to age well and to ensure that, whatever their circumstances, everyone should have the opportunity to make the most of later life.'

In a report produced by Age UK Oxfordshire in 2012 as part of the Campaign to End Loneliness, the charity presented a biological perspective on loneliness, pointing out that social species have evolved biological mechanisms that promote their gravitational pull towards each other. Penguins provide a good example. They rotate as they huddle together, taking turns to be on the outside of the group where it is coldest. This enables all to survive. Being isolated from others is unsafe for a social animal. In every animal species, including humans, death occurs earlier amongst those who are isolated. Loneliness also creates changes in the brain and body which can contribute to or precipitate ill health.

Their research also found that loneliness can be linked to cognitive decline and dementia in older people. There is evidence that socially engaged older people experience less cognitive decline and are less prone to dementia. The risk of

Alzheimer's disease more than doubles in older people experiencing loneliness.

In 2016, Alzheimer's disease and other dementias replaced ischaemic heart disease as the leading cause of death in England and Wales for the first time. Apparently, it has now become the leading cause of death due to our ageing population and better diagnosis. This is a sobering statistic.

So what does all this prove? We are an ageing population, and loneliness is a modern epidemic. And yet, as I hope this book proves, we can learn so much from the older generation. 'When you're eighty you're invisible. When you're ninety you may as well be dead. People don't see you,' a ninety-year-old woman called Eileen confided in me despairingly. 'History's going out the back door.'

The memories and rich tales of Britain's wartime men and women are the lifeblood of our country. So why don't we listen more? Why are they ignored, their stories lying forgotten like suitcases in a dusty attic? Once the gossamer light tread of youth has gone and the sinews stiffened, what remains? Wisdom!

Let's look at imaginative groups, like the Geezers of Bow, who go into sports clubs, youth groups and schools to share their stories, and, in doing so, bridge the gap between young and old.

Happily, one senses there is the beginning of a shift in attitudes to ageing. Andrew Scott, co-author of a fascinating new book, *The 100-Year Life: Living and Working in an Age of Longevity*, sets out a compelling argument as to why we need to radically rethink the way we approach life, in view of the fact that we are all living longer.

According to Andrew, a Professor of Economics at London Business School, about half the children born today in the West will live to be over 100. All of us are living longer than our parents. In short, we are being given a lot more time.

'Very few people born in 1917 lived to see a hundred,' says Andrew. 'If life expectancy trends continue then we can expect the majority of those born today to have a realistic chance to live to a hundred. The women in this book didn't expect to live a long life, so didn't plan for it, but today's generations need to think hard about how to structure a life over such a long time. Too often society interprets this increase in longevity as about ageing and end of life, but instead it is about having more time overall and so is about all of life. Just as the twentieth century saw the creation of new stages of life – teenagers and pensioners – so we are seeing new stages and new behaviours emerge. It's time to turn away from the generational stratification of a three-stage view of life.'

The 100-Year Life challenges society's outdated and tired attitude to ageing, encouraging us all to see longer life as an opportunity to reflect on what values we hold dear. Instead of chasing fleeting moments of happiness, perhaps we should all think harder about our identity and how we go about achieving deeper well-being as a meaningful member of our community. This is something that has always come naturally to the Stepney Doorstep Society and I suspect holds the key to their long life.

'Given the rarity of the ages of this group amongst their generation they clearly are blessed with good genetics,' says Andrew. 'But they also seem blessed in achieving a wisdom that comes from balancing being and belonging. As more and more people live longer, the hope is that we will become more interested in the wisdom of older people once again.'

Let's hope Andrew is right. How we go about achieving longevity is a hot topic right now. Acres of column inches are devoted to *how* to live longer, but not so much on *what* to do with your time if you did manage to achieve a 100-year life.

Will *you* live to be 100? Would you want to live to 100? And if you were given a guarantee of living to 100, would you make different choices today over how you spent the rest of your life?

When it comes to the women in this book, I get the distinct impression that looking back they wouldn't change a thing. Their strong identities are honed from their experiences in being raised in close-knit communities, drawn even tighter in the face of adversity.

I think this exchange between 100-year-old Beatty Orwell and her friends, Millie, also 100, Renee, 91, and Marie, 96, at Jewish Care's Brenner Centre at Stepney Community Centre, in December 2017, is perhaps the most illuminating when searching for the answers to their incredible longevity.

Me (aged 43) to the group: 'What are your secrets to living a long and happy life?'

Bursting into laughter: 'You want the truth?' Beatty asks. 'All right, we'll keep it clean!'

Millie (100 years old): 'I'm a hundred . . .'

Renee (91 years old): 'No, you're not.'

Millie: 'Wait a minute. I'm a hundred and eight months! It's like this. In this day and age, the young people live a different life to what we did when we were young. We led an ordinary, plain life. We didn't have money to go out and spend. You used to make the best of it and that's why we're different to young people today.'

Renee: 'You're right, Millie. And we enjoyed it more.'

Beatty: 'That's right. What we had, we shared. Also, I would say, going upstairs. I've always lived high and I've had to go up and down stairs, and that's kept me fit. I've worked

306

all my life, since the age of fourteen. Look at me now, I'm a hundred and a half,' she adds, tipping her head back and hooting with laughter.

'You're a baby,' Millie teases.

Renee: 'You know what I say? Not to worry about anything; worry is what kills you. As long as your family and friends are all well, just carry on.'

Millie: 'And don't forget friendships. Coming to this club, I've made friends. I've got friends all over the club and it is wonderful to have someone to speak to and laugh with, otherwise I'm all right. I live alone, I look after myself.'

'And you know what else?' adds Renee. 'She's got a lovely nature.'

'Thanks, Renee,' Millie shrugs, 'I'm not bad.'

Up bustles Marie, whose ninety-sixth birthday we are all here to celebrate, clutching an enormous bag. She hands round chocolates, oranges and crisps.

Me: 'Why are you handing these out? It's your birthday today!'

'I know, but I've got to look after these girls,' she says. 'Otherwise, they'll starve themselves. You gotta feed them.'

Renee grabs her hand and kisses it. 'You know how long I've known Marie for?'

'All our lives,' Marie cuts in. 'Since we were kids.'

'How's it feel to be ninety-six, Mar?' asks Renee.

'Great,' she replies. 'I've enjoyed myself, whatever I've done, I've enjoyed. We've all worked very hard. Maybe that's it. Hard work, community and friendship. And don't forget the chicken soup.'

After we've sung 'Happy Birthday' and Marie's blown out her birthday candles, I kiss her, wish her well and take my leave. I glance back as I reach the door. Millie's dancing with a younger man, Marie's busy handing round slices of cake, and Beatty and Renee are deep in conversation. That's the way to do it.

Four months after I wrote this, Millie Finger (born Millie Walvish on 30 March 1917) died in her own home, shortly after she made it to her 101st birthday. She is irreplaceable.

Notes and Further Reading

Preface

Details of Kate Thompson's life and family were pieced together from research conducted by Geoff Swinfield Genealogical Services and conversations with surviving members of her family. With thanks to Ronald Hilson and Sidney Harris who shared their memories of the Quinn Square rent strike and Gladys Harrison who used to run her nan's betting slips up to Quinn Square.

I also spent time reading about the strike at Tower Hamlets Local History Library & Archives, which holds material relating to the strike, including a pamphlet entitled the *Quinn Square Tenants' Rent Strike Victory*, published by the London District Committee of the Communist Party, No. LP.1948/331.5.

Politics and Persons, Father St John B. Groser, President of the Stepney Tenants' Defence League (STDL) (SCM Press, 1949).

I interviewed Henry Felix Srebrnik, author of *London Jews and British Communism 1935–45* (Vallentine Mitchell & Co. Ltd, 1995).

Full notes on the Bethnal Green Tube disaster can be found under Chapter Five notes.

Chapter One

Like many Jewish families, the Indersteins anglicised their name and became known as the Stones.

Our Flag Stays Red, Phil Piratin (Thames, 1948).

Battle for the East End: Jewish Responses to Fascism in the 1930s, David Rosenberg (Five Leaves Publications, 2011).

The Thirties, Juliet Gardiner (HarperCollins, 2009) is a fascinating look at this time.

I first visited Beatty, Millie, Marie and Renee at Jewish Care's Brenner Centre at Stepney Community Centre, a vibrant centre for older Jewish people living in East London and the City, in February 2016 and have returned many times. Beatty's 100th birthday celebrations were in July 2017. The centre has been at the heart of East London's Jewish community for many years: https://www.jewishcare.org/how-we-can-help-you/community.

Tower Hamlets Local History Library & Archives hold the trade directories for 1936, showing the amazing diversity of traders and stores in and around Whitechapel.

Chapter Two

Professor Martin Parsons, PhD, FRHistS, founder and former Director of the Research Centre for Evacuee and War Child Studies, University of Reading.

I met Marie (Girl Walker) when she answered an advert I placed in *Our East End* in 2016.

I met Kathy and her friend Vera in 2015 at the Sundial Centre, a community centre for Tower Hamlets and Hackney in Bethnal Green.

Chapter Three

The German airman who crashed in Kennington is buried at Brookwood Military Cemetery. The event was reported in the *South London Press* on Tuesday, 17 September 1940.

Passing the Flame: The Life and Work of Dr Joan Martin, Joy Puritz (Green Oak Publishing, 2011).

The Secret History of the Blitz, Joshua Levine, in partnership with the Imperial War Museum (Simon & Schuster UK, 2015).

Living Through the Blitz, Tom Harrisson (Penguin Books, 1978).

The Blitz: The British Under Attack, Juliet Gardiner (HarperPress, 2010).

London's East End Survivors: Voices of the Blitz Generation, Andrew Bissell (Centenar, 2010).

I met Gladys in July 2015 at the Imperial War Museum: http://www.iwm.org.uk.

Len, I tried to get hold of you but couldn't contact you. I hope you approve of this book.

Chapter Four

Read about the Canning Town school disaster in Juliet Gardiner's *The Blitz: The British Under Attack* (HarperPress, 2010).

Phil Piratin's account of the Savoy Hotel takeover is in the IWM sound archive, 10210.

Tower Hamlets Local History Library & Archives has a wealth of information on Bethnal Green Underground as a shelter and the Blitz in Bethnal Green, all of which I accessed for this chapter.

Bethnal Green's Ordeal 1939–45, George F. Vale, pamphlet held at Tower Hamlets Local History Library & Archives.

The Secret History of the Blitz, Joshua Levine, in partnership with the Imperial War Museum (Simon & Schuster UK, 2015).

Living Through the Blitz, Tom Harrisson (Penguin Books, 1978).

The Blitz: The British Under Attack, Juliet Gardiner (HarperPress, 2010).

John Drury, Chris Cocking and Steve Reicher, 'The Nature of Collective Resilience: Survivor Reactions to the 2005 London Bombings' (*International Journal of Mass Emergencies and Disasters*, 27(1), 66–95, 2009).

E. Pellicci in Bethnal Green: http://epellicci.com.

I was kindly introduced to Minksy by The Gentle Author, writer of the fascinating daily blog Spitalfields Life, http://spitalfieldslife.com.

I met Phoebe at a lunch club run by Neighbours in Poplar: https://www.neighboursinpoplar.com.

The Women's Voluntary Services, now known as The Royal Voluntary Service, has a comprehensive section on its wartime history on its website: https://www.royalvoluntaryservice.org.uk.

Chapter Five

For more information on the memorial visit:
http://www.stairwaytoheavenmemorial.org
http://www.bgmemorial.org.uk.

I interviewed Dr Joan Martin at her home in West London in July 2017.

I have interviewed Minksy Keeper many times but about the Tube disaster at her home in East London in September 2014 and again in October 2017.

I interviewed Alf Morris in Bethnal Green in November 2014.

I interviewed Sandra Scotting in January 2015.

I interviewed Babs Clark in Bethnal Green in September 2017.

I recommend you pay a visit to the stunning memorial, which has just won a National and London RIBA (Royal Institute of British Architects) 2018 award and also the London Project Architect of the Year 2018 award.

Chapter Six

The song 'Bless 'Em All' was first recorded in 1939 by George Formby. It was adapted for use by some war workers, who changed the lyrics. The bawdier version which opens this chapter was sung in some East End garment factories.

Millions Like Us: Women's Lives During the Second World War, Virginia Nicholson (Penguin, 2012) is a mine of information on the lives of women during the war.

I met Pat and Dolly in 2016 at St Hilda's East Community Centre in Club Row, East London: http://sthildas.org.uk.

For more information on the Basement Writers visit: http://bricklanebookshop.org/history/Our%20History%20-%20Writing.html.

Sally Flood's poem 'Small Cogs' and many other poems and original stories appear in *Tales by Eastenders*, a Sundial Book Project, available from the wonderful Brick Lane Bookshop: www.brick-lanebookshop.org.

Jennifer Daley is a PhD candidate at the Department of War Studies at King's College London: https://www.kcl.ac.uk/sspp/departments/warstudies/index.aspx.

Dee, fired for refusing to lug a typewriter about – I'm sorry, I tried contacting you but was unable to locate you. I hope you approve of this book.

Chapter Seven

I met Mary at the Sonali Gardens Day Centre, LinkAge Plus, based in Shadwell, East London in 2017. It is one of five such centres in Tower Hamlets, offering residents aged fifty and upwards a range of social and health-related activities to maximise their well-being and make the most of life: http://linkageplus.co.uk.

For a fascinating look at life in Wapping in the twentieth century, read *Between High Walls: A London Childhood*, Grace Foakes (Shepheard-Walwyn, 1972). Grace describes the poverty and richness of life in Wapping, as well as the rituals surrounding childbirth and the care of children.

Sister Christine of St Matthias Community Centre founded Neighbours in Poplar, which helps the elderly in Poplar and the Isle of Dogs, runs lunch clubs, Sunday dinners, leisure activities and organises celebrations at Christmas and other festivals, helping change lives over four decades for thousands living alone or isolated:
http://www.stmatthiascommunitycentre.com
https://www.neighboursinpoplar.com.

For more information on Jean Vanier, visit: http://www.jean-vanier.org/info/.

Chapter Eight

See Imperial War Museum website for information on V-1 and V-2 rockets: http://www.iwm.org.uk.

London's East End Survivors: Voices of the Blitz Generation, Andrew Bissell (Centenar, 2010) has a comprehensive chapter on V-1 and V-2 rocket strikes in East London as well as many fascinating interviews with wartime survivors.

I met Vi at the Sundial Centre, a community centre for Tower Hamlets and Hackney in Bethnal Green in 2016 and interviewed her at home in 2018.

https://www.peabody.org.uk/neighbourhoods/sundial-centre/sundial-centre-day-care-tower-hamlets.

Chapter Nine

For more information on the Kray twins, read *The Profession of Violence: The Rise and Fall of the Kray Twins,* John Pearson (Granada Publishing, 1984).

Statistics on women and war work and divorce can be found in Virginia Nicholson's fascinating look at women's lives during the Second World War, *Millions Like Us: Women's Lives During the Second World War,* published by Penguin, 2012.

I met Pat at the V&A Museum of Childhood in Bethnal Green in 2016: http://www.vam.ac.uk/moc/.

You can read more detail on Dr Joan's extraordinary life in the biography *Passing the Flame: The Life and Work of Dr Joan Martin,* Joy Puritz (Green Oak Publishing, 2011). I interviewed Dr Joan Martin in July 2017.

For more information on swimming for people with disabilities see the Halliwick Association of Swimming Therapy: http://www. halliwickpenguins.org.

Vintage Glamour in London's East End, Boris Bennett and Michael Greisman (Hoxton Mini Press, 2014) is a jewel of a book, filled with Boris Bennett's remarkable portraits.

Chapter Ten

Figures on the rise of illegitimate births and venereal disease in wartime can be found in Joshua Levine's *The Secret History of the Blitz* (Simon & Schuster UK, 2015) in an enlightening chapter entitled 'The First Sexual Revolution'.

The names of Polly and Frankie Barrett, Denise, Mrs Bryant and Danny have all been changed to protect Denise's identity. I interviewed Denise in 2017.

More information on the Abortion Reform Act can be accessed via the British Pregnancy Advisory Service. BPAS has been providing high-quality abortion care on behalf of the NHS for over forty years and is the UK's leading abortion care charity: https://www.bpas.org/abortion-care/.

For more information on the Family Planning Association (FPA), a sexual health charity: https://www.fpa.org.uk.

I interviewed Betty in 2017. Her story features in a wonderful pamphlet, *Poplar, Past, Present and Future,* supported by Neighbours in Poplar, which features a wealth of stories, memories and photographs: https://www.neighboursinpoplar.com.

Chapter Eleven

I first met Doreen in 2015 and interviewed her in December 2017. For more information on the London Pearly Kings and Queens Society Charity Fund please visit: http://www.pearlysociety.co.uk.

Family and Kinship in East London, Michael Young and Peter Willmott (Routledge and Kegan Paul, 1957). Updated version with introduction written by Kate Gavron and Geoff Mulgan, *Family and Kinship in East London* (Penguin Modern Classics, 2007).

The New East End: Kinship, Race and Conflict, Michael Young, Geoff Dench and Kate Gavron (Profile Books, 2006).

Find out more on the East End Preservation Society: https://www.facebook.com/EastEndPSociety.

For more information on St Matthias and Neighbours in Poplar run by Sister Christine, please visit: https://www.neighboursin-poplar.com.

I first visited the Geezers in January 2017. For more information or to contact the club please visit: https://www.ourbow.com/category/the-geezers/.

Report on housing crisis under headline 'Anger as 26,000 New Millionaire Flats are Given Green Light' by Rupert Neate, Wealth Correspondent, the *Observer*, 04.02.18.

Postscript

The 100-Year Life: Living and Working in an Age of Longevity, Lynda Gratton and Andrew Scott (Bloomsbury, 2016).

Age UK: https://www.ageuk.org.uk.

Link to study: https://www.campaigntoendloneliness.org/wp-content/uploads/Loneliness-The-State-Were-In.pdf.

Sources

Loneliness: Human Nature and the Need for Social Connection, conference presentation, John T. Cacioppo and William Patrick (W. W. Norton & Company, 2008).

'Late-life Social Activity and Cognitive Decline in Old Age', B. D. James, R. S Wilson, L. L. Barnes and D. A. Bennett (*Journal of the International Neuropsychological Society* 17(6), 2011): http://www.ncbi.nlm.nih.gov/pmc/articles/PMC3206295/.

'Loneliness and Risk of Alzheimer Disease', R. S. Wilson, K. R. Krueger, S. E. Arnold, J. A. Schneider, J. F. Kelly, L. L. Barnes, Y. Tang, D. A. Bennett (*Archives of General Psychiatry* 64(2), 2007): http://www.ncbi.nlm.nih.gov/pubmed/17283291.

Acknowledgements

A heartfelt thank-you to every woman and man who has shared their time and precious memories with me for inclusion in this book. I am always struck by the spirit, warmth, openness and hospitality of East Enders.

To every single historian, author, tour guide, professor, blogger, Facebook group, café owner, writer, resident and lover of the East End who has shared his or her knowledge with me and helped me to see beyond the sentimental clichés to the heart of the East End. Thank you.

Special thanks must go to Professor Dick Hobbs, Gloria Spielman, Peter Kurton and Sandra Scotting, true children of the East End, who patiently read my first draft and whose advice was warmly and gratefully received.

To Ron and Sidney, thank you for showing me round your manor. You're true gents.

Huge thanks and respect to the most imaginative East End tour guides in the business, Rachel Kolsky and David Rosenberg, for showing me your East End. Their tours take you beyond the Jack the Ripper cliché, to the true East End, revealing the extraordinary human stories and battles behind the buildings.
http://www.golondontours.com/GoLondonTours/Home.html
http://www.eastendwalks.com.

Enormous thanks to Diane Banks and Martin Redfern at Diane Banks Associates, whose enthusiasm, talent and expertise I have come to rely on, and the glorious Fenella Bates at Penguin for believing in this book.

Enormous thanks to all the staff at Jewish Care's Brenner Centre at Stepney Community Centre and everyone at East London Age UK, LinkAge Plus and Tower Hamlets organised groups who have allowed me to come along and meet their fascinating members over the years, and especially Vince Quinlivan, who volunteers at Jewish Care's Brenner Centre at Stepney Community Centre, for his support.

Thanks must go to the calm, efficient, ever-cheerful Sarah Richards, who has assisted me in the research of this book and been such a tremendous support, and Amy Condon for her grammatical guidance.

Enormous thanks to historical researcher Jennifer Daley from the Department of War Studies at King's College, and Joshua Levine, for their eagle eyes in ensuring wartime accuracy, and Terri Coates, consultant midwife on *Call the Midwife*, for reading the chapters on childbirth, death and abortion.

Enormous thanks to Malcolm at the Tower Hamlets Local History Library & Archives for his unrivalled knowledge of the East End.

Much respect and thanks must go to author Louise Raw, author of *Striking a Light: The Bryant and May Matchwomen and their Place in History*, for her unfailing support and for being such a colossal champion of women.

Finally, immense gratitude and respect to hard-working Sarah Jackson of the East End Women's Museum who, along with her

co-founders, Sara Huws and Judith Garfield, MBE, Director of Eastside Community Heritage, is a passionate supporter of magnificent East End women. The women the history books forgot.
https://eastendwomensmuseum.org
https://www.hidden-histories.org

- All interviewees' ages are correct as of time of interview. Some interviewees were happy to provide their full names; at the request of others, I have used first names or nicknames. All names are real with the exception of Denise and her family in Chapter Ten, where I have used a pseudonym to protect her identity.
- All streets, areas and place names are real.
- All events and stories are real to the best of my knowledge and research.
- Interviews were carried out between January 2014 and January 2018.
- Any inaccuracies are my own.

Picture Credits

We are grateful to the following for granting us permission to include their photographs in this book:

Page one, top: Tower Hamlets Local History Library and Archives; bottom: People's History Museum. **Page two**, top and bottom: Tower Hamlets Local History Library and Archives; **Page three**, top and bottom left side: Tower Hamlets Local History Library and Archives; bottom right side: Stairway to Heaven Memorial Trust. **Page four**, top: Gladys Harrison; bottom: Beatty Orwell; **Page five**, top and bottom: Beatty Orwell. **Page six**, top: Marie Joseph; bottom: Marie Butwell; **Page seven**, top and bottom: Marie Butwell. **Page eight**, top: Babs Clark; middle: Kay Coupland; bottom: Dr Evelyn Goldie. **Page nine**, top: Dot Smee; bottom: Dr Joan Martin. **Page ten**, top and bottom: Henrietta Keeper. **Page eleven**, Henrietta Keeper, **Page twelve**, top: Henrietta Keeper; bottom: Henrietta Keeper/Griffiths Photographers; **Page thirteen**, top: Sally Flood; bottom: Jessie Smith. **Page fourteen**: Marie Butwell; **Page fifteen**, top: Pat Spicer and Boris Bennett; bottom: Rene Stack and L&J Suss. **Page sixteen**, from top to bottom, left to right: Girl Walker; Minksy Keeper; Dr Joan Martin; Jessie Smith; Babs Clark; Gladys Hale; Sarah Ainslie.

Do you have a woman in your family whose story you'd like to share? Please do get in touch to tell me more, or simply to let me know what you think of the book. I'd love to hear from you.

katharinethompson82@gmail.com
@katethompson380
https://www.facebook.com/KateThompsonAuthor/

He just wanted a decent book to read ...

Not too much to ask, is it? It was in 1935 when Allen Lane, Managing Director of Bodley Head Publishers, stood on a platform at Exeter railway station looking for something good to read on his journey back to London. His choice was limited to popular magazines and poor-quality paperbacks – the same choice faced every day by the vast majority of readers, few of whom could afford hardbacks. Lane's disappointment and subsequent anger at the range of books generally available led him to found a company – and change the world.

'We believed in the existence in this country of a vast reading public for intelligent books at a low price, and staked everything on it'
Sir Allen Lane, 1902–1970, founder of Penguin Books

The quality paperback had arrived – and not just in bookshops. Lane was adamant that his Penguins should appear in chain stores and tobacconists, and should cost no more than a packet of cigarettes.

Reading habits (and cigarette prices) have changed since 1935, but Penguin still believes in publishing the best books for everybody to enjoy. We still believe that good design costs no more than bad design, and we still believe that quality books published passionately and responsibly make the world a better place.

So wherever you see the little bird – whether it's on a piece of prize-winning literary fiction or a celebrity autobiography, political tour de force or historical masterpiece, a serial-killer thriller, reference book, world classic or a piece of pure escapism – you can bet that it represents the very best that the genre has to offer.

Whatever you like to read – trust Penguin.

read more
www.penguin.co.uk